Critical Praise for Russell Dunn's Guidebooks

Adirondack Waterfall Guide

Many of the falls are well known, but this is an especially good guide to cataracts that hikers might otherwise miss. **Adirondack Life**

If you love waterfalls, you'll love the guidebook written by Russell Dunn. [It is] a ... readable and easy-to-use guide to a whole lot of waterfalls in the eastern Adirondacks that you'll want to see if you haven't. **Adirondack Explorer**

This book is indeed a joy to read. Dunn easily draws us into his world with graceful, inspired writing, and provides the kind of insights that may prompt us to keep a copy permanently in our cars. **Trailwalker**

It is the experience of discovering the unexpected that I treasure most about Adirondack waterfalls, and the fact that there are still such places to 'discover' in New York State in the twenty-first century is no small thing. **Bill Ingersoll**

Catskill Region Waterfall Guide

Dunn's directions are easy to follow, and he offers some nifty history on each of the cataracts. If that's not enough to make you jump in the car, the dramatic photos should cinch it. **Hudson Valley**

A must-own tool. ... This book fills a real need and is a key to a treasure house of beauty. Altogether the book is a winner. **Arthur G. Adams**

This book is highly recommended for its unique combination of appealing writing, strong research, intriguing destinations, and interesting history. **Kaatskill Life**

Hudson Valley Waterfall Guide

Will very likely open eyes to a world of the outdoors that would have passed us by otherwise. **Fred LeBrun, Times Union**

Those who pick up this extraordinary waterfall guide by Russell Dunn will find countless paths to these and other inspirational places in the Valley. **Ned Sullivan, president, Scenic Hudson**

Published by
Black Dome Press Corp.
1011 Route 296, Hensonville, New York 12439
www.blackdomepress.com
Tel: (518) 734–6357

First Edition Paperback 2006
Copyright © 2006 by C. Russell Dunn and Barbara Delaney

Dunn, Russell.
    Trails with tales : history hikes through the capital region, Saratoga,
    Berkshires, Catskills & Hudson Valley/Russell Dunn and Barbara Delaney.
    — 1st ed. pbk.
        p. cm.
    Includes bibliographical references and index.
    ISBN-13: 978-1-883789-48-0
    ISBN-10: 1-883789-48-6
    1. Historic sites—New York (State)—Guidebooks. 2. Historic sites
    —Massachusetts—Berkshire Hills—Guidebooks. 3. New York (State)
    —Tours. 4. Albany Region (N.Y.)—Tours. 5. Saratoga Region (N.Y.)
    —Tours. 6. Catskill Mountains Region (N.Y.)—Tours. 7. Hudson
    River Valley (N.Y. and N.J.)—Tours. 8. Berkshire Hills (Mass.)
    —Tours. 9. Hiking—New York (State) 10. Hiking—Massachusetts
    —Berkshire Hills.   I. Delaney, Barbara. II. Title.
    F120.D86 2006
    917.470444—dc22

                                                      2006008842

Maps created with TOPO! software © 2006 National Geographic Maps
To learn more visit http://www.nationalgeographic.com/topo
Outdoor recreational activities are by their very nature potentially hazardous and contain risk. See "Caution and Safety Tips," page 6.

Cover: *Morning, Looking East over the Hudson Valley from the Catskill Mountains,* Frederic E. Church (1826–1900), 1848. Oil on canvas: height 18"x width 24". Original gilt frame: height 26" x width 32". Signed and dated, lower left: "F E Church/1848". Albany Institute of History & Art. Gift of Catherine Gansevoort (Mrs. Abraham) Lansing. x1940.606.7

Design: Toelke Associates
Printed in the USA

10 9 8 7 6 5 4 3 2

Trails with TALES

History Hikes through the Capital Region, Saratoga, Berkshires, Catskills & Hudson Valley

Russell Dunn and Barbara Delaney

BLACK · DOME

Map 1: Capital and Saratoga Regions

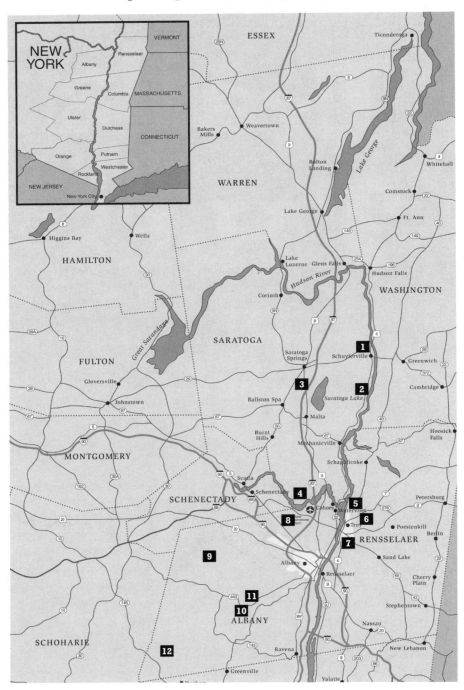

Map 2: Schoharie, Catskills and Hudson Valley

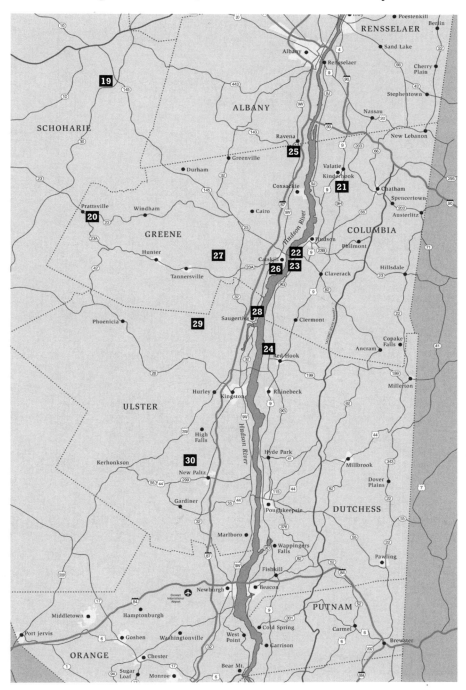

Map 3: The Berkshires

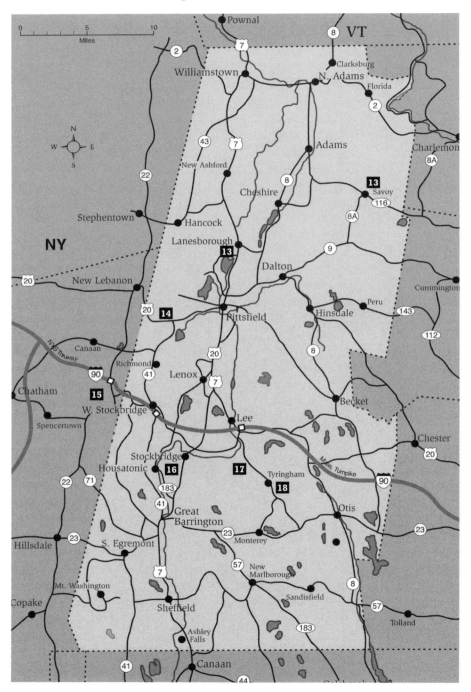

Map Key

1. Starks Knob & Schuylerville Champlain Canal Towpath
2. Saratoga National Historic Park
3. Geyser Park
4. Vischer Ferry Nature & Historic Preserve
5. Peebles Island State Park
6. Oakwood Cemetery
7. Burden Pond Environmental Park
8. Ann Lee Pond
9. Indian Ladder
10. Bennett Hill Preserve
11. Clarksville Cave Preserve
12. Edmund Niles Huyck Preserve
13. Balanced Rocks
14. Shaker Mountain
15. No Bottom Pond
16. Ice Glen & Laura's Tower
17. Tyringham Cobble
18. Ashintully Estate & McLennan Preserve
19. Vroman's Nose
20. Pratt Rock
21. Lindenwald & Martin Van Buren Nature Trail
22. Rogers Island
23. Olana
24. Montgomery Place
25. Ravena Falls
26. Hudson River School Art Trail
27. Catskill Mountain House Escarpment
28. Saugerties Lighthouse
29. Overlook Mountain
30. Sky Top & Mohonk Lake

To Thomas & Olive Delaney,
who instilled a love of walking in the outdoors
and reading books of adventure

Contents

Contents

Foreword

Always knowing where you are is a cardinal rule of hiking. When rambling in woodlands or mountains, it generally means "staying found," which is really just the affirmative way of saying "not getting lost." This is an essential ability, and it's fortunate that each of us has it innately, at least to the extent needed to navigate our everyday lives. Hikers usually build upon this ability by adding practice—and eventual skill— in combining the tools of map and compass, or perhaps GPS, with an open eye to their surroundings. What makes this book especially interesting is that it takes up directly from that last point, the open eye.

The authors relate their own "Aha!" moment. It came as they first drew the straight-line connection, true as the compass, between moss-covered traces found deep in the woods, a wonderful story unearthed in a library, and their own hearts and imaginations. Once that bright line was drawn, they were hooked. They found that knowing where you are can mean much more than the way that map symbols and compass bearings relate to the physical terrain. For them, hiking suddenly became far more than an exercise in moving from here to there, and the enjoyment of being outdoors. Now, everywhere they went, the landscape began to actually speak, and they became energetic listeners. That feeling is not a stranger to me, and if you have picked up this book and read this far, it is likely no stranger to you, either. It can find its way into us, regardless of age or experience.

I feel unbelievably fortunate to have grown up hiking and climbing in a part of our region where, as a friend once put it, "the bones and stories of the landscape cry out in the dark"—the Shawangunk Mountains. My parents took me blueberry picking in the wake of now-legendary forest fires and let me crawl around among the boulders beneath cliffs and waterfalls. Since that is as good as life gets, my affection for the outdoors was of course immediate. A formal introduction to map and compass came at age eleven, when two older hikers dragged me up and over two Catskill peaks on their quest to join the 3500 Club. One of the peaks was trailless, so (probably to keep me from whining) they let me sight the compass line as we bushwhacked from tree to tree through the steep tangles of woods and rocks.

The next fall, two of my own friends and I were surprised by an early snow as we camped beneath a rock overhang that was a reputed Indian shelter. As darkness grew with wind and snow, we began to fear that we would run out of dry firewood. To three young boys, the nighttime seemed a lot bigger, and we took turns foraging for dead branches in the nearby woods. Returning from one dark foray with a heavy limb, I looked up and was struck by the image of our place. Long and fearsome shadows danced on the broken cliff wall, while the surrounding trees shown hard and black in the swirling snow. And beneath a massive rock, a small silhouette squatted in a tiny island of light and warmth. Suddenly it seemed that this place and this night were probably just the way the Indians had known it, perhaps for thousands of years. At that moment, a band of them could easily have just returned from hunting mastodons in the valley below. And I was there.

That sense of connection has followed me through life. It has even guided my career with National Park Service, helping present-day communities to preserve their own special places and uncover the stories they have to tell. And why not? Trading stories and handing them down in various forms is one of the most powerful tools of culture. This is especially true when those stories are inexorably tied to something as indelible as the landscape. Starting from the deep bedrock and working its way up, it is the land and its stories that make us who we are.

To me, this book is full of old friends, whether places, people or stories. It also includes several distant acquaintances, and (especially pleasing) even a few complete strangers. To find such a wide and eclectic variety between the covers of one book, and also within an easy drive of home, is a wonderful gift.

This book invites you to walk in the steps of the artists, writers and other influential figures who first made the appreciation of the American landscape into an institution. Along the way, you can take in the very same views that inspired the Hudson River School of artists, who in turn inspired the formation of the American conservation movement. Their inspiration is readily within grasp because, thanks to the success of conservation so far, many of those views are as wild today as they were a century and a half ago.

This book also invites you to the now-quiet camps of British and Colonial armies as they labored and fought through a major turning point in the American Revolution. It points the way to the Hudson River island where, two decades after the *Half Moon* sailed by, the Mohawks, through a cunning deception, won a decisive victory in their territorial feud with the Mohicans.

Along the way, there are profiles of some local people who have helped make American history and folklore. There is the remarkably progressive woman who sought to dispel the idea of women as intellectually inferior by founding the first school of higher education for women in 1821. There is also the local meat packer whose work supplying troops with provisions during the War of 1812 seems to have set him as the original of the American icon, Uncle Sam. The home and farm life of the eighth president of the United States are further illuminated by nature trails. And then there is the mogul of the tanbark industry who is immortalized by a frankly odd monument carved into a sandstone ledge in the Catskills.

No single book can do justice to the full wealth of stories that abound in our area. This guidebook is simply a tool, a key for entry, a brief introduction to a future friend. Each trail described here offers its own facet of a particular place, a particular aspect of our region's landscape, and a particular slice of history.

In all, the authors invite you to know where you are, but not just in the sense of "staying found," with map and compass, GPS, or even trail guide in hand. More importantly, they encourage us to know where we are in the way of seeing the stories embodied in the landscape around us. They have selected a few special places within our region that have particular stories to tell. They invite us to use those stories for orientation in an ever-greater understanding of an ever-greater world, and once more find our place.

After all, every walk and every trail is a story of some kind. The landscape is entirely cloaked with them, waiting to be known. Their broad outlines are draped across the forms of the trees. Their details lie slightly overgrown with moss and ferns. Here and there a hard fact stands out in stone. The trials imposed by troubles and time are written in fields and foundations now grown into forests, perhaps threaded together with an old road now passable only as a footpath. From a high point, the sweeping view across today's landscape, forever changed and forever changing, is a touchstone of time. All of these will speak to you if you listen. You will become more connected to the landscape, where special places have special stories.

Soon you may begin to see and hear many more stories that need to be recaptured and retold, before they escape into placeless and faceless anonymity. Along with them, you may find many more special places that need to be listened to and protected. If you listen, and keep an open eye, you will stay found. What a wonderful thought!

Thinking this way makes me hungry for a story. Grab this book, and let's go for a hike!

Karl Beard
Kingston, NY
March 2006

Karl Beard is the New York Projects Director of the Rivers, Trails & Conservation Assistance Program of the National Park Service.

Introduction

Have you ever come across a crumbling wall, old stone foundations, half-buried artifacts, or rusted bits of machinery while walking in the woods and wondered to yourself, "What used to be here?" You are not alone.

Trails with Tales is the story of our experiences hiking to fascinating natural and geological areas, and then discovering through research the varied layers of history that underlie each hike. Since we are hikers who enjoy history, as opposed to historians who like to hike, the emphasis in this book is always on the hike first and the history second.

Each history hike falls within a radius of approximately seventy miles from Albany, New York, and is described in enough detail to allow you to duplicate our adventures with book in hand. All of the hikes are of moderate length and are accessible to any hiker who is reasonably fit. Many of the hikes are suitable for young children, with the usual caveats about maintaining strict supervision, especially in rocky, steep, or deepwater terrain. Some of the hikes involve short bushwhacks, but none of these off-trail adventures are extensive or overly demanding.

In our earlier hiking days we tended to forge ahead full speed. We were in search of waterfalls and unusual rock formations, and not necessarily interested in the history that was in evidence all around us. Then, one day, while exploring Griffin Falls and the surrounding terrain in the southern Adirondacks, we happened upon some curious pieces of rusted machinery in the woods. This aroused our interest to the point that on the way back to our camp on the Great Sacandaga Lake we stopped by the Northville Public Library. While there, we rummaged through the local lore on Griffin Falls. That was our "Eureka!" moment. The corroded metal we'd seen upstream from the falls was not just a rusty boiler from an old tannery; it was a remnant of an entire lost town!

Griffin is but one example of the kind of moss-covered puzzles you can encounter in the wild (a hike to Griffin Falls and the lost town of Griffin will be featured in the next volume of *Trails with Tales*). Since then, we have found many hikes with storied pasts. As we accrued more and more intriguing historical information about a variety of hiking locales within mid-eastern New York State and western Massachusetts, it occurred to us that other curious walkers might be equally fascinated by these hikes into history.

Trails with Tales retraces our footsteps as we follow those of Native Americans, European colonists, Revolutionary War combatants, Victorian gentry, and industrialists—the explorers and legendary figures of the region. These hikes reflect the American experiences unique to particular eras in the

Hudson and Schoharie valleys and the Berkshire, Adirondack, Catskill, and Helderberg mountains. The historical events that are chronicled span from pre-Colonial times through the Industrial Revolution and beyond. It is our intent to bring ghostly shadows and faint traces of long-ago events into a clear picture of what was once a vivid reality with vibrant people forging ahead in a new world, where the old stone foundations, pieces of machinery, and derelict dams you see along the trails were proud homes, mighty factories, and water-powered centers of commerce.

All of the walks we have selected have in common a natural, stand-alone beauty, enhanced by tangible silhouettes of a fascinating past. The hikes also cover a wide range of geological features including waterfalls, mountains, escarpments, lakes, sculpted rocks, ponds, rivers, islands, caves, balanced rocks, geysers, and deep gorges. Some of the areas described have had the good fortune of being recognized and saved by environmental conservancies. In some instances these conservancies have preserved not only the land, but the history as well, and have published their findings. These resources, when available, are listed in the endnotes.

The hikes in *Trails with Tales* have been organized by region and, within each region, by geographic proximity. This has been done to minimize driving time. Some hikes are short enough, or near enough to another hike, that you might enjoy doing more than one hike in a day's outing.

Each hike is organized according to Location, coordinates from Delorme's *New York State* or *Massachusetts Atlas & Gazetteer*, Fees, Hours, Restrictions (where applicable), Accessibility, Level of Difficulty, Highlights, Description of Hike, History, Side Bar (when warranted), Additional Resources (when known), and Directions. For those not familiar with the coordinate system in Delorme's *Atlas & Gazetteer,* the following is an example: "p. 32, AB1-2" means that you open the *Atlas & Gazetteer* to page 32, trace down the topographic map until you are halfway between letters A and B, and then trace across the page until you are halfway between numbers 1 and 2. At this intersection or close to it will be the hiking area you seek.

We hope you will find this book an interesting guide to new hikes or a source of enrichment to already familiar walks. Happy Trails!

Caution and Safety Tips

Outdoor recreational activities are by their very nature potentially hazardous and contain risk. All participants in such activities must assume responsibility for their own actions and safety. No book can be a substitute for good judgment. The outdoors is forever changing. The authors and the publisher cannot be held responsible for inaccuracies, errors, or omissions, or for any changes in the details of this publication, or for the consequences of any reliance on the information contained herein, or for the safety of people in the outdoors.

Safety Tips

1. Always hike with two or more companions. There is always safety in numbers. Should an accident occur, one or more can stay with the victim while another goes for help.

2. Bring a day pack loaded with survival items such as extra layers of clothes, matches, a compass, water, high-energy food (e.g., Gorp or Power Bars), mosquito repellent, an emergency medical kit, moleskin, duct tape (for quick repairs), rain gear, a whistle, and sun block. Very few hikers are ever "over-prepared."

3. When waterfalls are encountered, treat them with the respect they deserve. Don't get too close to the top, where an inadvertent slip can send you tumbling over the edge. Many waterfalls send up a spray, so keep an eye out for slippery rocks and maintain your footing. Whenever possible, approach waterfalls from the base.

4. Apply ample portions of insect repellent to prevent mosquitoes and black flies from targeting you, and don't be stingy with sunscreen if you are going to be exposed to the sun for any length of time. Remember that you can get sunburned even on a cloudy day if conditions are right. Wear a long-sleeved shirt and long pants.

5. Wear good hiking boots for proper traction and ankle support.

6. Be aware of the risks of hypothermia, and dress accordingly. Wear clothing that has the ability to wick away moisture (polypro, for instance), or dress in materials such as wool that will continue to insulate even when wet. Avoid wearing cotton. Keep in mind that the temperature doesn't have to be freezing to cause the onset of hypothermia. If you become

accidentally wet or immersed while hiking during the spring, fall, or winter, return to your car immediately unless the temperature is higher than 70 degrees. Also be cognizant of the dangers of hyperthermia (overheating) and always drink plenty of water when the weather is hot and muggy. Stay in the shade whenever possible, and use streams, ponds, and lakes to cool off in if you begin to feel overheated.

7. Stay vigilant for others who may not be attentive to those around them. During hunting season, wear bright colors and make frequent sounds so that you will not be mistaken for a wild animal (which you will be, if a hunter accidentally takes a shot at you and you get riled up!) If you are hiking to the base of a large waterfall, keep an eye out for people at the top, especially kids, who might impulsively toss a rock over the edge without first checking to see if there is anyone below.

8. Stay on trails whenever possible. When you head off-trail to explore old ruins and foundations, be sure to get your bearings first before you leave the trail.

9. Do not consider bushwhacking through the woods unless: you are an experienced hiker; you have a compass with you and know how to use it; you are prepared to spend several days in the woods if necessary; you are with a group of similarly prepared hikers; and you have notified someone as to your destination and your estimated time of return from the hike.

10. Don't presume to be a master rock climber by trying to free-climb rock walls in any deep gorge you may encounter. Many gorges have walls made of shale or slate—not particularly stable rocks to grab hold of if your life is depending on a firm support. Stay on trails. When the going is steep, maintain three points of contact whenever possible.

11. Heed all signs and trail markers. Be on the lookout for possible changes in topography or trails following the date of this book's publication. Trails may be rerouted because of blowdown, heavy erosion, the sudden appearance of a lake or bog because of beaver activity, or any number of other unanticipated events. Trails, or portions thereof, occasionally become closed off. If you see a posted sign, go no further.

12. Always let someone back home know where you are hiking and your expected time of return. Clearly discuss with him or her what actions should be taken if you are not back at the appointed time.

13. Always know where you are. Guidebooks, topographic maps, and compasses are essential if you venture out into the wilderness. A GPS unit is also worth bringing along. Nothing, however, is a substitute for good judgment and basic common sense.

14. When you visit waterfalls, never jump or dive off rocks or ledges into inviting pools of waters around waterfalls. Too many people have slipped and tumbled onto the rocks below, or have collided with unseen and unknown hazards below the water's surface.

15. Stay away from overhanging precipices of ice. People have died when blocks of ice have suddenly broken off from the rock face.

16. After the hike, check yourself thoroughly (and your partner, also!) for deer ticks, which can carry Lyme disease. Removing the tick within the first twenty-four hours after contact effectively minimizes your chances of contracting the disease.

17. Avoid cornering any wild animal. If the animal has nowhere to retreat and feels threatened, it may seek a way out that goes right over you.

18. Do not drink untreated water. Giardia is not a pleasant memento to bring back from your hike.

19. Be extra careful if you are making your way over terrain where freezing rain has fallen or melting snow has frozen into ice. This is particularly dangerous along abandoned roads, which are more likely to be covered with ribbons of ice than are trails within the shelter of woods. In warmer weather always be on the lookout for that inevitable slippery tree root, or loose gravel that can give way as you walk downhill.

20. Exercise caution around old ruins and foundations. Crumbling bricks, potholes, broken glass, and other debris can cause you to lose your footing and fall. Make sure that you are up-to-date with your tetanus shots.

And remember: If you carry it in, carry it out!

Acknowledgments

A book never comes into existence fully formed. Although the authors receive the credit, a tremendous amount of dedicated work occurs behind the scenes. For this assistance we are eternally grateful to our diligent, always genial editor, Steve Hoare, and to our energetic publisher, Deborah Allen, who are never content to let us rest until we have gotten everything just right. Their efforts were aided immeasurably by the careful scrutiny of proofreaders Matina Billias, Natalie Mortensen, Christl Riedman, and Ed Volmar. We are indebted to Ron Toelke and Barbara Kempler-Toelke for bringing the book visually to life with their talented and creative design.

No book of history can be infallible. In an attempt to achieve the greatest possible accuracy, we enlisted the aid of a number of knowledgeable individuals who generously gave of their time and expertise to review specific chapters in this book. For this we are indebted to: Chuck Porter, former Hudson Valley Community College geology professor, caver, hiker, kayaker, and mountain biker; Jim Moore, who provided directions to some of the ancillary rock formations at Balance Rock State Park; Thom Engel, local authority on Indian Ladder and its geology, and eminent regional caver; Thomas Wood, historian, Town of Saratoga; Jeff Anzevino of Scenic Hudson; Carolyn Barker, who provided her insights on the Edmund Niles Huyck Preserve; Irene Olson, Rensselaerville historian; Gerald Grant, Director of Research, Shaker Museum; Linda McLean, Director of Olana State Historic Site; Nancy Boulin, who reviewed the chapter on Pratt Rock; Dick Voloshen, who reviewed the text on Overlook Mountain; Robert A. Gildersleeve, author and Executive Director of the Mountain Top Historical Society; Joan LaChance, archivist, for reviewing the chapter on Sky Top and Mohonk Lake; Evelyn Trebilcock, Curator of Olana State Historic Site; and Elizabeth Jacks, director of the Thomas Cole National Historic Site.

Special thanks also go to Sue Lasker, Fritz Traudt, Susan Traudt, and Colleen Grzesik, and to Bob Drew for postcard contributions and consultations.

All postcards used in this book are from the private collection of Russell Dunn. All photographs were taken by the authors.

List of Hikes by Theme

Ponds
8 Ann Lee Pond
7 Burden Pond
Environmental Park
15 No Bottom Pond

Mountains
10 Bennett Hill
Preserve
27 Catskill Mountain
House Escarpment
26 Hudson River
School Art Trail
29 Overlook Mountain
14 Shaker Mountain
17 Tyringham Cobble
19 Vroman's Nose

Waterfalls
7 Burden Pond
Environmental Park
12 Edmund Niles
Huyck Preserve
26 Hudson River
School Art Trail
9 Indian Ladder
24 Montgomery Place
6 Oakwood Cemetery
25 Ravena Falls

Caves
11 Clarksville Cave
Preserve
9 Indian Ladder
16 Ice Glen &
Laura's Tower
15 No Bottom Pond

Lighthouse
28 Saugerties
Lighthouse

Islands
5 Peebles Island SP
22 Rogers Island
28 Saugerties
Lighthouse

Mansions, Houses, & Estates
8 Ann Lee Pond
18 Ashintully Estate &
McLennan Preserve
21 Lindenwald & MVB
Nature Trail
24 Montgomery Place
23 Olana
28 Saugerties
Lighthouse
14 Shaker Mountain
1 Starks Knob &
Schuylerville
Champlain Canal

Notable Ruins
8 Ann Lee Pond
18 Ashintully Estate &
McLennan Preserve
7 Burden Pond
Environmental Park
12 Edmund Niles
Huyck Preserve
24 Montgomery Place
29 Overlook Mountain
5 Peebles Island SP
20 Pratt Rock
25 Ravena Falls
14 Shaker Mountain
1 Starks Knob &
Schuylerville
Champlain Canal
4 Vischer Ferry
Nature & Historic
Preserve

Gorges
16 Ice Glen &
Laura's Tower
24 Montgomery Place

Lakes
12 Edmund Niles
Huyck Preserve
26 Hudson River
School Art Trail
24 Montgomery Place
23 Olana
30 Sky Top &
Mohonk Lake

Rivers & Scenic Views
27 Catskill Mountain
House Escarpment
26 Hudson River
School Art Trail
16 Ice Glen and
Laura's Tower
24 Montgomery Place
23 Olana
29 Overlook Mountain
5 Peebles Island SP
22 Rogers Island
2 Saratoga NHP
28 Saugerties
Lighthouse
30 Sky Top &
Mohonk Lake
1 Starks Knob &
Schuylerville
Champlain Canal
Towpath
4 Vischer Ferry
Nature & Historic
Preserve

Trails *with* Tales

Part I: Saratoga Region

Each of the three hikes in this region illustrates the struggles of early colonists as they formed settlements along the Hudson River north of Albany (then called Beverwyck) and attempted to develop the area in and around Saratoga. As you follow these hikes you will be walking along trails that in some cases were well worn by Native Americans long before Europeans laid claim to the land.

Two of the hikes—Saratoga National Historic Park and Starks Knob— take you through famous battle sites of the American Revolution. Images of American patriots, British soldiers, Tories, and Iroquois enmeshed in deadly battles for territory can be easily conjured as you walk these paths.

When you walk on the Champlain Canal towpath or stroll through Geyser Park, you will be transported back in time to a more genteel period of history in Saratoga County. These hikes are on pathways where American patriots, having won the war, were eager to develop the land and its natural resources. The towns of Saratoga and Schuylerville were becoming important nineteenth-century communities. Included in this section are some of the most historically significant hikes to be found anywhere in the United States.

Starks Knob & Schuylerville Champlain Canal Towpath: Hike up to the top of a strategically located, rocky mound whose presence assisted in foiling the southward march of the British towards Albany during the American Revolution; then walk along a grassy, former towpath that was built in 1823 to expand trade from the Hudson River to Lake Champlain.

Saratoga National Historical Park: Hike or bike ride through rolling hills that were sites of crucial battles that determined the outcome of the American Revolution.

Geyser Park: Walk through a park with geysers and springs that were used in early times by Native Americans and later developed as medicinal waters for nineteenth- and twentieth-century health-seekers.

1 STARKS KNOB & SCHUYLERVILLE CHAMPLAIN CANAL TOWPATH

Location: Schuylerville (Saratoga County)
New York State Atlas & Gazetteer: p. 81, CD5

Fees: None

Hours: Starks Knob is open daily, dawn to dusk; the Champlain Canal towpath is open daily from dawn to dusk; the Schuyler House is open from Memorial Day through Labor Day, 9:30 AM–4:30 PM, Wednesday through Sunday, and is part of Saratoga National Historic Park, U.S. Department of Interior.

Accessibility: Starks Knob—short, level walk to bottom of hill, with a short but very steep climb up to top of rocky promontory; Champlain Canal towpath—1.0-mile walk on level ground

Level of Difficulty: Starks Knob, easy to moderate; Champlain Canal towpath, easy

Highlights:
- Scenic views from Starks Knob of Hudson River and Green Mountains of Vermont
- Old Champlain Canal, and ruins of the aqueduct and dry dock along towpath walk
- Schuyler House—former home of General Philip Schuyler— at end of towpath walk

Description: *Starks Knob* is a small hill formed out of an unusual volcanic rock, called pillow basalt. Equally unusual is the unique role this rocky hill played in deciding the fate of the American Revolutionary War.[1,2]

The "knob" is approximately seventy feet high. It was much taller at one time, before quarrying, and one side of the knob contains a rocky depression caused by former quarrying activities. This feature has caused some to mistakenly refer to the mound as an extinct volcanic cone because of its close resemblance to a volcano and the fact that the knob is composed of volcanic rock.[3]

Starks Knob is promoted and maintained by The Friends of Starks Knob and the Saratoga National Historical Park.

The Champlain Canal towpath is an unpaved stretch of the old, original Champlain Canal towpath. It connects the Schuyler House, on the southern end, with a small park at Champlain Barge Canal Lock 5 adjacent to the Canal Visitors Center located on Ferry Street. The Canal was built in 1823 to connect the Hudson River with Lake Champlain. The Schuyler House is the former residence of General Phillip Schuyler, Revolutionary War hero.

Directions: *To Starks Knob:* From the junction of Rtes. 29W & 4/32, drive north on Rt. 4/32 for 1.1 miles. Turn left onto Starks Knob Road and park immediately in the area on your right. Walk 0.05 mile up Starks Knob Road to the entrance to Starks Knob.

To the Champlain Canal towpath: From the junction of Rtes. 4/32 & 29E, drive approximately 0.1 mile east on Rt. 29 (Ferry Street). Parking for the towpath can be found to the right, behind the post office.

View of Hudson River from Starks Knob.

The Hikes

Hike #1—Starks Knob

There are two interesting short trails at the Starks Knob site. One trail leads to the base of Starks Knob and provides an excellent view of the scooped rocks, called pillow basalt. This trail begins on the north (right) side of Stark's Knob Road a short way uphill above the parking area. The trail is level and grassy, no more than several hundred feet in length. Seasonal wildflowers such as daisies, Queen Anne's lace, and day lilies border this broad trail. At the beginning of the trail there is a marker that describes the military and geological significance of Starks Knob.

The second trail begins on Starks Knob Road less than 0.05 mile west of the flat trail. This trail is short and steep, climbing rapidly through woods until you reach the narrow, rocky top. There are lovely views of the Hudson River and Northumberland Bridge to the north. The Green Mountains of Vermont can be seen in the distance.

Hike #2—The Champlain Canal Towpath

The walk begins about 0.1 mile east on Rt. 29 East (Ferry Street) from its junction with Rt. 4. There is parking to the right behind the post office. The grassy towpath is about 1.0 mile in length, with a plaque at the trailhead describing some of the features you will see. The trail ends on the property of the Schuyler House, which is worth a visit in itself if you are doing the walk between Memorial Day and Labor Day.

The first point of interest as you head south along the path is the large pond to your right. The pond is the former boat basin, which in its day was large enough for a canal barge to turn around.

West of the pond you will see, immediately to your right, the remains of an early dry dock. The dry dock was an area of the pond where boats navigating the canal in the 1800s could be floated in, positioned over racks, and repaired as needed. You will also observe the stone foundation remains of the old dam that was used to regulate the water level, and a stone drain.

Continuing south past the end of the pond, at about 0.2 mile, you can see the remains of the stone supports and abutments of the original Schuylerville aqueduct. The aqueduct was built to carry the canal and towpath over Fish Creek.

A footbridge now takes you across Fish Creek, where rapids can be viewed below. The path passes through a wooded area and then veers to the right to enter the lawn of the Schuyler House. This house was used as a summer residence for General Philip Schuyler and for later generations of his family.

History: *Starks Knob.* The two short trails up and around a rather small protrusion of rock provide a mountain of history, both military and geological.

Starks Knob was a key to winning the American Revolution. If this upthrust of rock had not been commandeered by General Stark (1728–1822)[4] and his men, the world might be very different today. On October 11, 1777, one of Burgoyne's German troops wrote, "This undertaking is still feasible, as the road on this side of the river is still unoccupied." The writer was not aware, however, that Colonial forces had just moved in overnight to occupy the strategic position of Starks Knob. The next morning the British troops awoke to discover that they were suddenly trapped, with no means of escape, in a bottleneck created by General John Stark. This maneuver has been referred to by historians as "corking the bottle."[5]

The Schuyler House

The Schuyler House is on property that was owned by the Schuyler family and dates back to the early 1700s. It is now a designated National Historic Site and part of Saratoga National Historic Park. The Schuyler House was burned by the British forces under General John Burgoyne during the final days of the Revolutionary War. The house that is now standing, with some modest renovation over the intervening years, was built by General Philip Schuyler in just seventeen days after the British surrendered. It was visited by George Washington, Benjamin Franklin, and Alexander Hamilton, among other notables.

General Philip Schuyler's House, circa 1930.

Field of Grounded Arms

The Field of Grounded Arms is located in Fort Hardy Park on Ferry Street. It is historically significant as the place where the British forces under General John Burgoyne laid down their arms and surrendered to the American forces under General Philip Schuyler during the Revolutionary War.

Saratoga Monument

The Saratoga Monument is a 155-foot-high obelisk located on a small hill overlooking the Hudson Valley. It marks the spot where the British forces made their last stand during the Battle of Saratoga.[9,10] Superb views of the Taconics and Green Mountains to the east and the Adirondacks to the northwest can be obtained from the top of the monument.

Near the bottom of the monument are four niches. Three are occupied by statues, while the fourth is empty. A statue of General Schuyler looks to the east. A statue of General Horatio Gates faces the north. A statue of Colonel Daniel Morgan faces the west. The empty niche, facing south, serves as a reminder of Benedict Arnold's treason. Arnold was a true American hero at the Battle of Saratoga and would have earned his rightful spot on the monument had it not been for his later attempt to deliver West Point into British hands.

The monument can be accessed from the south end of town, along Rt. 32, by turning west onto Burgoyne Street and driving uphill for 0.6 mile to where Cemetery Road comes in on the left. From there, the monument is on the left. From the west—driving east towards Schuylerville from Saratoga Springs—turn right onto Rt. 338, which leads to Burgoyne Street in 0.6 mile.

Saratoga Monument in Schuylerville, circa 1900.

Stalled at Schuylerville on October 13, 1777, General Burgoyne and his troops lost a large enough number of soldiers and the necessary forward momentum to reach and take Albany. On October 17, 1777, Burgoyne's army met final defeat at the Battle of Saratoga.

In addition to his success at Starks Knob, General Stark distinguished himself in other battles, including the Battle of Bennington where he is quoted as saying, "There are the Red Coats, and they are ours, or this night Molly Stark sleeps a widow"—an indication of his willingness to fight to the death.

Stark retired in 1783, having achieved the rank of major general. Thirty-two years later Stark was asked to speak at an anniversary celebration. He was unable to attend, but he sent a message to be read, in which he said: "Live free or die. Death is not the worst of evils." To this day his home state of New Hampshire has as its official motto, "Live free or die."

Starks Knob's geological history is equally fascinating.[6,7] The knob is formed from volcanic rock, a rather rare occurrence in eastern North America. The hill is formed out of a submarine pillow lava called pillow basalt.[8] The "pillows" formed when basalt lava flowed up from deep cracks in the earth, erupting under water and creating a ridge along the surface of the vent, 460 to 440 million years ago. As the lava continued to flow through the vent and cooled, ball-like "pillows" were formed. These formations are of such significance that classes of geology students and working geologists continually visit the site to study this geological phenomenon.

Champlain Canal Towpath. The Champlain Canal, sixty-four miles in length, was completed in 1823, two years before the Erie Canal was inaugurated. The Champlain Canal connected the Hudson River with Lake Champlain and was a commercial success until the twentieth century, when railroads became the primary means for commercial transport. The canal towpath is a remarkably well-preserved remnant of canal history.[11]

There is a direct historical connection between the Champlain Canal towpath and the Schuyler House at the southern end of the towpath. Both General Philip Schuyler and his son, Philip Schuyler II, played instrumental roles in the concept and construction of the Champlain Canal. When General Schuyler was in Europe from 1761–1762, he became interested in canals and studied their construction. He was principally interested in how they might be used in developing the internal resources of a country. If it had not been for the eruption of the American Revolution, he would have proceeded to muster support for building the canal immediately upon his return from Europe.

In 1776 General Schuyler told Benjamin Franklin that an uninterrupted water carriage between New York and Quebec could be accomplished by constructing a canal. It wasn't until the 1790s, however, that Schuyler and New

York Governor George Clinton laid out serious plans for a project to connect the Hudson River with Lake Champlain. Unfortunately, General Schuyler died in 1804 and the project stalled.

General Schuyler's son, Philip II, who lived with his uncle, Alexander Hamilton, was only sixteen years old when his father died. The young Philip proceeded with his education and graduated from Columbia College. Then, with the political tutelage of his eminent uncle, he lobbied for the construction of the Champlain Canal. Thanks to his tireless efforts, construction on the Champlain Canal began in 1817 and was completed in 1823, two years before the Erie Canal was opened.

SARATOGA NATIONAL HISTORICAL PARK   2

Location: Stillwater (Saratoga County)
New York State Atlas & Gazetteer: p. 81, D4-5

Fees: None for visitor center; modest day-use fee for hiking and biking

Hours: The visitor center is open year-round except for Christmas, Thanksgiving, and New Year's Day; the park roads are closed December through March.

Accessibility: There is easy access to all of the tour road stops, which total 9.0 miles in length; many of the paved pathways are wheelchair accessible.

Degree of Difficulty: Easy to moderate

Highlights:
- Buildings that date back to the American Revolution
- Monuments to Revolutionary War heroes
- Battlefield sites
- Views of the Hudson River and Green Mountains
- Visitor center with informational material on the Battles of Saratoga, including a short video; gift shop with books and souvenirs

Description: The Saratoga National Historical Park is the site of the Battle of Saratoga, a pivotal Revolutionary War American victory. The park encompasses 3,500 acres. The 9.0-mile tour road, which has ten marked historical sites, can be driven, biked, or hiked. As a bike adventure, the tour is ideal. You can travel to various historical points, secure your bike, and then hike at will. There is an off-road, 1.0-mile loop trail that passes the traditional gravesite of the British General Fraser, who was mortally wounded during the second battle of Saratoga.

The park visitor center, which includes a bookstore and a museum, is open year-round. The visitor center provides a brochure and a map highlighting the significant stops along the historical tour road. There is also an excellent videotape portraying the battles and providing an overview of the Revolutionary War period.[1]

Directions: The Saratoga National Historical Park is located forty miles north of Albany and approximately fifteen miles southeast of Saratoga Springs.

From the Adirondack Northway (I-87), get off at Exit 12 for Malta. Turn east onto Rt. 67 and continue for 0.4 mile. At a traffic light, cross over Rt. 9 and continue straight. You are now on Rt. 108. Continue east on Rt. 108 for 2.2 miles. When you come to Saratoga Lake, turn right onto Rt. 9P and drive east around the lake for 2.1 miles. Turn right onto Rt. 423 and drive east for 3.8 miles, then turn left onto Rt. 32. In just over 2.0 miles, turn right into the entrance to Saratoga National Historic Park. After 0.1 mile turn right again into the visitor center parking lot.

From Mechanicville, at the junction of Rtes. 4/32 & 67, drive north on Rt. 4/32 for over 5.0 miles. Turn left onto Rt. 32 where Rtes. 4 and 32 split. Drive west on Rt. 32 for 2.2 miles. Turn right onto Rt. 32 and drive north for just over 2.0 miles. The park entrance will be on the right.

The Hike

The main hike, bike, or auto trip is on a 9.0-mile, one-way road that wends its way through rolling hills. There are nine designated historical stops with parking areas along the way. These points of historical interest are tastefully interpreted by written plaques and sometimes by audiotapes. The one surviving structure—the Neilson house—is usually not open to the public, but its interior can be viewed through the windows.

The striking thing about this trek is the preponderance of natural fields and woodlands, including lovely overlooks of the Hudson River. Because of its primarily natural state, the park is home to a variety of wildlife, plants, and trees. It is common to see herds of deer in the fields at early morning or dusk, as well as rabbits, red fox, porcupines, and squirrels. Hawks, chickadees, red-winged blackbirds, and bluebirds have been noted, in addition to wrens, sparrows, and robins. A variety of wildflowers abound with the seasons, both in the woods and in the fields. Commonly seen are trout lilies, day lilies, violets, foam flower, hobble bush, daisies, chicory, Queen Anne's lace, and loosestrife, depending on terrain and time of year. It is the kind of place to which you will want to bring binoculars.

In the winter the roadway is closed, making for good cross-country skiing and snowshoeing. Snow trails are usually well defined, though not formally groomed.

Top of Middle Ravine, Saratoga Battlefield, circa 1930.

Brief descriptions of the nine historical tour stops are as follows:

1. Freeman Farm Overlook. On September 19, 1777, major battles between the British and American soldiers took place in these fields. John Freeman, a loyalist who fought with the British, was the owner of the farm. General Burgoyne and his troops appropriated the farm as their quarters. Morgan's Virginia riflemen opened fire on Burgoyne's troops, killing, among others, General Simon Fraser. The loss of General Fraser caused the British forces to retreat. There is no longer a building standing at this site.

2. Neilson Farm. Both before and after the war, this farm was maintained by John Neilson, who fought as an American patriot against Burgoyne's forces. Remarkably, the house still stands, although it has changed over time. About 30 percent of the house is original construction. Today, you will see a simple, one-room home that is furnished as it might have been during the time of the battle, when it was used as American officers' quarters. You can see the furniture and implements through the windows, but the building is rarely open to the public.

After the battles ended, the Neilsons resumed residence—all eleven of them! You may wonder how they managed when the entire family was indoors at the same time, such as at bedtime. Even with a sleeping loft, it would have been cramped. In 1926, New York State purchased the Neilson farm to create a state historic site. In the process of making the site, they removed portions of the house that were built in the 1800s. In 1938, New York State gave this building and the acreage known as "the battlefield" to the National Park Service, the current administrators.

3. American River Fortifications. This is the site of the military position established and maintained by Col. Thaddeus Kosciusko, a Polish engineer and volunteer for the American army. It was because of the barrier constructed by the patriot army and the cannons stationed here that the British forces under General Burgoyne were unable to proceed downriver to Albany. Instead, they attempted an attack on the American encampment at Bemis Heights—a strategic blunder.

4. Chatfield Farm. This site was an American outpost. Looking out from the ridge on Asa Chatfield's farm in 1777, the Americans saw the British moving toward the Barber farm. Beyond the ridge is the ravine across which Americans and British exchanged musket fire during the first and second battles.

5. Barber Wheat Field. This was the site of one of the pivotal battles. On October 7, 1777, American troops mortally wounded British General Simon Fraser and drove back the British and German soldiers who were attempting to outflank the American regiment stationed to the left. Burgoyne's troops were forced back to Freeman's farm.

6. Balcarres Redoubt. This battle fortification was named for Lord Balcarres, who commanded the British light infantry. This site was the most significant fortification of the British army between the Hudson River and the Breymann redoubt. The position of the redoubt is outlined by posts.

Driving through the park, circa 1940.

7. Breymann Redoubt. The site of this former battle fortification is also outlined by posts. It was named for Lt. Col. Henrich Breymann, commander of the German troops that were stationed here to guard the right flank of the British army. It was at this site that Benedict Arnold received a severe leg wound while bravely battling the British soldiers. Arnold ultimately captured this desirable military position. It was a decisive battle of the American Revolution, commemorated by Benedict Arnold's nearby "boot monument."

8. Burgoyne's Headquarters. The path at this stop leads to the site of Burgoyne's headquarters, which was a tent encampment.

9. The Great Redoubt. This site on top a hill overlooking the Hudson River was built by the British to guard their hospital, boat bridge, and supplies on the river flat. Burgoyne withdrew his troops to this site after the famous battle of October 7 when they were driven from the Freeman farm.

Each of the nine sites is described in greater detail on the site plaques and in the visitor center.

10. Loop Trail. In addition to the nine road stops already described, there is a one-mile loop trail on grassy terrain that begins at stop #10, the Fraser burial site. General Fraser was mortally wounded during the second battle of Saratoga, and was buried on the hill as he wished. It is said that shots flew through the air and landed near the mourners. Later, after the surrender, General Schuyler said that he would have called a ceasefire had he known of the funeral.

Beyond the gravesite the trail continues past markers indicating the placement of the former British hospital, Artillery Park, baggage area, and the Taylor House, where Fraser died. The remnants of the old Champlain Canal, constructed in the early 1800s, can also be seen along this trail.

History: The battles of Saratoga are acknowledged to be the turning point of the Revolutionary War. It was here on October 17, 1777, that the American army defeated an army of British forces led by General John Burgoyne, who had expected to march from Canada to Albany, thus conquering the upper Hudson Valley before joining with Sir Henry Howe to secure the rest of the valley all the way to New York City. The American forces under generals Schuyler and Gates, however, proved themselves adept at military strategies that impeded and finally defeated the British on the Saratoga battlefield. This defeat and the loss of momentum created a weak point in the plan of conquest for Burgoyne, who at battle's end commanded only 6,000 troops. On the other hand, the Saratoga victory vastly increased the morale of the patriots. By

American Headquarters, circa 1930.

October 1777, 20,000 American troops had rallied in Saratoga to defeat the British. Most important, once and for all, the Americans had secured the Hudson River corridor.

Brigadier General Thaddeus Kosciusko, a military engineer from Poland, is given credit for designing the strategic fortifications that assisted in bringing victory to the Americans.

Benedict Arnold distinguished himself during the battle at the Breymann Redoubt. Unfortunately, he later turned traitor and plotted to have West Point fall to the British. For two centuries his name has been synonymous with treason. Today, his reputation is a little less tarnished, but he is still an enigma.

It is interesting to note that the Continental Army was not racially segregated. Men of African descent fought alongside Caucasians. Some were still slaves, however. In 1819 some African-Americans who had fought in the war received government pensions.

The letters and journals of Baroness Friederike von Riedesel relating to the American Revolution and the battles of Saratoga eloquently describe the British encampment and the surrender of General Burgoyne to General Gates.[2] The baroness had traveled from Germany with her three very young children to join her husband, General Riedesel, who fought on the side of the British. A noblewoman by birth, she traveled across the ocean to Quebec and then down the Hudson Valley to be by her husband's side, come what may. It was to her temporary residence, the Taylor cabin, where the gravely wounded General Simon Fraser was brought for medical care. The baroness recounted assisting in his care until he died the following day. Meanwhile she watched as the Americans set fire to her new residence, which was visible in the near distance.

Fortunately for historians, Baroness von Riedesel related in some detail her experiences—from leaving Germany by coach, to setting sail from England to Canada, and finally her journey on to Saratoga. She also described the experiences she and her family encountered as prisoners of war after the surrender. It seems that as a woman of good standing and the wife of a general, she and her family were generally treated with deference. In fact, she and her children stayed in Albany as guests of General Philip Schuyler after the war.

3   GEYSER PARK

Location: Saratoga Springs (Saratoga County)
New York State Atlas & Gazetteer: p. 80, D3

Fees: Nominal fee charged during season, Memorial Day through Labor Day

Hours: Daily, dawn to dusk

Accessibility: Hike #1—0.1-mile stroll along a level path; Hike #2—0.1-mile walk down into a ravine

Degree of Difficulty: Easy for both hikes

Highlights:
- Spouting geyser
- Interesting tufa formation
- Historic springs

Description: Geyser Park is a 250-acre tract of land contained in the Saratoga Spa State Park, a 2,545-acre, state-owned reservation that in addition to Geyser Park contains a performing arts center (SPAC), the Gideon Putnam Hotel, Little Spa Theater, Lincoln Mineral Baths, an 18-hole championship golf course, and the Museum of Dance.

The hike through Geyser Park follows Geyser Brook along two sections of its length.[1,2] The main part of the hike starts from Hayes Spring and culminates upstream below the high bridge that leads visitors to the performing arts center. The second part of the hike begins upstream by Geyser Lake.

Directions: From I-87 (the Adirondack Northway), get off at Exit 12 for Ballston Spa and Malta. At the end of the exit ramp, turn left onto Rt. 67 and drive west for 3.4 miles. When you come to the traffic light at the south end of Ballston Spa, turn right onto Rt. 50 and proceed north for nearly 5.0 miles. Turn right at a sign indicating the entrance to Saratoga Spa State Park.

If you are approaching from Saratoga Springs (junction of Rtes. 50 & 9), drive south on Rt. 50 for 2.3 miles and turn left into the entrance for Saratoga Spa State Park.

As soon as you turn east into the park, you will see Hathorn Springs # 3 directly on your left. Proceed straight through the tollbooth and drive east for

0.1 mile. Turn left onto Geyser Loop Road, where a sign points the way to the geysers. The road quickly takes you past the Coesa Pavilion, on your left, and then the Hathorn Pavilion, to your right. Within 0.4 mile the road leads down to the bottom of a short hill. When you see the sign on your right for the Karista Pavilion, turn left immediately into a parking area on the opposite side of the road. You have reached the tiny parking lot for the Hayes and Orenda Springs.

To get to Geyser Lake from the entrance to Saratoga Spa State Park, turn onto Rt. 50 and drive north for 0.7 mile. When you come to a traffic light, turn right onto the Avenue of Pines. If you are approaching from Saratoga Springs (junction of Rts. 9 & 50), drive south on Rt. 50 for 1.6 miles and turn left at the traffic light onto the Avenue of Pines.

Proceed east. In slightly over 0.1 mile, you will see the left-hand turn for State Seal Spring. On the opposite side of the road is an old bottling plant that now houses the Saratoga Automobile Museum. Turn right as soon as you pass by the east side of the bottling plant. Once you are behind the bottling plant, turn right into a huge parking area and park in the far southwest corner.

The Hikes

Hike #1, from Hayes Spring:

The hike begins at a small parking lot next to Hayes Spring and follows a well-maintained walkway that parallels Geyser Brook and takes you along its south bank.

The first point of interest is Hayes Spring, which was established in 1938–1939 by the Camp Saratoga Works Progress Administration. The spring is located right at the beginning of the trail. You will see a square-shaped spring house, out of which two spigots issue. If you cup your hands and sip the water, you will notice a very strong mineral taste and smell. The water flowing from the spigots drops into a drain and is channeled underground to where it exits from the side of the creek bank. Walk over to the stone wall that forms the side of the stream next to the spring and look down. You will see not only where the spring waters exit, but also a huge deposit of minerals that has built up over the decades from the draining mineral waters.

As you look upstream, you will observe a spout of water shooting up well over ten feet into the air on the opposite side of the creek. You are looking at the Island Spouter, a geyser that is located on its own, self-created island, with the creek sweeping by on both of its sides. The entire island is one huge mineral deposit and is shaped like the shell of a dinosaur-sized turtle. As you walk past the Island Spouter, you will notice that parts of the island have been undercut by the stream.

Hays Spring and Coesa Creek with Island Spouter, Saratoga Spa, Saratoga Springs, N. Y.

The Island Spouter, circa 1940.

A short distance upstream from the geyser is a natural fall where the creek drops one foot over a ledge that spans the entire stream. Just beyond, you will reach an old dam about five feet high. Take note of the rusted section of pipe lying on the east bank of the stream just downstream from the dam.

To the left of the dam can be seen an enormous formation of tufa flowstone whose lower section crosses directly across the trail. The formation stands over thirty feet high and has been created by the outflow of Orenda Spring, located above the top of the embankment. This formation is without doubt the park's most distinctive and colorful attraction, for it is more indigenous to the hot springs of Yellowstone National Park than to anywhere else in northeastern New York. Although the formation looks like a brownish-orange mudslide, it is solid rock, called tufa or travertine, and is formed by deposits of colored minerals, mainly carbonates, that have been left behind by the water flowing over it.

Geologists estimate that the Island Spouter and Orenda Spring formation, both made out of tufa, are thickening at the rate of about two inches per year.[3] According to Strock, a research chemist at Simon Baruch Research Institute, this rate of deposit translates to roughly two tons of tufa per million gallons of water.[4] If you look closely, you will see that twigs and leaves have been instantly fossilized by this process.

Follow the main path, which takes you over and across the base of the formation. Look to your left and you will see numerous tiny openings, like post office boxes, in the flowstone.[5]

A short distance further you will come to the end of the path, at a point where the streambed suddenly bears left and then passes through a large pipe. A six-foot-high, stair-like waterfall, artificially created, can be seen at this point. This is a pretty spot, and there are enough large boulders around for you to find an unoccupied one to sit on and enjoy the view for a moment or two.

The stream and ravine did not always end at this point. At one time the creek made its way unencumbered by drain pipes until an embankment was created across the ravine to allow for the installation of a road.

If you were to follow the stream further northwest, you would eventually reach the dam at Geyser Lake near the junction of Rt. 50 and Gideon Putnam's "Avenue of Pines."

Hike #2, from Geyser Lake:

From the end of the parking lot behind the Saratoga Automobile Museum (a former bottling plant), follow a path southwest that leads immediately to Geyser Lake and the dam at the pond's outlet.[6] You will notice, just down from the trail, a tiny cement structure of more recent vintage next to the pond.

The path takes you along the edge of the ravine, where excellent views of the fifteen-foot dam can be obtained.[7] You will need to watch your footing, however, as the trail goes very close to the edge of the ravine.

If you look across the stream to the opposite bank, directly below the dam, you will see a pile of cement slabs as well as an intact cement building that once served as either a powerhouse or pump station.

Follow the path as it leads down to the bottom of the ravine. In days gone by, a tiny bridge crossed Geyser Brook in this general area.[8]

There is not much else to see at this point—only the cement relics of several old picnic tables next to trailside. The path quickly ends at an artificial embankment, where the stream continues through a large drain pipe. An old road crosses over the stream at the top of this embankment. It is possible to climb up out of the ravine here and continue following the creek downstream until you reach the Hayes Spring trail, below.

Back at the parking lot, you can walk northeastward around Geyser Lake for a short distance and enjoy the impossibly tall pines that reach high into the sky. There is nothing else to see by the pond, however, except for the former bottling plant (now the Automobile Museum) near where you parked.

History: The name "Saratoga" is derived from the Iroquois word *Sarach-togue,* meaning "place of swift water."[9] The word "Springs" was appended to Saratoga in recognition of the several naturally occurring bubbling springs that led to the early fame of the city.

Native Americans knew of the springs long before European settlers arrived. The location of the springs and their reputed curative powers were a carefully guarded secret, one which the natives did not wish to share with the Europeans.

The first known white man to visit the springs was Sir William Johnson, who was led to High Rock Spring. Johnson suffered from the aftereffects of an old musket ball injury to his leg and could barely get around. The Mohawks, having taken a liking to Johnson because he was fair-handed with the tribe (as well as being consort to the sister of a Mohawk chief), carried Johnson by stretcher to the springs in 1767, where he camped out and partook of the spring waters. Supposedly, within a short length of time, Johnson recovered enough that he was able to walk part of the way back under his own power.

Presumably, Johnson was not able to keep the spring a secret for long. High Rock Springs was subsequently visited by such famous eighteenth-century men as General Philip Schuyler, General George Washington, Alexander Hamilton, and Governor George Clinton in 1783.[10] By 1793, Dr. Valentine Seaman of New York had published a treatise on the springs of Saratoga and Ballston.[11]

Gideon Putnam came to the area in 1795 and settled near High Rock Spring. Putnam purchased lands near Congress Street and was instrumental in the development of Saratoga Springs, eventually building a tavern and board-inghouse in the village.

The medicinal properties of the various Saratoga springs were taken very seriously in the nineteenth century. William Stone, in his book *Reminiscences of Saratoga,* written in 1875, says of Hathorn and Champion springs: "Physicians, I believe, are passing favorably upon both; and from my own practical, rather than scientific, experiments, I am inclined to think that they will be found as reliable in a medicinal point of view as any other spring in this remarkable place."[12]

In 1833, Saratoga Springs began to become a prosperous destination when railroad passenger service was extended to Saratoga. The first engine with a train of carriages traveled from Schenectady to Saratoga on July 4, 1833. It was said by Mr. Gideon M. Davison, in his paper on July 7, 1833, that the number of strangers in the village "cannot be less than 1,000—at least twice as many as are here at this season of the year."[13]

Geyser Brook: Geyser Brook rises from two tributaries west of Saratoga Springs—Slade Creek and Hollow Creek—and flows into Kayaderosseras Creek north of Pelton Hill. The stream is impounded by a dam near the intersection of Route 50 and Gideon Putnam Road, where a small lake is formed. In the past, the creek was called Coesa Creek and the lake, which was once much larger, was known as Coesa Lake. At that time a pretty footbridge spanned the creek just downstream from the dam, allowing visitors to explore the area in an easier manner than is possible today. This was part of a trail system that once wound around the lake, enabling Victorians to stroll from one geyser and spring to the next.

It was in the area of Geyser Lake—called Ellis Corner in the nineteenth century—that the seeds were sown for the future spa city of Saratoga Springs. In the 1860s a small factory on the edge of Geyser Lake was established to produce nuts, bolts, and iron hardware. In the 1870s, while in the process of expanding the factory, the owners uncovered a spring. Realizing the commercial potential of the spring's uniquely flavored waters, they sunk a well, and thus sprouted Geyser Mineral Springs—the first of many springs that would eventually be discovered. Quickly the area became known as The Geysers. One spouting geyser was so spectacular that it was allowed to gush at full volume periodically so that incoming passengers on the Delaware & Hudson train would be enthralled as they passed by it.

The area around Geyser Lake was changed in the 1960s when Route 50—a highway running from Scotia to Saratoga Springs (and beyond)—was built, causing the demise of old structures near the lake including the building at Geyser Mineral Spring, which the state had been using as a warehouse. Even part of the lake was reclaimed in order to construct the road. The waters from Geyser Mineral Spring were not lost, however. Underground pipes transport the spring water to the nearby State Reservation Bottling House.

Geyser Lake: Geyser Lake, also known as Coesa Lake, was artificially created by the impoundment of a fifteen-foot-high dam. Today, a swamp-like section of the lake continues along the west side of Route 50, but it is hardly noticeable to travelers as they drive by.

At one time a number of springs and geysers, gas companies and bottling plants, could be found near and around the lake. Today, the State Seal Pavilion, housing Ferndell Spring, is directly across the road from the Saratoga Automobile Museum. Issuing from the spring are two spigots—one gushes noncarbonated water with low mineral content, while the other discharges

Geyser Brook, circa 1940.

carbonated mineral water from the former Geyser Spring on the south side of Geyser Lake. The noncarbonated waters are still in favor. You can often see people filling jugs from this spigot.

In 1872 the Triton Spouting Spring was created on the east side of Geyser Lake by the drilling of a 192-foot well. It was protected by a small-framed building that also served as a tiny bottling plant. Nearby was the Adirondack Spring (also known as Kissingen Spring and Hyperion Spring). This spring was drilled in 1872 and was also 192 feet deep. Along the west side of Geyser Brook, directly below the dam at Geyser Lake, was the Geyser Spouting Spring. A prominent well-driller named Jesse Button drilled it in 1870. Close to Geyser Lake was Aetna Springs, drilled in 1872 at a depth of 180 feet. The owners changed the name of the spring to Vichy Springs to capitalize on the French spring whose mineral waters were supposedly similar in taste. Twenty-five years later the French initiated a lawsuit, but they had allowed too much time to elapse and their suit failed.

Avenue of Pines: This spectacular lane is sixty feet wide, one mile long, and contains four rows of white pine trees. It connects Geyser Park with Lincoln Park, and Route 50 with Route 9.

Geyser Park: Geyser Park is the largest of four Saratoga parks developed by the State Conservation Commission. The other three are Congress (which is on village-owned land), High Rock, and Lincoln Park.

What made Geyser Park so special was that its springs consistently produced the largest flow of mineral water and the greatest gas content. Except for the bottling plant (which now houses the Saratoga Automobile Museum), all of the other structures related to the production of bottled mineral water and carbonated gas have been demolished over the years.

Other springs in Geyser Park[14]

Hathorn Spring #3, discovered in 1905, is located at the west entrance to the Saratoga Spa State Park. Water flows from a Tennessee marble foundation, which has become coated with minerals over the years.

Polaris Spring (also known as Ravine Spring) is a spouter that still gushes east of Geyser Brook and south of the Island Spouter.

Vale of Springs. Native Americans loved this part of what is now Saratoga State Park. They called it Dandaraga. When SPAC (the Saratoga Performing Arts Center) was created in 1966, however, the Vale of Springs was essentially paved over.

Part II: Capital Region

The nine Capital Region hikes showcase the rich cultural history of the Albany area and its environs. Some of the hikes contain intriguing natural features such as waterfalls, caves, and escarpments with stunning views, in addition to fascinating histories spanning from the pre-colonial period to the post–Industrial Revolution era. You can walk in the footsteps of early Native Americans at Indian Ladder and Peebles Island, imagine the daily struggles of the families who worked in the early-nineteenth-century mills at Rensselaerville and Troy, ponder what it must have been like to live in one of the most famous nineteenth-century Shaker communities, and tread the ground where Revolutionary War soldiers fought and died. The following areas are explored in this section:

Vischer Ferry Nature & Historic Preserve: Take a journey along the towpath of the Erie Canal, observing ruins of the old dry dock, the historic Whipple Bridge, and the scenic Mohawk River.

Peebles Island State Park: Hike on an island that was home to pre-colonial Mohicans and Mohawks, and that later became Dutch colonial farmland and a fallback position for colonials during the Revolutionary War.

Oakwood Cemetery: Meander through tombstone-lined rows where many famous Americans, including Uncle Sam Wilson, General Wool, and Emma Willard, are buried on rolling hills near magnificent waterfalls overlooking Lansingburgh and the Hudson River.

Burden Pond Environmental Park: Trek through a quiet, urban nature preserve, past a series of small cascades on the Wynantskill and remnants of machinery that once supported the bustling nineteenth-century Burden Iron Company.

Ann Lee Pond: Walk around an artificially created pond that was part of the earliest Shaker community in the country and near the home of Mother Ann Lee, founder of the Shakers.

Indian Ladder: Take a scenic walk along the base of a towering escarpment with waterfalls and caves that was once frequented by both Native Americans and early European settlers.

Bennett Hill Preserve: Climb to the top of a scenic hill overlooking the Helderbergs that rose above a once-prominent colonial farm.

Clarksville Cave Preserve: Explore the fascinating limestone karst above the roof of one of the Capital District's premier caves replete with intriguing lore and legends.

Edmund Niles Huyck Preserve: Hike on intersecting trails through lovely woods past an awe-inspiring waterfall and old stone ruins that mark a time when the area was teeming with mills.

VISCHER FERRY NATURE & HISTORIC PRESERVE

Location: Vischer Ferry (Saratoga County)
New York State Atlas & Gazetteer: p. 66, B3

Fees: None

Hours: Dawn to dusk

Accessibility: 4.0-mile trail that can be done in sections. The towpath provides a flat, fairly level surface and is used by both hikers and bicyclists.

Degree of Difficulty: Easy; moderate if you walk the entire length at one time.

Highlights:
■ Sections of the Erie Canal
■ Historic dry dock
■ Ruins of Lock 19
■ Historic Whipple Bridge

Description: The Vischer Ferry Preserve, cooperatively managed by the New York State Department of Transportation and the Town of Clifton Park, offers a unique opportunity to walk along a towpath that parallels the old historic Erie Canal. It is a memorable excursion via a trail over 4.0 miles long that takes you past old bridge abutments, an abandoned dry dock, a well-preserved lift lock, and various sections of stonework that form parts of the canal's old walls.[1–3]

Directions: From the Adirondack Northway (I-87), get off at Exit 8 for Vischer Ferry & Crescent. At the end of the exit ramp, turn right and drive east for nearly 0.4 mile. When you come to Dunsbach Road, turn right and drive south for over 0.7 mile. Turn right onto Clam Steam Road and drive southwest for 0.6 mile. When you come to Riverview Road, turn right. You will immediately cross over the Adirondack Northway, at 0.1 mile.
    Clutes Dry Dock Entrance: After nearly 0.8 mile from the beginning of Riverview Road, you will come to the parking area on your left for Clutes Dry Dock. This is the eastern terminus of the nature preserve.

Male Drive Entrance: Proceed west from Clutes Dry Dock for 0.4 mile. Park in an area on your left opposite Male Drive for access to the towpath trail.

Access to Clifton Park Water Authority: In over 0.3 mile from Male Drive, you will see a secondary park entrance that also serves as an access road to the Clifton Park Water Authority. From here, if you walk southwest you will reach the Whipple Bridge; going east will take you to the end of the preserve at Clute's Dry Dock.

There are also secondary trail options, including a loop that will take you south to the Mohawk River and then back up to the Whipple Bridge.

Whipple Bridge Entrance: From the Clifton Park Water Authority entrance, proceed west on Riverview Road for nearly 0.4 mile (or 0.8 mile from Male Road). Parking for the Whipple Bridge can be found on both sides of the road. If you hike southwest, you will reach historic Lock 19; if you go east, you will arrive at Clute's Dry Dock.

Ferry Drive Entrance: From the Whipple Bridge, continue west on Riverview Road for over 1.8 miles. Turn left onto Ferry Drive and proceed south for over 0.1 mile to a parking area. If you walk northwest from the cul-de-sac, you will reach the power plant and dam spanning the Mohawk River. From here there are wonderful views of the Mohawk River, Lock 7, and Goat Island.

If you walk southeast, you will reach the remnants of Lock 19 within 1.0 mile.

Vischer Ferry Hydroelectric Project: From Ferry Drive, continue west on Riverview Road for nearly 1.2 miles. Turn left opposite Sugar Hill Road and drive south for 0.2 mile to an overlook provided by the Vischer Ferry Hydroelectric Project. The overlook affords a tantalizing view of the Mohawk River, along with Lock 7 (near the southern bank), Goat Island (nearly one-half of the way across the river from the northern bank), and a long dam extending across the full width of the river. Although the overlook is not part of the hiking trail that parallels the Mohawk River and the old Erie Canal, it is near the preserve's western terminus, which ends just east of the power plant.

Park in the designated area. No unauthorized motor vehicles are allowed any further, but you are permitted to follow the paved road on foot as it goes steeply downhill. When you come to the point where the road does a U-turn, bearing west to the power plant gate (where no access is permitted), continue straight ahead to the western entrance to the hiking path. This access is made available through the civic-minded generosity of the New York Power Authority.

Vischer Ferry, circa 1940.

The Hikes

The hike has been broken up into five sections.

Hike #1—Clute's Dry Dock

Only the stone walls of the dry dock remain. Gone are the various buildings that once existed in close proximity.

The dry dock was built in 1825 by a man named Volvyders. It was later re-established in 1852 by Nicholas J. Clute. From that point on it served as a focal point for a settlement that grew up around the dock, servicing, repairing, and building boats. According to a historic marker at the site, the settlement was abandoned in 1907. Two of the homes in this settlement survived when they were relocated to nearby Male Road. A wonderful picture of Clute's Dry Dock prior to the creation of the Barge Canal can be seen in Washington & Smith's *Crossroads and Canals: The History of Clifton Park*.[4,5]

The dry dock is rectangular-shaped, measuring roughly eighty feet by sixty feet. Across from the entranceway to the dry dock, on the opposite bank of the Erie Canal, is a stone wall where boats needing repairs presumably moored while waiting to enter the dry dock. Just west of the entranceway can be seen a smaller channel.

Hike #2—Whipple Bridge

The iron truss Whipple Bridge, which originally crossed the Mohawk River at Sprakers, was completed in 1869 by Squire Whipple, an 1830 graduate of Union College. In 1919, when the Erie Canal was abandoned, the bridge was moved to Fonda, where it then spanned the Cayudatta Creek, a medium-size stream that rises near Gloversville. Eventually, the bridge went into decline.

With its demise imminent, the Whipple Bridge was salvaged by Dr. Francis E. Griggs, Jr. who, along with students and faculty members of Union College and other benefactors, rehabilitated it and set the bridge across the old Erie Canal in its present location, where it now provides ready access to the towpath from Riverview Road.

In earlier days, Public Bridge #46 crossed over the Erie Canal at the point where the Whipple Bridge now stands, extending VanVranken Avenue further south to the old settlement of Fort's Ferry. It was later replaced by a culvert, and that is how things remained until more recent times.

Hike #3—Old Lock 19

According to an historical marker adjacent to Lock 19, this double-chamber lock was constructed in 1842 during a period of canal enlargement.[6] The lock had three compartments and provided a lift of 8.5 feet. Some forty-three years later, further enlargements were made so that a minimum of two boats could be accommodated on each side. The lock's stonework remains intact and essentially as it looked during the heyday of the Erie Canal, with the exception of the wooden timbers, which have long since rotted away. The stones were quarried at Rotterdam Junction, west of Schenectady.

According to historical accounts, up to ninety-five boats a day passed through the lock.

Hike #4—Old Ferry Route

At the south end of Ferry Drive, you will come to a cul-de-sac where an historic marker serves to bring the present roadway and its dead end into historical perspective. The marker explains how Eldert Vischer operated a rope ferry, taking passengers across the Mohawk River at this site.

In 1900 a toll bridge was put up to facilitate river crossings, but it only endured until 1902, a victim of the Mohawk River's ferocious unpredictability. You can see the surviving bridge abutments on opposite sides of the river, with the abutment along the north bank being directly in front of the cul-de-sac at the river's edge.[7]

Just west of the cul-de-sac can be seen the continuation of the Erie Canal, which is surprisingly deep and intact. Old limestone blocks line the beginning of the northern wall of the canal.

Just upstream from Vischer Ferry, the canal system ultimately brought boats to a height of 196 feet above the Hudson River, nearly the equivalent of a twenty-story building.[8] Over sixty-five feet of this total was the result of having to bypass Cohoes Falls, located in the city of Cohoes.

The fixed dams constructed at Crescent and Vischer Ferry were each over 2,000 feet long, with powerhouses to harness the tremendous energy of the Mohawk River. If you wish to undertake a side trip, the long dam at Crescent can be accessed by driving up Waterford Flight A Road from Waterford and following a trail that leads from the road's terminus to the north bank of the dam.

Hike #5—Vischer Ferry Hydroelectric Plant

At the western terminus of the preserve can be seen the Vischer Ferry Hydroelectric Plant, as well as a 2,000-foot-long dam, Goat Island, and Lock 7 (which is located across the river along the southern bank).

The hydroelectric plant was constructed in 1925 and is still serviceable.

Goat Island is a sprout of land near the northern bank whose upper level of shale steps forms a series of cascades when sufficient water is flowing over the Lock 7 Dam, which rises above the island.

The Niskayuna lock and dam were completed in 1913 and remain a vital link in the modern barge canal system.

If you look across to the other side of the river from the pathway, you will see the scenic Mohawk–Hudson Bikeway, which connects Albany with Rotterdam Junction and provides an excellent outing for walkers, joggers, rollerbladers, and bikers.

At one time a substantial Native American village existed along the south bank of the Mohawk River, between the Niskayuna Isle peninsula and the confluence of the Lisha Kill and Mohawk River.

Between the Vischer Ferry Hydroelectric Plant and Ferry Drive, the pathway follows a very deep and pronounced section of the old Erie Canal.

History of the Erie Canal: Most of the hiking paths parallel the old Erie Canal. Work on the Erie Canal was begun locally in 1822 and completed in 1825. Almost immediately, the size of the canal proved to be too narrow and shallow to meet the requirements of boats, which were growing in both size and number. As a result further enlargements were made in the Capital Region section of the canal in 1842.

The canal provided a navigable system for transporting goods and people from Albany to Erie (a town that came into existence only because of the canal's terminus, and namesake, at Lake Erie). Informally known as "Clinton's Ditch," after New York State Governor Dewitt Clinton, it was a marvel of engineering in its time and remains impressive even by today's standards.

The canal started from the Hudson River at Waterford, bypassed Cohoes Falls, and crossed the Mohawk River via a 1,188-foot-long aqueduct over to Crescent. From there it proceeded to Rexford, where it again crossed over the Mohawk River—this time across an aqueduct 748 feet long—and on into Schenectady. From Schenectady it continued west to Buffalo following preexisting east-west waterways—such as the Mohawk River, Oneida Lake, Seneca River, and the Clyde River—to avoid mountainous obstructions. It is said that if the canal had to be built in a south-north orientation, the project might never have been finished, since the canal would have had to cut across the geological grain of numerous mountains and hills.

The boats and small barges traversing the canal were pulled along by sure-footed mules and horses trotting the towpath adjacent to the waterway. (The trees now adorning the towpath at the water's edge were not in existence when the canal was bustling with traffic.)[9]

More about Ferries: Eldert Vischer didn't establish the first ferry in this area. That honor goes to the Fort family, who set up the first river crossing in 1728 at Fort's Ferry—a tiny community that once existed south of the Whipple Bridge. Eldert Vischer, however, did have the good fortune to be located next to the community of Vischer Ferry, which continued growing and prospering as time went on. In its prime the village contained three stores, a blacksmith shop, a hotel, two schools, a carriage maker, a harness shop, three mills, and a post office. As the village prospered, so did Eldert Vischer.

The ferry was located next to a brick house that Eldert's father, Nicholas Vischer, had built earlier. Both Vischer's ferry and Fort's ferry were used by farmers and their families to get to Schenectady or Albany to buy or sell produce and goods.

The ferries were simple, flat barges with hinged ends that could be raised and lowered so as to assure solid footing on each bank of the river. A rope, stretched across the river between two rigid poles, passed through a pulley on the boat, thus allowing the ferrymen to pull the boat from one shore to the other.

PEEBLES ISLAND STATE PARK 5

Location: Cohoes (Saratoga County)
New York State Atlas & Gazetteer: p. 67, B4-5

Fees: Vehicle fee, currently $6.00/day, weekends from May 1 to Memorial Day, daily from Memorial Day to Labor Day, and weekends from Labor Day to Columbus Day

Hours: Year-round, 7:30 AM to sunset

Accessibility: Fairly level walk along old roads and well-groomed trails

Degree of Difficulty: Easy

Highlights:
- Views of the Hudson and Mohawk rivers from island cliffs
- Breastworks dating back to the American Revolution
- Old factory, now home to the historic preservation unit of the New York State Department of Parks, Recreation, and Historical Preservation

Description: Peebles Island (also spelled Peobles in times past) is an oasis of natural beauty and history that rests between the once heavily industrialized cities of Cohoes and Troy. The island is one of several small bodies of land formed at the confluence of the Mohawk River and the Hudson River—New York State's two most dynamic river valley systems.

A marvelous trail system extends around the perimeter of the island along the edge of a steep escarpment and past old dams, rapids, a whirlpool, and even a small, broad cascade. It also passes by breastworks (old defense fortifications) from Revolutionary War days and an area of low-lying land near the confluence of the Hudson and Mohawk rivers that was once occupied by Native American villages. In addition there are multiple trails crisscrossing the island. When added to the length of the perimeter trail, these crisscrossing trails give the avid hiker a chance to negotiate more than three miles of paths and walks.[1]

The 132-acre island is listed on the National Register of Historic Places. The state park contains 190 acres and includes Peebles Island and a narrow strip of land on the northeastern section of Van Schaick Island. Several historic, abandoned buildings that once constituted the Matton Shipyard may be found on this section of Van Schaick Island.

The kiosk at the north end of the parking area provides interesting information on the history of the island.

Directions: From Albany, proceed north on I-787 and turn right onto Ontario Street (Rt. 470) just before you reach the end of Rt. 787 at Cohoes. Drive east on Ontario Street, crossing over several small islands in the process. At 0.6 mile, turn left onto Delaware Ave. Go north on Delaware Ave. for 0.9 mile, crossing over an old railroad bridge and onto Peebles Island. Park in the parking area, next to the old Cluett, Peabody & Company Factory.

Peebles Island can also be accessed from Waterford. From the junction of Rtes. 4 & 32 in the center of Waterford, drive east on Rt. 4 for less than 0.05 mile, then turn right onto Second Street. Proceed south on Second Street for 0.2 mile. You will come to a one-lane bridge with a traffic light. The bridge (an old, converted railroad bridge) will take you from Second Street directly over to Peebles Island.

The Hikes

The main walk starts from the parking lot at the old Cluett, Peabody & Company factory and follows a path that leads along the fenced-in northern border of the property. This is the beginning of the yellow-blazed perimeter

A number of islands have formed at the confluence of the Hudson and Mohawk rivers. Photograph circa 1900.

trail. All of the trails are color-coded, following a fairly logical system: yellow indicates the perimeter trail; the white trails lead across the island's length; and the red trails connect the perimeter to the interior of the island.

Before embarking on the trek, however, take a few minutes to walk over to the northeast end of the island, which is close at hand. You will notice a series of grassy mounds that were once part of the breastworks for the colonial army during the Revolutionary War. The breastworks are located directly next to the southeast end of the bridge that leads over to Waterford. Also take note that the land just below the breastworks is noticeably lower in elevation and closer to the water level than other sections of the island, which is why it is so unusually fertile. Its low elevation made it subject to periodic flooding in times past.[2] Basing their conclusions on the numerous shards of pottery and Native American artifacts that have been found in the area, archeologists believe that Mohawk villages once occupied this site. In 1630 Kiliaen Van Rensselaer made note that Mohican tribes had a settlement at the confluence of the Mohawk and Hudson Rivers.[3] Van Rensselaer purchased this land from them.

If you walk over to the outdoor pavilion southeast of the breastworks, you will be rewarded with excellent views of the Hudson River landscape from an observation platform located directly at the river's edge. Should you return to this platform at different times of the day, it will become readily apparent that the Hudson is a tidal river. The shoreline contracts and expands on a regular, periodic cycle. Next to the pavilion is a plaque that explains how the Hudson River was known to Native Americans as "the river that flows two ways" because of its tidal variations.

Return to the parking lot and follow the yellow-blazed trail that parallels the metal fence, proceeding west. You will immediately pass by additional grassy mounds on your right, which were also part of the early Revolutionary War fortifications.[4]

When you clear the north side of the old factory, look to your left and you will see an old farmhouse next to the factory and enclosed by the same high, metal fence. The farmhouse was built in the 1840s. It is said that Herman Melville once rowed out to the island with one of the elder Peebles (probably Garret Peebles, who was married to Maria Van Schaick, a relative of Melville's) in order to court a female member of the Peebles family. It would seem that Melville ultimately met with little success, for nothing further is mentioned about this courtship.

Once you reach the end of the field behind the factory, you will come to a fork where two roads/paths diverge. The path to the left leads towards Van Schaick Island; the one to the right continues straight ahead and then turns right several hundred feet further uphill, heading towards to the west side of the island. Both of these roads/paths are marked with yellow blazes and eventually follow the perimeter of the island. These are the trails of choice to take if you want to enjoy continuous views from the top of a high escarpment. These trails will lead you past shadblow trees, along steep bluffs, and through a profusion of flowers that vary in brilliance depending upon the time of the year. In late May, red and yellow columbine bloom on the rocky escarpment.

Hike #1—Nature Hike:

At the fork in the road at the end of the field behind the factory, follow the yellow-blazed trail leading off to the left, going southward. Within 0.3 mile, after a dip in the road, you will come to a junction. Take the red-blazed side path to your left, which leads quickly to the escarpment trail. From here you will obtain exciting views of the Mohawk River's middle sprout, as well as Buttermilk Falls, off in the distance. The middle sprout is one of five sprouts formed as the Mohawk River makes its way into the Hudson River through a series of islands that act like strainers.

As you follow the trail along the edge of the escarpment, you will be impressed not only by the views, but by how high up you are and how vertical the escarpment wall is. Very quickly the yellow-blazed trail enters on your right, which means that the red-blazed path was simply a side spur, getting you down to the escarpment edge in a more expedient fashion. Near the southeasternmost extension of this trail, 0.1 mile from where the red-blazed trail rejoins the yellow-blazed trail, you will arrive at Buttermilk Falls (which one of the park's kiosks refers to as Horseshoe Falls). Buttermilk Falls is a fairly low, but

Farmhouse built in the 1840s. Photograph 2005.

broad cascade. You will also observe how a large whirlpool has eroded a stupendous, semicircular pothole into the escarpment base of Van Schaick Island's northwest perimeter. When you stand on the top of the escarpment overlooking Buttermilk Falls, be sure to look back at the side of the bluff (above which you were walking earlier). You will see large, almost cave-like depressions in the escarpment wall.

Just past this high point overlooking the falls, you will come to a small path that leads down to the bedrock at the top of the falls. Once you have reached the level of the stream, you will be able to see just how sharply inclined the bedding of the river is at this point. At the southeastern point of Peebles Island, you can make out the south sprout of the Mohawk River as it makes its way down between Van Schaick Island and Simmons Island. There are good views there looking south at the various islands, which are interconnected by short bridges.

Continuing wst around the knobby head of Peebles Island and over to its southwest side, you will observe a huge, long dam just below the Rt. 32 bridge that spans the Mohawk River. The dam is far longer than the bridge. Over 1,000 feet farther up the Mohawk River from the Rt. 32 bridge, but not visible because of the intervening gorge containing it, is Cohoes Falls—a mighty, sixty-five-foot-high waterfall.

As you proceed north along the western perimeter trail, you will end up paralleling the north sprout of the Mohawk River, a section that contains several distinct islands. The first body of land encountered is Second Island, followed by Goat Island. Look closely at their shorelines and you will notice tiny, camouflaged shelters used by duck hunters for concealment. The low areas visible to the east, some containing intermittent pools, are sections of an old river channel that was abandoned as the river cut down to its present level.

Continue walking along high bluffs that overlook the river. Just after you pass by Goat Island, you will see, directly below, a long dam that stretches all the way across the Mohawk River past the prow of one island and on to a tiny island just north of Goat Island. The dam starts up again on the west side of this tiny island and continues straight over to the west bank of the Mohawk River, although this section of the dam is not easily visible from Peebles Island.

When you reach the part of the escarpment overlooking the dam, take note that you are now standing on the highest portion of the trail, nearly ninety feet above the level of the river. The dam itself is quite impressive. It is made of cement, with the upper section consisting of wooden slats. In one part of the dam, a huge tree dangling over the edge of the barrage has punched out one of the slats, allowing the water to come through in full force.

In less than 0.1 mile from the dam overlook, you will come to a kiosk on your right that provides information on the bald eagle and the 1976 New York State Bald Eagle Restoration Project.

Peebles Island is steeped in history. Photograph 2005.

Continuing further north along the escarpment trail, you will see Bouck Island, just south of Waterford. Shortly thereafter, the trail bears to the right and pulls away from the escarpment. When you come to a junction, bear left, following the yellow blazes. Then turn left again onto a main road/path that quickly returns you back to the factory and the parking lot.

Hike #2—History Hike:

Starting at the parking lot, continue past the west end of the old Cluett, Peabody & Company factory. When you come to the fork at the end of the field, go straight (to your right) and then take your first right, following the yellow blazes. You will now be proceeding north.

Within 0.05 mile you will notice to your left a number of large depressions in the earth. (These depressions may be difficult to see except in the late fall or early spring when vegetation is sparse.) These are the remnants of gravel pits that were short-lived attempts at mining the island in the early 1900s. These pits were easily excavated because they were already pre-existing holes in the bedrock that had been filled in with glacial till during the last ice age.

Continue a short distance farther and then turn right where the path forks. This is a continuation of the yellow-blazed trail. Very quickly you will arrive at a point where the escarpment begins. Look down from the bluffs and you will see what looks like a tiny creek flowing between Peebles Island and another, small body of land. Several centuries of sedimentation have virtually filled in what at one time was a channel between Peebles Island and a distinct and separate segment of land.

As soon as you begin following the top of the escarpment south, you will come to a point where a faint trench crosses the path. Pay close attention; you can easily walk by it without noticing. You will observe that the trench continues into the woods and creates a rather large, U-shaped pattern. This is the outline of an artillery fort.

When you return to the parking lot, walk over to the northeast end of the island next to the old railroad bridge (now converted to accept vehicular traffic) that comes across from Waterford. Look west up the Mohawk River to where the New York State Barge Canal (the old Erie Canal) comes in, near the Mohawk's confluence with the Hudson River. Take note of how Waterford has developed the north bank of the Mohawk River into a marvelous little port.

Geology: According to Chuck Porter, regional geologist, "The black rocks making up much of the area are Ordovician Canajoharie Shale—mostly black shale with some sandstone beds. Deposited in deep oceanic water on the edge of ancient North America around 450 million years ago, they have been tilted and crumpled in several mountain-building episodes. Large faults are visible, often with white quartz infillings."[5]

History: Because of its unique location, Peebles Island has played a vital role in the history of the Capital Region. A kiosk by the parking lot provides ample historical background on the island.

It is believed that the Mohawks first occupied the island in the early 1200s, erecting a small village (called a "castle") on the island's north side where the land was most fertile. Native Americans typically constructed their villages along rivers, and often at the confluence of two major streams. In the case of Peebles Island and the islands adjacent to it, the shallow waters provided a convenient ford for crossing the Hudson River (which is how Waterford—"water ford"—came to be named). Before the Federal Dam was built between Troy and Green Island, a ford to Waterford existed just north of the Troy city limits. A road still goes down to the east side of the ford.[6]

In 1630, Kiliaen Van Rensselaer purchased from the Mohicans a sizable tract of land on the west side of the Hudson River. This tract of land extended from Beeren Island (south of Albany), to Smack's Island.[7]

In 1668, Philip Pietersen Schuyler and Goosen Gerritsen van Schaick were granted three small islands, one of them being Peebles Island. Van Schaick Island, named after Goosen van Schaick, is in close proximity to Peebles Island. Van Schaick Island is further north and forms the eastern perimeter of the whirlpool by Buttermilk Falls. It is Van Schaick Island that

47

Delaware Avenue traverses, leading you across an old, renovated railroad bridge to Peebles Island. The Peebles, for whom the island is named, were descendants of Goosen Van Schaick. It is likely that crops were raised and cattle were herded on Peebles Island during the Colonial era.[8]

The Van Schaick house, originally built in 1735 and still standing, is located on Van Schaick Island near the intersection of Van Schaick and Delaware Avenue. This home was probably used as Colonial army headquarters by General Philip Schuyler and General Horatio Gates between August 18 and September 8, 1777.

General Schuyler's main army occupied Van Schaick Island during the Revolutionary War. Peebles Island was assigned to a Polish patriot and military engineer named Thaddeus Kosciusko (1740–1817), who supervised a small corps of men and built three redoubts (small forts) on the island.[9] At that time Peebles Island was known as Haver Island.[10,11] (Haver is the Dutch word for "oats," presumably at one time a main crop on the island.) Kosciusko's name has not been forgotten in the Capital Region. The bridge spanning the Mohawk River at Crescent on the Adirondack Northway (I-87) is now named the Thaddeus Kosciusko Bridge.[12]

The outcome of the Revolutionary War turned on the Battle of Saratoga. If that fateful battle had gone awry for the Americans—if General Burgoyne and the British army had been victorious over General Gates and the Colonials—then Peebles Island would have played a much larger role in the history of this country. Peebles Island was the next line of defense against the British, whose goal it was to drive south down the river. Grassy mounds that were a part of the breastworks constructed by Kosciusko are visible on the northeast end of the island near the bridge connecting Waterford and Peebles Island, and may be found at the beginning of this hike, next to the old Cluett, Peabody & Company factory.

The Cluett, Peabody & Company factory is a reminder of Troy's role as a thriving center of the textile industry in the nineteenth century. The Cluett, Peabody & Company factory was a bleachery (a building where textiles were bleached) that began operating in 1909[13,14] to assist the main factory in Troy in turning cotton cloth arriving from the South into collars and shirts.[15] When New York State purchased Peebles Island in 1972,[16] the island was converted into a state park. Today, the old factory building serves as the warehouse for the historic preservation unit of the New York State Department of Parks, Recreation, and Historical Preservation, and as a workshop for conservators. It is open to the public each spring.

The abandoned buildings of the former Matton Shipyard can be seen 0.2 miles south of the Peebles Island / Van Schaick Bridge along the east side of Delaware Avenue. Approaching from the south, the shipyard buildings will be the first historic structures you will see before reaching Peebles Island. The shipyard was started in 1916 by John E. Matton, but this was not his first venture. Prior to that, Matton had been running a boat building and repair shop on the original Champlain Canal in Waterford. Reputedly, the Matton Shipyard built more barges, tugboats, and sailing craft than any other business on the canal system.[17] Altogether, it manufactured 345 vessels, including Navy sub-chasers. The web site of the State Council of Waterways (SCOW) has a photo gallery with a picture of the Matton Shipyard.[18] It is interesting to note that it wasn't until 1938 that the Matton Shipyard's manufacturing process changed from wood to steel. The shipyard was eventually sold to Bart Turecamo of Oyster Bay in 1964. In 1983 the shipyard was closed for good. It was acquired by New York State in 1990, and is now part of the Peebles Island State Park.

6 OAKWOOD CEMETERY

Location: North Troy (Rensselaer County)
New York State Atlas & Gazetteer: p. 67, BC4-5

Fees: None

Hours: Year-round, dawn to dusk; cemetery gates open at 9:00 AM and close at 4:30 PM sharp

Restrictions: No thoroughfare allowed; trucks and commercial vehicles prohibited

Accessibility: Slightly hilly terrain crisscrossed by roads. The walk is fairly easy; the hike to the waterfall on Gould Creek does require a bit more effort because of the trail's steady descent.

Degree of Difficulty: Easy

Highlights:
- Waterfalls
- Views overlooking Lansingburgh, Troy, and the Hudson River
- Tiffany windows in the Gardner Earl Chapel
- A variety of monuments and mausoleums commemorating notable people who are buried in the cemetery

Description: Although graveyards are generally not sought after for hiking excursions, there is much to recommend the Oakwood Cemetery—wild areas of dark, foreboding ravines and supple waterfalls, as well as the history contained in its sprawling monuments of marble and granite.

The natural areas consist of several small ponds. Small streams drop into deep-cut gorges from the outlets of two of these ponds, producing several waterfalls. The most notable waterfalls are located in an area called the Devil's Kitchen, formed at the northwest side of the cemetery.[1]

The cemetery contains nearly 60,000 gravesites and provides a fascinating tour of how some of the more illustrious residents of Troy and nearby communities have been commemorated.[2]

Directions: From I-787, take Exit 9E for Troy / Bennington. As soon as you cross over the Hudson River, you will come to a stoplight. Get in the left-hand lane. Within 0.1 mile after starting up the hill, you will come to another stoplight. Turn left onto Rt. 40 and drive north for 1.1 miles. Turn left into the entrance for Oakwood Cemetery. In slightly over 0.1 mile you will pass by the Gardner Earl Chapel & Crematorium on your left. You will come to the huge Vanderheyden Bell (also on your left) at approximately 0.2 mile. The bell was cast in 1893 by the McNeeley Bell Company of Troy and weighs 3,000 pounds. The bell serves as a natural starting point for the various treks.

To the Nature Trail: From the Vanderheyden Bell, proceed north through the cemetery for approximately 0.6 mile. As soon as you pass between two ponds, turn left and drive west for 0.2 mile, staying as close to the edge of the pond (called Long Lake) as you can. Park at the outlet end of Long Pond, close to the escarpment edge overlooking Lansingburgh.

To the waterfall near the Gardner Earl Chapel & Crematorium: Park off the road close to the Vanderheyden Bell. You will notice a small pond between the Vanderheyden Bell and the crematorium. The waterfall is just downstream from the top of this pond. Follow the road downhill from the Vanderheyden Bell for several hundred feet for views of the cascade, looking back. If you follow the stream further downhill, you will see several additional cascades before you reach the Uncle Sam Bikeway, but these are minor falls and fairly insignificant.

To the Tombstone Trail: You can either drive or walk this route. From the Vanderheyden Bell, follow the directions given above in Hike #2 to each tombstone, mausoleum, and gravesite.

Scene in Oakwood Cemetery, circa 1940.

The Hikes

Hike #1—The Nature Trail:

The main hike begins from the west end of Long Lake at the pond's outlet (refer to "Directions" to reach Long Lake). Take note that both Long Lake and the smaller pond to the east are artificial bodies of water created by the impoundment of Goulds Creek. You will notice at the outlet a small, but very pretty cascade created where the waters of Goulds Creek drop into a narrow, deep ravine. As you proceed to the edge of the escarpment, which overlooks the town of Lansingburgh, you will discern a trail proceeding downhill, going north and paralleling both the edge of the escarpment and Goulds Creek.

In less than 0.2 mile the trail takes you around a bend and you will suddenly find yourself going west. You will observe at this point a fairly long, flattened cascade to your right. This will look increasingly more like a waterfall when you look back as you descend down the trail. This is the scenic area referred to as the Devil's Kitchen.

If you continue to the bottom of the gorge, you will encounter the Uncle Sam Bikeway, which parallels the east side of Lansingburgh.

A secondary hike begins at the northeast side of the Gardner Earl Chapel & Crematorium, where you can follow the stream downhill, walking along the descending road. Within several hundred feet you will have a clear view, looking back, of a medium-sized cascade that is formed just below the tiny, artificially created pond next to the crematorium.[3]

If you continue downhill a short distance further to the point where the road crosses over the stream, there are several small, but pretty cascades located downstream before the bikeway is encountered, in the "Q" section of the cemetery.

Hike #2—The Tombstone Trail:

To the Russell Sage Mausoleum: From the Vanderheyden Bell, go north (straight ahead), following a green marker that points the way to Uncle Sam's grave. At 0.2 mile you will come to an oval circle where the road divides. Bear to the right. Immediately you will see the William E. Yourt monument on your left. Turn right opposite this monument at a tiny sign that says "Sect. I-1." Drive up the hill for less than fifty feet. The Russell Sage Mausoleum, unnamed, is directly on your right. Next to the mausoleum, on the west side, is a monument to Marta Winne, wife of Russell Sage, and on the east side is a stone bench with the head of Medusa carved into its back. Just up the hill from Russell Sage's mausoleum, to the left, is the Warren Family Mortuary Chapel, which is an imposing structure many times the size of Sage's mausoleum.

To General George H. Thomas' tombstone: From the Vanderheyden Bell, drive north (going straight). At 0.15 mile, turn right at a sign reading "Sect. N" and drive uphill. In another 0.05 mile, turn left. Almost immediately you will come to the grave site of General Thomas on your left, enclosed with a number of other graves by a black iron fence.

To Emma Willard's grave site: From the Vanderheyden Bell, turn left as if to head down the steep hill to the main cemetery office. Just before you start down the steep hill, turn right at a small sign for "Sect. M." At approximately 0.1 mile from the Vanderheyden Bell, you will see Willard's tombstone to your left, directly across the road from the Maullin/Swartwout monument. Willard's tombstone is easy to miss because it is neither large nor conspicuous.

To the Burden family site: From the Vanderheyden Bell, drive north (going straight), staying on the main road. At nearly 0.6 mile you will pass between two small ponds. Bear to the left. After passing by the "Sect B-1" sign on your left, you will quickly come to a fork in the road at the Everingham/Kimball monument. Turn right. In less than 0.1 mile you will see the Reynold monument straight ahead. Turn left. Within 0.2 mile you will come to the Tracy Mausoleum, which looms large on your right. Turn right onto the small road next to the mausoleum, which comes to a dead end in fifty feet. Directly to your right, at the end of the road, is the Burden Mausoleum, which is different from what the name might suggest—the graves are enclosed by four walls only, and no roof. (For the history of the Burden family in Troy, see the chapter on Burden Pond Environmental Park.)

To Uncle Sam Wilson's grave site: From the Vanderheyden Bell, drive north (straight ahead) and follow the tiny green signs indicating "Uncle Sam's Grave." At 0.4 mile, after driving down a small hill, turn left where you see a "Sect. D-1" marker. Immediately, just as you start uphill, turn right at marker "F." Follow the road up and around as it bears left. Within less than 0.1 mile you will see Uncle Sam's burial site on your left, easily located by the flagpole behind it.

To the Robert Ross Monument: From the outlet to Long Lake (see directions for the Nature Trail), drive south along the edge of the escarpment for 0.2 mile. The Ross monument will be directly to your right. Superb views can be obtained from there of Lansingburgh, distant Cohoes Falls, the Hudson River, the Empire State Plaza, the Helderbergs, and—on a clear day—the very distant Catskills.

To General Wool's Monument: From the outlet to Long Lake (see directions for the Nature Trail), follow the edge of the escarpment south for 0.2 mile. When you reach the Robert Ross Monument on your right, veer left at a fork in the road. Then immediately turn right, which will promptly bring you up to a tall obelisk that is the Wool monument.

History: Oakwood Cemetery was built in 1849, designed by landscape architect J. C. Sidney of Philadelphia. The cemetery acquired its name from the oak forest that it replaced. Oakwood was one of the first rural cemeteries in the United States to incorporate natural geology such as gorges and waterfalls. Previous rural cemeteries throughout the nation had been laid out in fairly monotonous flat or rolling hills of green grass. The crematorium and chapel, built to honor Gardner Earl, has beautiful stained-glass windows designed by Louis Comfort Tiffany, prominent nineteenth-century artist and heir to the Tiffany merchant enterprises.

The Gardner Earl Chapel was designed in 1888 by an Albany architect named Albert Fuller. It contains mosaic floors, onyx and marble columns, eight grand Tiffany windows, and carved oak furnishings of extraordinary beauty. The chapel was commissioned by Gardner's father, a prosperous manufacturer of shirt collars and cuffs in Troy. The exact cost of building the chapel is unknown, but at the time no expense was spared in its construction.[4,5,6]

The Gardner Earl Chapel and Crematorium, 2005.

The cemetery is the final resting place for a number of historically significant individuals, including "Uncle Sam" Wilson, General Wool, Emma Willard, and Russell Sage.

"Uncle Sam" Wilson: Long before the caricature of a tall, gray-bearded man dressed in a red, white, and blue-striped costume was created by political cartoonists, there was an actual person who lived in Troy, worked initially as a bricklayer, and then later as a butcher, who many believe was the original Uncle Sam. His name was Sam Wilson (1766–1854).[7,8]

During the War of 1812, Wilson supplied pork and beef to a government contractor named Elbert Anderson for troops who were stationed at an army cantonment at Greenbush. Sam would faithfully stamp each piece of meat with the initials "U.S.—E.A." for "United States—Elbert Anderson." Seeing the letters, the troops began to personalize the initials, and before long, "U.S." became "Uncle Sam."

Sam Wilson's grave and his wife's are unadorned. Wilson's tombstone would be truly inconspicuous were it not for a much larger, granite monument that was erected near the graves in 1936 to commemorate this historically significant person, and for a flag flying atop a flagpole to designate the spot.

Emma Willard: Emma Willard (1787–1870) is best known for having founded a school for women in 1821. Willard's school was predicated upon her progressive ideas published in a manuscript entitled *A Plan for Improving Female Education.* At that time women were considered intellectually inferior to men. Willard's goal was to begin the process of dispelling this notion by showing, through proper education, that women were the intellectual equals of men.

When Willard's Female Seminary opened in 1821, ninety girls enrolled, arriving from as far away as Georgia. The school rapidly achieved national prominence, becoming a model for all future schools of higher learning for women.

After Emma Willard's death in 1870, the school moved uphill to a campus created in 1910 through money donated by philanthropist Margaret Slocum Sage, a graduate of Willard's school and the wife of Russell Sage (a man whose name lives on through the Troy institution of higher learning named after him).

There is a bronze statue of Emma Willard on the Russell Sage Campus (near the Hudson River in Troy) marking the former site of Willard's school before moving to its new campus in 1910.

Russell Sage: Russell Sage was an American financier who came from humble beginnings as an errand boy for his brother's grocery store in Troy. From 1853 to 1857, he was a Whig representative in Congress. He made his fortune as an associate of Jay Gould in the development of elevated railways in New

York City. It is said that he and Gould were involved in the manipulation of vast stock holdings in order to create large profits for themselves.

In 1891 an attempt was made by Henry Norcross to assassinate Sage with a dynamite bomb after Norcross' demands for a large sum of money were ignored. The bomb failed to injure Sage, but succeeded in killing Norcross.

Upon his death Sage was worth $70–80 million, which his wife, Margaret Olivia Slocum, used to benefit various institutions, including Russell Sage College in Troy.

History remembers Sage as a "robber baron." Sage's wife may not have thought all that much better of him. Next to Sage's mausoleum is a stone bench with the head of Medusa carved into the back.

General Wool: General John Ellis Wool was a distinguished soldier who served in the War of 1812 and was second-in-command to Zachary Taylor during the Mexican War.

Years later, Wool and a number of his troops were traveling through Vermont near Lake Dunmore when they came upon an absolutely gorgeous waterfall towering above the lake. The fall was formed on a large stream that the locals had named Sucker Brook. The idea of such a noble waterfall being named Sucker Brook Falls was too much for Wool's men to bear. They renamed it Falls of Lana in honor of General Wool, whose name translates to *lana* in Spanish. To this day the Falls of Lana remain one of Vermont's most gorgeous, as well as most beautifully named waterfalls.

Scene in Oakwood Cemetery, circa 1910.

Most people, however, remember Wool for his war exploits. The general was such a die-hard soldier that he came out of retirement at age seventy-five to assist in the Civil War. He died in 1869 at the age of eighty-six, and a sixty-foot-high monument commemorates his grave.[9,10,11]

General George H. Thomas: George H. Thomas was a major general in the U.S. Army who was born in Virginia in 1816 and died in California in 1870. Thomas was known as the "Rock of Chickamauga" for his Civil War exploits. A plaque set in the ground in front of Thomas' plot describes these details and others about his life. Although he may be a relatively obscure figure today, more than 10,000 people, including President Grant, attended the funeral at his gravesite. At that time it was the largest assemblage of people ever for an event in upper New York State.

Robert Ross: Robert Ross was murdered in March 1894 while trying to protect a ballot box in Troy. The ballot box had been stolen at gunpoint and stuffed with fraudulent ballots.

Preservation: Cemeteries are history frozen in time for "eternity." Unlike so many buildings of historical significance that are demolished to make way for new development, cemeteries, for the most part, remain untouched by human hands. They stay as they are, with the exception of new graves being added.

Still, cemeteries are subject to the ravages of time. They are exposed to wind, rain, snow, sleet, and ice. Tombstones inevitably begin to disintegrate; inscriptions fade away. Occasionally acts of vandalism take their toll. In April 2005, Uncle Sam Wilson's grave and several other monuments were desecrated.

Preserving cemeteries has become a new field of specialization, and many cemeteries now consult with preservationists on how best to stave off the ravages of time. Historical societies work with cemeteries to maintain not only the physical structures and monuments, but the history they contain. Oakwood Cemetery and Albany Rural Cemetery, for example, both have active societies that conduct tours and nature walks on the grounds. For this we are deeply indebted to the individuals and groups that strive to ensure that the dead *do* live on in our collective memory.

7 BURDEN POND ENVIRONMENTAL PARK

Location: South Troy (Rensselaer County)
New York State Atlas & Gazetteer: p. 67, C4-5

Fees: None

Hours: Open year-round, dawn to dusk

Accessibility: 0.5-mile hike along a fairly easy-to-follow trail system

Degree of Difficulty: Easy

Highlights:
- Waterfalls
- Urban nature sanctuary
- Ruins of old powerhouse, pipes, and machinery

Description: The Burden Pond Environmental Park consists of a small pond, a large area of marshlands, a number of small but pretty cascades, and the ruins of an old, abandoned powerhouse that in the mid-1800s generated electricity for the Burden Iron Company.[1] Additional historical artifacts relating to the Burden Iron Company are located across Mill Street (Rt. 4) in an area of the Wynantskill downstream from the pond. At present this area can be accessed only by a bushwhack, and this approach is even more problematic because the property is owned by Rensselaer County and is archaeologically sensitive.

Directions: *To the Burden Pond Environmental Park:* From I-787, take Exit 7E (South Troy and Watervliet) to Rt. 378 east. Route 378 east quickly crosses over the Hudson River and then veers to the left. At the second stoplight, turn right onto Mill Street (Rt. 4 south) and drive uphill for 0.4 mile. As soon as you cross over the Wynantskill, turn left at a stoplight onto Campbell Avenue and park immediately on your left next to the south end of the Burden Pond Dam.

Alternative Parking: Just before you cross over the Wynantskill and reach the stoplight at the junction of Mill Street (Rt. 4) & Campbell Avenue, turn sharply left onto Delaware Avenue. Drive uphill for 0.1 mile and park in a large lot on your right immediately after the road bends sharply left. From here you can either walk back down the road to the Burden Dam to start the hike, or you can follow an eroded path that leads east downhill from the parking area and intersects the main trail farther up from the Burden Dam.

To the Burden Iron Works Museum: From the junction of Rtes. 378 & 4 south (Mill Street), drive north on Rt. 4 (Burden Road) for less than 0.3 mile. When you come to a traffic light, turn left onto Main Street and drive 0.1 mile west, crossing over railroad tracks in the process. Then turn right onto East Industrial Parkway and drive north for 0.1 mile. Turn right, and then immediately right again. This leads around the back of the Burden Iron Works Museum. Keep going around until you reach the front, east entrance to the museum.

The Hike

The hike at Burden Pond Environmental Park begins from a small parking area at the junction of Campbell Road and Mill Street, directly next to the south side of the Burden Pond Dam.

From the parking lot, walk over to the pond and take a moment to reflect on the view in front of you. Curiosity may drive you to wonder what function the Burden Dam originally served, for its current purpose seems to be strictly aesthetic. At one time, however, the pond was intimately linked to South Troy's industrial development. Look closely at the cement wall along the shoreline next to the dam and you will notice the outline of a sluiceway gate. Up until the late nineteenth century, water was ushered through this penstock, carried under Mill Road (Rt. 4), and then down through a raceway along the south bank of the Wynantskill to the Burden Iron Company where the world's largest waterwheel turned.[2]

The Burden Iron Company is now nothing more than a shadowy memory and the subject of old photos in history books, but it can still come alive in your mind's eye if you visualize how the landscape once looked as the raceway carried water away from the pond to power a number of large mills and factories downstream from where you are standing. Instead of the houses and trees that you see now, there were nothing but walls of brick and stone with huge chimneys belching smoke into a darkened sky.

Burden Pond was not always as small as it is today. During its heyday it was a good-sized pond, but years of sedimentation have turned it into a marshy swamp. As more time elapses and additional fill accumulates, there may be little left of the pond to see. Today, the dam and the swamp provide a wetland area for geese and mallard ducks, which seem to thrive in the marshlands, perhaps encouraged by throngs of visitors who feed them.

From the parking area, follow the sidewalk north. You will immediately cross over the Mill Street bridge in front of the dam. Once you are on the north side of the bridge, walk east across the lawn towards the dam. The trailhead for the Burden Pond Environmental Park begins here.

Burden Falls,
circa 1910.

The trail immediately takes you into a jungle-like thicket of brush. It becomes readily apparent that a great deal of work initially went into creating the park, for there are wooden walkways and wall supports along the first 0.2 mile of the hike. Unfortunately, the guardrails and walkways have deteriorated markedly, perhaps accelerated by vandals. As a result, some care must be taken as you negotiate the pathways.

You will notice that the trail leads around the perimeter of the pond (which looks more like a swamp than an actual pond). You will also notice that trails begin to proliferate the farther in you go. For this you can thank the myriad of dirt-bikers and ATV riders who not only ride on the existing trails, but add some more of their own each year. The number of trails may seem confusing at times, but you won't go astray if you remember to keep to your right, gradually making your way towards the Wynantskill, which flows through the center of the swamp. Some of the trails that head up the steep wall of the ravine to your left take you right out of the gorge. These should be avoided.

If you continue circling the perimeter of the swamp, veering right, you will eventually come to the Wynantskill and, just upstream from the inlet to the swamp, an old cement building on the opposite side of the stream at the bottom of a steep ravine. These are the ruins of the powerhouse for the former Burden Iron Company. If it is summer and you don't mind getting wet, you can ford the stream and take a look at the old machinery housed inside the building. The machinery is rusted solid and unusable, but it will give you an idea of the kind of technology that existed in the early 1900s.

Take note of the huge pipe over three feet in diameter that follows along the side wall of the ravine and then plummets all at once down to the powerhouse. It was through this enormous pipeline that water was transported from an upper, dammed body of water called Paper Mill Pond (also known as Lower Smart's Pond) down to the powerhouse, where potential energy was converted into kinetic energy before the waters were returned to the Wynantskill.

Leaving the powerhouse behind, continue following the creek upstream along the top of the escarpment as the valley narrows and turns into a rugged looking ravine. In less than 0.05 mile you will come to a set of small cascades encased in the deep walls of the gorge. The falls are pretty, but fairly flat in appearance as you look down from the top of the ravine.

Continue along the top of the ravine for another 0.05 mile. You will arrive at continuous overlooks of the stream as it zigzags, twice changing direction dramatically. A pretty, eight-foot-high waterfall is located at the upper bend in the creek, and another, tiny cascade is just below. On the opposite side of the gorge, the pipeline has reappeared. Between here and the downstream powerhouse, large sections of the pipeline are gone, presumably knocked apart by weathering and landslides from construction work along the top of the south bank.

If you look at the top of the main waterfall, you will notice that the pipeline now crosses the stream, having gone through an opening blasted out in the side wall. Although this perspective doesn't allow you to look beyond the top of the cascade, the pipeline rapidly comes to an end at a breached dam immediately upstream from the fall. The breached dam can be reached by following the trail up towards the top of the ravine, and then back down again going slightly east. This descending trail, in turn, branches off in two directions. The main branch takes you to the streambed and the pipeline just above the top of the fall, where you can examine the pipe close-up and observe the cement dam that is just a short distance upstream. Take note of the oblong block of cement lying in the streambed—a relic from the breached dam.

Stop for a moment to examine the integrity of the metal pipe. Although sections of it have holes in them and look likely to crumble, there is still quite a bit of strength left in the metal. Take a look inside the pipe where the pipeline has split apart. You will see that one section of the pipe contains several inches of silt from days when the pipe carried water (and silt) down from the dam. Look closely at the near wall of the bank, and you will see a brick or two from the paper mill that once stood downstream from the dam along the north bank.

If you take the other branch (to the left) from the descending trail, it will quickly lead you to the breached dam. The section of the dam along the north bank is relatively intact, but the section that abutted the south bank is gone, having been washed away years ago. Another dam was further upstream, past the point where Campbell Road crosses over the Wynantskill, in years past. It also held back a pond of water, called Smart's Mill Pond, and it, too, had a paper mill along its north bank, directly downstream from the pond.

History: Troy has occupied a favorable strategic position throughout its history, taking advantage not only of the natural waterways provided by the Hudson and Mohawk rivers, but also of the Erie Canal, Champlain Canal, and land routes as well, including the Mohawk Valley Turnpike (Rt. 5) and the Cherry Valley Turnpike (Rt. 20). Troy's roots date back to 1651, when Kiliaen Van Rensselaer purchased land in the area of the Wynantskill from the Native Americans and established a mill on the creek by 1656.[3]

Iron and steel industries were quick to see Troy as a suitable site for foundries. Raw pig iron was easily transported from the Adirondacks, processed in Troy, and then shipped by barge or rail across the country. The power of the Wynantskill as a dependable source of energy was recognized early on by emerging industries. In 1807, Brinckerhoff's Nail Factory, a rolling mill, was established by John Brinckerhoff. In 1809, John Converse and several associates set up a rolling and slitting mill on the upper Wynantskill.[4,5]

It is the name Henry Burden, however, that has become virtually synonymous with South Troy's nineteenth-century industrial growth. In 1822, Burden began working at the Troy Iron and Nail Factory as a superintendent. A native of Scotland, Burden had been trained as a draftsman and engineer. Though not university educated, he proved to be extremely creative and innovative. In 1825, Burden patented a machine that could make wrought-iron railroad spikes. In 1834 the machine was revamped to produce hook-headed spikes. Then, in 1835, Burden patented a machine for making horseshoes, whose timeliness can not be overstated, for it is said that the U.S. Army Cavalry and field artillery rode to victory in the Civil War on the horseshoes made in Burden's factory. In fact, at its peak the factory produced enough horseshoes for 12,000,000 horses.

In 1838, Burden began construction on a sixty-foot-diameter overshot waterwheel to provide additional power to increase the efficiency and power of the machinery at the nail factory. At the time it was reputed to be the largest waterwheel in the world.

By 1840, Burden had become sole proprietor of the iron works, which came to be known as the Burden Iron Company. At this time the combined Burden factories extended for nearly the entire length of Mill Avenue and also occupied vast sections of buildings at the bottom of the hill near the river and railroad tracks. One of the buildings at the bottom of the hill, the former business office, now houses the Burden Iron Works Museum.[6,7]

Burden's creative genius led him to explore the use of iron sheeting in the construction of steamboats, and in 1833 he built a steamboat named after his wife Helen. Unfortunately, *Helen* ended up grounded on the Castleton dam and had to be scrapped. Undaunted, Burden continued to perfect and patent his boat designs. It is said that many of his ideas for improvement were used in the building of the successful steamer *Henry Hudson.* In 1846, Burden presented a prospectus for Burdens Atlantic Steam Company. Although this company never came to fruition because of the demand on Burden to divert his resources to the production of horseshoes for the Union Army, his boat ideas were subsequently used by major oceanic transporters such as the Cunard Line.

The Burden Iron Company lasted until 1938. In 1940 the company was bought by Republican Steel, but within several years it, too, had gone out of business.[8]

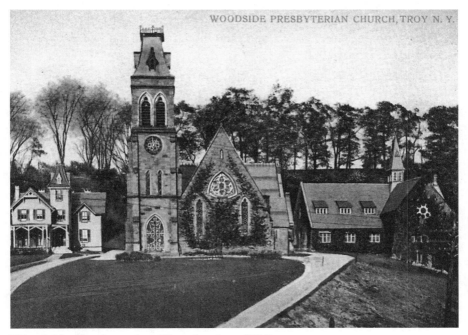

Woodside Presbyterian Church, circa 1910.

The Burden Waterwheel

The Burden waterwheel was constructed in 1838–1839. Called "The Niagara of Waterwheels" by the renowned hydraulic engineer Edward Dean Adams, the wheel was sixty feet in diameter, twelve feet wide, and contained thirty-six buckets, each over six feet deep.[9] When it was running at full speed, the wheel could deliver 482 horsepower.[10] There were problems with the wheel right from the start, however, and it was either rebuilt or reconstructed in 1851.

It is surmised that George Washington Ferris, Jr., a graduate of Rensselaer Polytechnic Institute (RPI), Troy, New York, used Burden's waterwheel as a model when he exhibited his famous Ferris wheel at the 1893 World's Columbian Exposition in Chicago. Ferris' wheel also utilized thirty-six buckets, only this time for seating, and not for harnessing power.[11,12]

Unfortunately, no attempt was made to preserve the Burden waterwheel after the upper works was dismantled in 1899, leaving the wheel fully exposed to the elements. By 1914 the great wheel had collapsed. Eventually reduced to pieces during the decades that followed, the waterwheel was salvaged and used as scrap metal during World War II to help the war effort.

Burden's waterwheel was at one time the largest in the world. Photograph circa 1920.

Additional Points of Interest:

The Woodside Presbyterian Church, located on Mill Street just downhill from the junction with Campbell Avenue, was built by Henry Burden in honor of his wife, Helen, whose initial, "H," is part of the design in the front stained-glass window. World-famous McNeely bells were installed in the bell tower. The building functioned as a church for many years, but it is presently closed to the public because of structural weakness. Efforts are currently underway to raise money for repairs and to ensure historical preservation.

The Burden Iron Works Museum is located on One East Industrial Parkway in South Troy and is housed in the former administrative building (circa 1880s) of the Burden Iron Works. The museum consists of several rooms of historical artifacts, including written materials and displays that depict the iron industry in nineteenth-century Troy.

The Burden Museum, 2005.

8   ANN LEE POND

Location: Colonie (Albany County)
New York State Atlas & Gazetteer: p. 66, BC3

Fee: None

Hours: Dawn to dusk, year-round

Accessibility: The 1.5 miles of trails around Ann Lee Pond are level and well-maintained.

Degree of Difficulty: Easy

Highlights:
- Ruins, including preserved Shaker buildings
- Cemetery with gravesite of Mother Ann Lee
- Pond with footbridge

Description: Ann Lee Pond is named after Mother Ann Lee, founder of the eighteenth-century Shaker religious community. The nature preserve is maintained by Albany County, as are the contiguous properties at the site of the old Watervliet Shaker community and the Ann Lee Nursing Home.[1]

This once-rural community now lies directly across from the bustling Albany International Airport. Nearby, former Shaker farmlands have been subdivided to create industrial parks. Despite these distractions, however, the pond, trail, and surrounding woods remain pretty and abound with wildflowers in the spring.

The seven, somewhat derelict, surviving Shaker buildings, now owned by Albany County, have descriptive plaques explaining their former use. The main building—the former Shaker meetinghouse—is open year-round, although the schedule varies according to the season.[2,3]

Directions: Ann Lee Pond is opposite the Albany International Airport. Going north on the Adirondack Northway (I-87), take exit 4, turn left onto Wolf Road, and drive north for less than 0.1 mile. Turn left onto Rt. 155 (Albany Shaker Road) and drive west for 1.6 miles.

From the Northway south, take Exit 4 and turn right onto Rt. 155 (Albany Shaker Road) at the end of the ramp. Drive west for 1.5 miles.

When you come to the stoplight, turn left onto Heritage Road. You now have two choices:

To the Shaker Heritage Society Museum & Gift Shop: Drive south on Heritage Road for 0.2 mile. Turn left and follow the blue-colored signs pointing the way to the museum and gift shop. Along the way, you will notice old surviving Shaker buildings.

To Ann Lee Pond: Drive south on Heritage Road for 0.3 mile from the stoplight. When the road veers to the right, either proceed straight ahead into a small parking area next to Ann Lee Pond's outlet, or continue right around the curve and park in a large area immediately to your left.

The Hike

The hike begins from the parking area at the end of Heritage Road. While there isn't a printed map available of the nature trails that circumnavigate the pond and lead through wooded areas, the paths are clear and well marked. The pond was created by the Shaker community to drain wetlands so that they could access more land for crops and buildings.[4,5] You will see a plaque by the trailhead explaining how the Shakers used the pond for ice-cutting in the winter.

At the trailhead by the northern shore of the pond, it is possible to begin the hike by following the trail either to the left or right. For this hike, take the trail to the right. At this point you will be standing directly in full view of the pond, which is home to ducks seeking refuge in the warmer seasons. You will see water lilies, marsh marigold, purple loosestrife, cattails, and duck weed at the perimeter of the pond.

Veer left at the western shore of the pond and walk through an open grassy area before heading into the woods. In about 0.5 mile the trail turns left as you approach the bridge across the pond. From the middle of the bridge, you can survey the entire pond. You may see ducks and even heron from this vantage. Across the bridge, as you enter into the woods, are a variety of trees including maple, red oak, beech, pines, and hemlock. In the spring, trillium, trout lily, foam flower, and violets blossom. In the summer and early fall you will see Queen Anne's lace, chicory, hobble bush, daisies, and black-eyed Susans, to name a few. A variety of mushrooms sprout as well, depending on the vagaries of weather.

Shortly after you cross the bridge and head east, you will come to a right-hand turn. Should you take that turn, you will head away from the pond and continue on the woods loop—a 1.3-mile-long trail through a pleasant hardwood forest.

To continue on the pond loop, stay on the main trail, which soon veers left. This loop is about 0.7 mile long. You may be amazed at how secluded and peaceful these woods are, despite being so near the airport and major roadways. You will return to the trailhead after completing the loop.

Across the road, to the west of the trailhead, is the old Shaker cemetery where Ann Lee is buried. There are 400 Shaker graves here. All of the grave markers are simple in design, as is to be expected.

If you walk 0.2 mile further on the roadway perpendicular to the pond, you will see the old Shaker buildings. Although the buildings are kept closed, you can walk around them and read the plaques that describe at length their former functions. In the summer an herb garden is planted to illustrate the kinds of herbs that the Shakers cultivated there until the early twentieth century.

History: Ann Lee Pond was named after Mother Ann Lee, who founded the Shaker religious community in Watervliet around 1778.[6] Mother Ann Lee and her followers lived on the properties contiguous to Ann Lee Pond. At the community's peak, the Shakers had acquired extensive land holdings and included a number of families. (In Shaker terms, "families" designated a group of individuals, not necessarily related, who lived together.) These families lived and worked in separate clusters of buildings. Each family interacted with the others on social, economic, and spiritual issues. The families at the Ann Lee Pond community were known as the Church Family, South Family, West Family, and North Family. The preserved buildings adjacent to the pond were part of the Church Family. There are also some privately owned former Shaker dwellings on South Road that were part of the South Family complex. These buildings lie southwest of the Church Family preserve. Sad to say, these buildings are in a poor state of repair. All in all, there were four to five square miles of property owned by the Watervliet Shaker community in the 1800s.

In the early 1900s the dwindling Watervliet Shaker community sold some of its land. In 1926 the Church Family property was sold to Albany County for use as the Ann Lee Home and county hospital. The Ann Lee Home, a nursing home, is still in operation. That same year the North Family buildings were extensively damaged by fire. The land that these buildings were on is currently the site of the Shaker Ridge Country Club. In 1928 another tract of Shaker land was purchased by the county to create the Albany Municipal Airport (now the Albany International Airport). It is said that the Shakers' own tractor was used to level the ground for the airport, and that the remaining Shaker community stood by and watched.

There are eight remaining Shaker structures across the road adjacent to the pond. These lands were designated in 1973 as the Watervliet Shaker Historic District. The old Shaker meetinghouse now serves as an office, library, and gift shop promoting Shaker history. The office is open most days and provides visitors with maps to the outbuildings. A booklet sold in the gift shop provides descriptions of the flora and fauna to be found by the nature trail.

Who was Mother Ann Lee? Ann Lee was originally a religious enthusiast from Manchester, England, who was persecuted and imprisoned in England because of her divergent religious views.[7] She and a small band of followers left their homeland in 1774 and settled in Niskayuna around 1778. Initially they were not welcomed by the community at large, for their pacifist views precluded them from fighting during the Revolutionary War and they were branded as Tories.[8]

Mother Ann, as she was affectionately called, was given to visions and evidently was a charismatic leader. She gathered a number of converts throughout New England, eventually amassing approximately 5,000 members.[9]

More about the nineteenth-century Shakers: The Society of Believers in Christ's Second Appearing, known simply as "Shakers," believed in living communally to create "heaven on earth." They lived simply, but well. Sexual abstinence for men and women was a basic tenet of their faith. They were industrious and creative, and credited with innovations in agriculture and household crafts. The men and women had equal rights, and lived communally but separately. They were racially integrated and home to some former slaves after the Civil War. Their one spiritual and emotional outlet was dancing, which was incorporated into their religious services. The practice of dancing with religious fervor was what led them to be called "Shakers."[10]

The Watervliet Shakers were adept at providing for the needs of their community. They grew crops, processed canned goods, wove cloth, made clothes, built houses, and made furniture. Their simple, well-made furniture is still highly prized. Like the Shaker communities in Hancock and Tyringham, Massachusetts (see chapters on "Shaker Mountain" and "Tyringham Cobble"), the Shakers not only provided for their own needs, they were also entrepreneurs who did a brisk business with the community at large. The Watervliet Shakers sold canned goods and fresh produce on the open market. There is a note on one of the building plaques that says that the Shaker cannery was productive until 1921. Local Native Americans also traded with the Shakers and participated in some of their community events.[11]

They also commercially produced and sold brooms, seeds, and pipes for smoking. The Shakers at Watervliet are credited with many inventions, among them the first flat broom (invented by Theodore Gates), a machine for filling seed bags, printing presses for printing on seed bags and herb packages, a pipe-making machine, a pea-sheller, and a butter worker, to name but a few.[12]

The Shakers had a policy of helping the poor and needy. During a severe epidemic in 1798, the Shakers pooled large resources of food and money to offer assistance. Their donations included beef, mutton, flour, beans, and other vegetables. Governor Dewitt Clinton sent a letter of thanks to the Watervliet Shaker community acknowledging this large gift.[13]

The Shaker way of life attracted attention in America and abroad. This idealistic, "intentional community" generated a great deal of interest in many eighteenth-century intellectuals.[14] Presidents James Monroe and Andrew Jackson visited Shaker communities. Charles Dickens, on his trip to America, visited the Shakers in New Lebanon. References to the sect even showed up in the literature of the time. Herman Melville in *Moby-Dick* writes, "The archangel Gabriel came from the crazy society of Neskyunna Shakers."

The Shaker way of life became less popular in the late 1800s, dwindling after the Civil War when there were fewer orphans and fragmented families seeking livelihood, community, and shelter. Since the Shakers practiced sexual abstinence, they depended on new recruits for membership. When new recruits began to diminish, so did the Shaker society.

The Shakers have not completely vanished, however. There are still a few Shakers today living in a community at Sabbathday Lake in Maine.

9

Location: New Scotland (Albany County)
New York State Atlas & Gazetteer: p. 66, CD1-2

Fees: Modest seasonal fee to enter picnic areas and swimming pool grounds

Hours: The Indian Ladder trail is open from May 1 to November 15, 8:00 AM to sunset. It is closed during the winter. John Boyd Thacher State Park is open year-round.

Restrictions: Rock or fossil collecting is prohibited.

Accessibility: 0.5-mile hike along base of escarpment, requiring an initial 100-foot descent

Degree of Difficulty: Easy

Highlights:
- Views of Albany and the distant Berkshires
- Towering cliffs
- Two large waterfalls
- Caves (pack a flashlight!)
- Huge natural amphitheater

Description: Indian Ladder consists of a 0.5-mile-long trail that takes you down to the bottom of a huge escarpment, along its base, and then back up again. During the hike you will pass by several small caves, a huge rock amphitheater, a sweeping cathedral arch, and two towering cataracts on streams of limited flow.[1]

Indian Ladder is located at John Boyd Thacher State Park, a nature and recreational area that contains 2,300 acres of hiking trails, vistas, picnics areas, pavilions, and an Olympic-sized swimming pool. Prior to 1914 the area was known simply as Indian Ladder Park. The park is located in the Helderbergs, which is a Dutch corruption of the German word *helle-berg. Helle* is German for "clear" or "bright," and *berg* means "mountain" (as in ice-*berg*).

Directions: From I-90 in Albany, take Rt. 85 south towards Slingerlands. In approximately 4.0 miles the highway ends. Turn right onto New Scotland

Road and continue west on Rt. 85 for nearly 8.0 miles. Near the top of a long, winding hill, turn right onto Rt. 157 and drive northwest for 4.0 miles, entering Thacher Park in the process. Turn right on Hailes Cave Road into the main activity area where a sign indicates "Hailes Cave, park office, swimming pool, and Indian Ladder." As soon as you drive past the entrance booth, turn right and park at the end of the parking lot.

Follow the signs that point to the Indian Ladder picnic area. The short sidewalk leading to the Indian Ladder trail begins here.

It is also possible to access the east end of Indian Ladder from the LaGrange picnic area, approximately 0.6 mile from the Hailes Cave Road entrance.

The Hike

Indian Ladder has both an east and west entrance. To follow this hike, start at the west entrance, where an opening in the escarpment wall was blasted out by nineteenth-century engineers. Look for a historical marker near the entrance steps that gives information on Tory Cave, a curious geological and historical site that is nearby but unfortunately off-limit to visitors.[2,3,4]

As you walk down the stone stairway through the road cut, stop for a moment to look at the marker on your left, which provides information about the Old Indian Ladder Road, a section of which you are walking. At the wooden platform at the bottom of the stone stairway, look straight ahead (north). You can make out the faint outline of this once-viable road that led up to the top of Indian Ladder from the valley below. The road is now impassable and has probably been so since the early 1930s.

At the bottom of the stone stairway is a flight of metal steps, divided into two sections, which will take you down the remainder of the way to the base of the escarpment. When you get to the bottom of the upper stairway, look straight ahead at the cliff face. You are looking at Upper Bear Path, which is formed out of a two- to three-foot bed of eroded Manlius limestone. Do not try to set foot on this path! It is dangerous and off-limits. Continue down the second flight of stairs to the bottom of the escarpment.

The hike now follows along a path at the base of the one-hundred-foot cliff face. This trail is called the Lower Bear Path and is formed out of a three-foot bed of Rondout dolomite, which, like the Manlius limestone, eroded more quickly than the surrounding rocks.

After a short walk you will come to a huge cathedral arch with a fissure-like passageway leading off from the east side of the arch. This archway is known as the Bridal Chamber. It has also been called the Giant's Castle in the past.

The Bridal Chamber is a huge, cathedral-shaped, rock arch that dwarfs the curiosity-seekers stepping up to it. The arch is referred to by geologists as a pseudo-karstic cave. The cave was formed by frost-wedging and gravity-sliding, which caused a huge section of limestone to drop off.

Bridal Chamber, 1998.

Passageways appear to go off from both sides of the arch. The one to the west rises steeply, but immediately goes nowhere. The passageway on the east (left), however, continues for quite a few feet. It is narrow, but tall enough to allow a visitor to walk stooping through its entire length. It is one of the more interesting side trips as you hike along Indian Ladder trail. Just be sure to bring a flashlight.

Back on the main trail you will come to a tiny footbridge that crosses over a small stream. You are at the entrance to Fool's Crawl, a long cave that extends into the bedrock.

Fools Crawl (also known as Bob's Crawl) is a 1,000-foot-long, tight, mud-filled crawl leading northwest along a streambed corridor. Presumably the cave received its name after the first person to reach its end realized just how miserable and unrewarding the effort had been. Fools Crawl was visited in the mid-1800s by Verplanck Colvin, who found "no deep water, lakes, or large rooms" for his efforts. Imagine if you will what Colvin experienced, pulling himself along this crawlway in total darkness, with bedrock pressing against his back, knees rubbing against the streambed, and water rushing by under his chest!

You may imagine, but do not attempt to imitate Colvin's exploration. Fool's Crawl is off-limits to the public. The park prohibits unauthorized entry.

Continuing on the main trail will take you next to Outlet Falls. If you are visiting in the early spring or after a period of heavy rainfall, you will see a huge, towering cataract. If you are visiting during the middle of summer, you may see only a small stream issuing from the base of the escarpment, with nothing falling from above. This is why Outlet Falls has also been called Dry Falls. The seasonally minimal amount of water carried by the streambed at the top of the escarpment is frequently diverted into an underground passageway.

The trail takes you on past a number of large boulders that fell as sections of the cliff face broke off. Soon you will hear Minelot Falls as you round the bend and enter a huge amphitheater of rock. This section, along with Outlet Falls, is known as Indian Ladder Gulf.[5] Generally there is always some water flowing over the top of Minelot Falls, although the cataract can be quite diminished in the summer. You can watch the water spin through the air as it falls onto huge boulders below.

Minelot Falls, at a height of 116 feet, is the largest waterfall on the Helderberg escarpment. According to Verplanck Colvin in an 1869 article: "From the edge of the overhanging precipice, more than a hundred feet above your head, streams down a silvery rope of spray, with a whispering rush, sweeping before it damp, chilling eddies of fugitive air that swap the watery cable to and fro." In contrast, during the winter, the fall appears— according to Colvin again—as: "one huge icicle from the cliff brink to its base; the water pours down—an unceasing stream—through the huge frost- proof conduit it has formed for itself. A pyramid of pure green-white ice, glittering, resplendent with icicles, which in fringed sheets, strange and fantastic shapes, adorns the translucent column."[6]

The waterfall was named for the fact that prospectors once mined iron pyrite near its base. The top of the falls is known as Lover's Leap.

You can walk behind the waterfall and under a wide, cavernous space, passing beneath millions of tons of rock.

Minelot Falls in early spring, 2000.

*Indian Ladder Gulf is one of the better-known geological features
of the hike. It was formed during an interglacial time.*

*This amphitheater behind Minelot Falls is very dramatic. In the words
of Verplanck Colvin, at the "back of the fall at the base of the precipice is a
low, horizontal cavity in the rock, from four to six feet in height, fifty or
sixty feet in length, by fifteen in depth." This space resulted when a narrow
strip of Rondout dolomite was eroded away. Although the bedding formed
out of Rondout dolomite is exceedingly thin at Thacher Park, it can be
thicker elsewhere, such as at Kingston, where it is forty feet in depth.*

*There are tiny
apertures along
the base of the
escarpment where
water exits after
being bled away
from the
streambed above.
Some of these
small openings
represent the
halfhearted
attempts by early
prospectors to
mine veins of
iron pyrite.*

*Many years
ago, visitors were
allowed to camp
along the trail
under the
sheltering rocks.*

**Indian Ladder,
circa 1900.**

Continuing east, you will finally come to the end of the escarpment trail at a place known as Craig Court, where a flight of metal stairs takes you back up to the top of Indian Ladder. You will notice another educational marker by the stairs. A colorful postcard reproduction shows a ladder propped up against the escarpment ledge. The marker explains that the ladder was actually positioned at the opposite end of the trail, at the point near where you first came down the stone stairway. There is also a mural by an unknown artist in the Delmar, New York, post office depicting the trail and the ladder.

Arriving at the top of the escarpment, you can follow a trail back to your starting point that will take you along the escarpment, from where on a clear day you can see as far away as the Adirondack foothills, the Taconic and Berkshire mountains in western Massachusetts, and the Green Mountains of Vermont.

Better yet, just turn around and hike back the way you came. You'll be surprised at how different and new everything looks in reverse.

History: The Helderbergs were known to Native Americans long before the arrival of colonists, but no records have survived from these earlier times. When the Hudson Valley was being settled by Europeans in the late 1600s, the Helderbergs were a vast area of wilderness and remained so up until the early 1700s. At that time Albany was merely a wild frontier town near the confluence of the Hudson River and the Normans Kill, a trading post frequented by early explorers, trappers, Native Americans, and merchant ships that ventured up the Hudson River.[7]

Once colonization began expanding westward, however, a trail developed across the plains of the Mohawk Valley between Albany and Schenectady. For Native Americans journeying back and forth from Schoharie to Albany or Schenectady, the Indian Ladder escarpment posed a natural barrier. According to legend they solved the problem by cutting down tall trees, trimming the branches to fashion makeshift ladders, and propping them up against the escarpment wall at low points. Out of this the name Indian Ladder arose. Some sources claim that there were as many as eight or nine different places where Native Americans felled trees and shored them up against the escarpment to serve as ladders, and that these tree ladders (or later generations of them) were still in place as late as 1820. All of this may be apocryphal, of course, and merely the grist of legends and tall tales.

At some point conventional ladders were set in place, but even these proved unsuitable because visitors occasionally fell off and suffered serious injury. The current metal stairways provide a safe way to access Indian Ladder.

Europeans began settling the region in greater numbers in the 1700s. Most of the farms were manor lands, meaning that the farmers and landowners had to pay tribute to a feudal lord—a concept taken directly from the Old World and applied to the New World. These lands were part of the Van Rensselaer Patent. The farmers were considered peasants, and their tribute was often collected in the form of chickens, wheat, or services rendered. Such servitude became untenable after the Revolutionary War and was gradually replaced by the system of taxation that we now have in place. The transition did not occur smoothly, however, and the new system was ushered in through the Anti-Rent Rebellion.

From the seventeenth through the nineteenth centuries, the Helderberg plateau was extensively stripped of trees for farming and logging, a fairly common practice throughout the entire region. What you see now is primarily second-growth forest.

In 1828 a crude roadway was constructed up from the valley to the top of the Helderberg escarpment. This was done by widening the original footpath that was used by early travelers and then blasting out a road cut in the escarpment wall at the low point against which the main Indian ladder had once been propped. Today, the old Indian Ladder Road has become obscured through disuse, but its outline is still clearly visible from the top of the escarpment if you look when the foliage is gone or when a dusting of light snow has fallen. The west entrance to Indian Ladder uses the top of this old road cut.

The names of the various groves and picnic areas in John Boyd Thacher State Park have interesting historical origins. Pear Orchard and Hop Field were named after specific crops grown by early settlers. Knowles Flat and LaGrange Bush were named after early settlers, and Hailes Cave was named after Professor Theodore C. Hailes, an early educator and explorer.

Life at Indian Ladder in the 1800s: Most of the people who lived in the region were engaged in some form of farming, raising dairy herds, sheep, hogs, or planting a variety of crops including rye, buckwheat, oats, corn, or potatoes. The work was labor-intensive and demanding, made particularly so by the rocky Helderberg soil and the fact that the limestone bedrock was so close to the surface.

Hops became an important crop around which social gatherings revolved. From these early community gatherings involving music, dancing, and gaiety, modern "dance hops" arose.

The Indian Ladder community was very close-knit. Farmers would rush to each other's assistance in times of emergencies, and, unfortunately, emergencies were frequent. Bad weather or pestilence caused crop failures. Fires occasionally consumed a barn or farmhouse.

Most of the old farms and buildings have vanished. The forests have reclaimed the area, giving the impression that nothing but wilderness ever existed here.

Geology: The Helderbergs are an area of raised land that was once at the bottom of an ancient, shallow ocean. Powerful geological forces lifted it to its present elevation eons ago. The height of its cliffs varies from 800 to 1,300 feet above sea level.[8,9,10]

Indian Ladder is at the northern end of this ancient, elevated seabed. It has a sharply defined cliff edge because of the composition of its rocks. The top forty-five feet of the cliff bedrock is Coeymans limestone (named for a town near Albany, where it was first described), a rock that resists weathering far better than any of the other rocks comprising Indian Ladder. The lower part of the cliff, roughly fifty-five feet in thickness, is composed of Manlius limestone (named after a small town near Syracuse), a rock that is not as durable and resistant to weathering. Manlius limestone is actually very dark in color, but it looks grayish at Indian Ladder because its exterior has been weathered. Because the lower section of the Helderberg escarpment is made up of Manlius

bedrock, the lower section erodes quicker than the upper layer, leaving the more durable, upper section of Coeymans bedrock overhanging and unsupported. When parts of the Coeymans section finally collapse, they break off in large blocks because of their vertical joints. This leaves the cliff face smooth and nearly vertical. The talus from this breakdown is what you see strewn about near the Indian Ladder Trail and down the long slope that extends from the trail into the valley.

The lowest part of the escarpment, the Rondout dolomite, began supratidally. The upper layers formed later, generally as the depth of the ocean kept increasing. When you climb up the metal

Minelot Falls in winter, circa 1910.

stairway back to the top of the escarpment, you are figuratively walking into deeper water.[11]

The large expanse of flatlands in the valley directly below was once part of the lake bed of Lake Albany, a post-glacial body of water.

At one time it was thought that the Helderbergs contained veins of gold. It turned out, however, that the "gold" was actually iron pyrite, better known as "fool's gold." The iron pyrite is contained in the Rondout dolomite that forms the bottommost three to five feet of the main escarpment. The mined iron pyrite did not go to waste, however. It was used to make paint during Revolutionary War times, and has also been used for the manufacture of sulfur and sulfuric acid.

The Helderbergs contain one of the richest beds of fossil-bearing rocks in the world. Here are the remains of univalves, bivalves, and brachiopods that lived over 420–425 million years ago during the Paleozoic era. These tiny creatures died and fell to the bottom of the ancient, shallow ocean, and their collective fragile bodies and calcium-rich shells became hundreds of feet thick over the eons. With time, the tremendous pressure exerted by the weight of the ocean and the upper layers of silt and sediment caused these beds of compressed calcium remains to become rock hard.

Enjoy looking, but please bear in mind that fossil or rock collecting is not allowed in the park.

Indian Ladder is a geologist's dream, and was visited by Sir Charles Lyell (father of modern geology), James Dwight Dana (founder of modern mineralogy), and Amadeus Grabau (father of modern stratigraphy), as well as a host of other famous scientists.

Other Historical Sites:

Hailes Cave is over 3,700 feet long, but not easily negotiated. Parts of its interior are only two to four feet high, and fifteen to twenty feet wide. The cave has been closed to the public for several decades now, for two reasons: it is located in an area totally separate from Indian Ladder and now off-limits; and its permanent resident—the Indiana bat (Myotis Sodalis)—is an endangered species and cannot be disturbed during hibernation. Years ago, however, the cave was a popular public attraction. Visitors would make their way to the cave from the Hailes Cave parking area and down a stairway through a fissure in the escarpment bedrock called Fat Man's Misery. Most visitors would congregate around the entrance; few would enter.

The cave was named after Theodore C. Hailes, an instructor at the old Albany High School who visited many of the larger, well-known caves in Albany and Schoharie counties. In earlier times Hailes Cave was known as Stuphen's Cave, Thacher's Cave, and Helmus Pitcher's Cave.

Tory Cave, now closed to the public as well, is formed along an old roadway that once led up to the top of the escarpment. It is named after Jacob Salisbury, a Tory spy during the Revolutionary War who used the cave as a hideout after leading raids on patriot farms in the valley. According to accounts, Salisbury was captured around the time of the Battle of Saratoga while hiding out in the cave. Apparently, smoke issuing from his campfire gave his location away. Salisbury was tried, convicted, and hanged, quite possibly right on the spot, although another version has Salisbury taken to Albany and then hanged.

Plans existed at one time to open up Tory Cave to the public, but those plans have not been acted on yet.

John Boyd Thacher: Born in 1847, Thacher served as a New York State senator from 1883–1886, and then mayor of Albany from 1886–1887 and 1896–1897. He had a keen interest in conservation and ecology. Thacher was concerned that the Helderberg escarpment might be sacrificed to industries that wanted to harvest its limestone, so he posthumously donated 350 acres of land along three miles of the Helderberg escarpment to the State of New York.

10   BENNETT HILL PRESERVE

Location: Clarksville (Albany County)
New York State Atlas & Gazetteer: p. 66, D2

Fees: None

Hours: Daily, dawn to dusk

Accessibility: 3.0-mile hike round-trip, with a 400-foot change in elevation

Degree of Difficulty: Moderate

Highlights:
- Old farmlands
- Partial views of Clarksville

Description: The trail at the Bennett Hill Preserve leads uphill to a partial overlook of Clarksville. Along the way, the trail passes by several sinkholes near the parking area and a tiny spring halfway up the mountain. Although there are views from the top of the hill year-round, the vistas are considerably more scenic during the winter and spring when there is less foliage.

The preserve is operated by the Albany County Land Conservancy—a private, not-for-profit land trust that was founded in 1992.[1,2]

Directions: From Albany (junction of Rtes. 9W and 443), drive southwest on Delaware Avenue (Rt. 443) for roughly 11.0 miles until you reach the village of Clarksville. At the center of town you will pass by Rt. 301 on your left. Continue west on Rt. 443 for 0.5 mile and turn left onto Rt. 312 (Clarksville South Road), immediately crossing over Onesquethaw Creek. Within fifty feet turn left onto Bennett Hill Road. Drive southeast for 0.5 mile. Pull in at the sign for the Bennett Hill Preserve on your right and proceed up the grass-covered road for 100 feet to the parking area.

To drive by the historic Bennett Hill Farm, continue southeast on Bennett Hill Road for over 0.2 mile until you reach the intersection with Rowe's Hill Road. The Bennett Hill Farm, now owned by the Saidels, is on your left, and the barns are to your right. The owners request that their privacy be respected, so please do not get out of your car to look around.

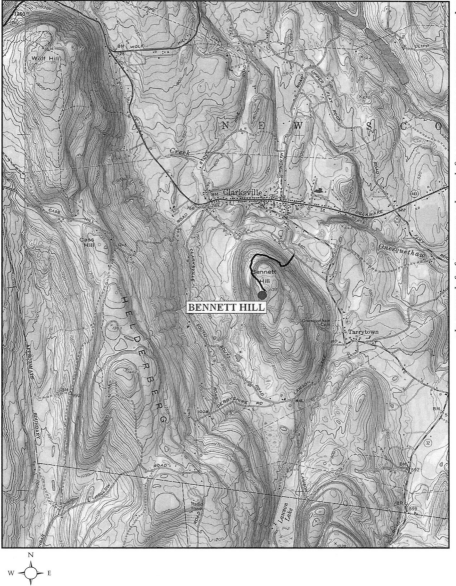

The Hike

The yellow-blazed trail begins at the kiosk next to the parking area and immediately passes by several sinkholes to your right and left. What makes sinkholes so fascinating is that they are frequently conduits into underground drainage systems far beneath the Earth's surface. Bennett Hill is no exception. If you visit during times of heavy rainfall, you will see a tiny rivulet coming down the hill and quickly disappearing into the sinkhole on your left. Further downhill the stream resurfaces at Onesquethaw Creek.

Continue on this trail, which is an old farm road that in earlier days led to pastures on top of the hill. The trail has eroded considerably since then. Follow the road gradually downhill along the west shoulder of Bennett Hill. During this part of the hike, you will have continuous views of dairy farmlands to your right, and of Cass Hill further off in the distance. Near the back of Bennett Hill, the trail finally starts to climb uphill, which it does dramatically. Along the way you will cross over two broad gullies. At one point the trail becomes so steep that it is hard to imagine oxen pulling a wagon up the grade without tumbling head over heels.

The first portion of the climb leads you to a lower area of flatlands—called Twin Juniper Plateau—on the west shoulder of Bennett Hill. You will see double yellow markers on a tree at this point, meaning that the trail turns right. If you continue straight, you will proceed directly onto the plateau, where prickly bushes have reclaimed the road in many places and make the walk less than pleasant. The walk across the plateau leads to no points of particular interest, nor to any overlooks. Therefore, it is best to follow the main trail as it veers right and continues uphill.

Within 0.2 mile from the plateau, you will pass by a spring with a rusted, inverted bathtub next to it—hence the name, Bathtub Spring. The spring, like the sinkhole at the base of the hill, is evidence of the porosity of the limestone and sandstone forming the mountain and surrounding lands. You can see the water issuing out of the hill just above and to the right of the bathtub.

After hiking for roughly 1.3 miles from the parking area, you will reach the top of Bennett Hill, which is surprisingly flat and expansive. You will know that you've arrived when you pass by a large tree—called Nancy's Pitch Pine—on your left. The tree is distinguished by its long, arm-like branches and blocks of rock at its base. Here the trail, which forms an oblong loop around the summit, is blazed with green colors.

When you reach the northern end of the plateau, which faces Clarksville, you will be at an elevation of roughly 1,120 feet. There are good views, intermittently, of the village of Clarksville, the Helderbergs to the north and west, and Albany to the east. The plateau also contains a wetland north of Nancy's

Pitch Pine. It is not possible to see this marsh from the trail, but you can bush-whack to it (just be mindful of deer ticks).

The highest point on the plateau, at 1,135 feet, stands south of the wetlands.

History: The 137-acre preserve is a gift to posterity from Dr. Jerry Bilinski of North Chatham, who donated the land in 1998.

Tribes of Native Americans were living in the area in the 1600s and probably earlier. Europeans arrived and settled the area by the early 1700s and coexisted with the Mohawks. Jonas T. Bush was the first recorded European settler on the property. He acquired the land in 1791, leasing it from Stephen Van Rensselaer, a patroon who typically granted leases for twenty-year periods. It is likely that Jonas Bush lived there for the entire duration of his lease.[3]

According to an historic marker,[4] the great barn directly opposite the end of Rowe's Hill Road was erected around 1740. It is now on the National Register of Historic Places. The barn is a magnificent example of early Palatine barn architecture.

The present homestead, located at the intersection of Rowe's Hill Road and Bennett Hill Road, was built in 1821 by William C. Hewitt for William Chapman.[5]

In 1834, Rushmore Bennett (for whom the farm, road, and hill is named) started an apple farm. Apple orchards are still visible on both sides of the road. Bennett also built a large gristmill on Onesquethaw Creek.

Onesquethaw Creek at Indian Head, circa 1900.

By the 1890s a summer boardinghouse was built adjacent to the main house. Called the Bennett Hill House, it provided room and board for up to forty guests. Many of the patrons were of Scandinavian descent and traveled from as far away as New York City. The boardinghouse lasted into the 1920s.

In the late nineteenth and early twentieth centuries, many urban families left the crowded cities in the summer to enjoy the country air of upstate New York. The cities, with their rudimentary sanitation and crowded conditions, were especially unpleasant and unhealthy in the heat of summer.

In the early 1900s the Bennett Hill property was part of a 200-acre parcel of farmland run by Mrs. W. H. Rowe (Rushmore Bennett's daughter) and her husband.[6] The farm was entirely self-sufficient, producing fruits, vegetables, dairy products, and poultry. The farm has passed through several owners in the years since. It is currently owned by the Saidels, who lovingly maintain the property and its history. It is private property and out-of-bounds for hikers who visit the Bennett Hill Preserve.

The landscape in the area around Bennett Hill has seen its share of change over the years. In the 1890s it was possible to leave the Bennett farm and immediately cross over Onesquethaw Creek via a tiny bridge that led into Clarksville.[7] The bridge was located in a remarkable section of the stream known as Indian Head, where the limestone bedrock had been modified by Onesquethaw Creek to produce small falls and even caves in the side walls. During drier months of the year, people crossing the bridge would be struck by the fact that the stream had disappeared, going underground to emerge again further downstream. This section, unfortunately, is not part of the preserve and is not open to the public.

Of historical interest is the Onesquethaw Union Cemetery, established in 1816 and located at the base of the east shoulder of Bennett Hill.

Geology: Bennett Hill is formed out of sandstone and shale—sedimentary rocks that were created 400 million years ago. Underneath this upper mound is Onondaga limestone, out of which numerous caves in Albany and Schoharie counties have formed, including the nearby Clarksville Cave (see chapter "Clarksville Cave Preserve").

The hill's distinctive appearance is reminiscent of the cobbles of Massachusetts, where rounded bumps rise steeply from relatively flat areas of land. Geologists believe that the hill's present smooth shape is the result of glacial modification.

The top of Bennett Hill presents as a fairly flat, 1,120-foot-high plateau, roughly 400 feet above the trailhead parking area. In the middle of the plateau is a small area of wetland. You will find the expanse of land on the summit to be surprisingly broad with many areas to explore for those who enjoy bushwhacking.

CLARKSVILLE CAVE PRESERVE 11

Location: Clarksville (Albany County)
New York State Atlas & Gazetteer: p. 66, D2

Fees: None

Hours: Year-round, daily from 7:00 AM to 11:00 PM

Accessibility: Short hike across an area of limestone bedrock that has dissolved in places along its joints, forming blocks with wide, gaping cracks. Care must be taken not to twist an ankle while traversing this area.

Restrictions: There are guidelines posted that should be followed. Camping, fires, wood cutting, and parties (without permission) are not permitted on the property. Anything carried in must be carried out. Alcohol, firearms, coolers, glass bottles, spray paint, and other objects that could damage the cave or create unsafe conditions are not permitted. Groups larger than fifteen people are not allowed in the cave.

Degree of Difficulty: The hikes to the cave entrances are easy; if you plan to enter the cave, please heed the special advisement below.

Special Advisement: It is strongly recommended that you contact a local caving organization if you plan to enter the cave. Area contacts are:

> **Helderberg–Hudson Grotto**
> P.O. Box 804
> Schoharie, NY 12157

> **Rensselaer Outing Club**
> Attn: Caving Chair
> RPI Student Union
> Troy, NY 12180

If you enter the cave, it is important that you wear a helmet with chin-strap, knee pads, sturdy boots, layers or coveralls, have at least three dependable sources of light, and go with several other people. Expect the temperature inside the cave to be between 45–50° Fahrenheit regardless of the season.

Highlights:
- Caves
- Interesting karst-formed terrain
- Sinkholes

Description: The main hike follows a series of trails that crisscross the karst terrain (a bedrock surface that is highly dissolved and cracked) above Clarksville Cave. Although the hike doesn't take you underground, it does lead you past the two main entrances to the cave and past interesting surface features, including deep fissures that extend into the bedrock.

The Clarksville Cave is nearly a mile long and consists of two main sections—Ward Cave, named after a local farmer, and Gregory Cave. At one time the two caves were thought to be separate and distinct, but they are now known to be joined. Part of the hike will lead you across the roof of this sizeable cavern. It is fun, as you hike along, to imagine what lies deep below the surface on which you are walking.

The Clarksville Cave is formed in Onondaga limestone (named after a particular limestone bed first found near Syracuse) that was formed in shallow tropical waters nearly 400 million years ago. Contained in the limestone are millions of fossils—corals, crinoids, and brachiopods—which are visible both in the cave and on the surface.[1] Clarksville Cave is unique because of its large size; most other caves formed in Onondaga limestone are considerably smaller and contain little relief. The cave's total relief—measured from its highest to lowest point—is 106 feet, and its length, including sections that are under water, has been pushed by hard-core cavers seeking "virgin passages" to 4,800 feet,[2] which is a respectable distance for a northeastern cave. The stream essentially follows the entire length of the cave and ultimately flows into Onesquethaw Creek just west of Rt. 443.

In 2004 the process began for a half acre of land surrounding the Gregory entrance to be donated by Albany County to the Northeastern Cave Conservancy. At nearly the same time, eleven acres of land, including the Ward entrance, was purchased from the Alberts-McNab family, who had owned it for over fifty years. The cave is now managed by the National Cave Conservancy (NCC), whose intent is to preserve the integrity of the cave and to maximize the safety of those who enter the cave.[3]

Directions: From Albany (junction of Rtes. 9 & 443), go southwest on Rt. 433 (Delaware Ave.) for roughly 11.0 miles until you reach the village of Clarksville. When you come to Rt. 301 on your left, continue southwest on Rt. 443 for about 0.1 mile further, and then turn right when you see a small, cement-block structure that is currently a restaurant called June's Place. Just behind and uphill from the restaurant is a parking area for the cave.

Fissure Cave, 2004.

To Ward Entrance & Karst Area: Walk up a path from the west side of the parking lot. Immediately, you will come to a kiosk containing guidelines for using the preserve, information on the cave, and some fascinating pictures of various sections of the cave's interior. There is a small changing room on the lower level to the right of the trail. From the kiosk, follow the path as it proceeds through the woods for approximately 0.1 mile. Along the way you will notice sandpits off to your right. After you pass the sandpits, you will see a main path coming in on the right. Continue straight ahead. Within a hundred feet you will arrive at another main path coming in on the right. At this point follow a trail that goes off to the left up a small hill. Within 100 feet you will be at the large sinkhole containing the entrance to the Ward section of the Clarksville Cave.

This is the beginning point for exploring the area of karst above the cave. If you walk 200 feet north-northwest from the sinkhole, following a faint but discernible trail, you will reach the next surface feature—a large fissure surrounded by a circle of limestone rocks. From here, continue following a faint trail that soon leads to various other trails that crisscross the karst surface. If you stray too far from the roof of the cave, you will know it because the surface features begin to taper off.

One interesting feature that is well worth visiting is a fifteen-foot bluff along the western perimeter of the preserve. To get there, pass by the path leading up to the Ward cave entrance and stay on the main trail for 0.05 mile. When you come to a junction, turn left and follow a jeep road west for 0.05 mile. You will see a high bluff towering above you close to where the trail turns markedly to the right.

To Gregory Entrance: From the parking area, walk down the gravel road to Rt. 443. Continue west along Rt. 443, staying to the side of the road. In several hundred feet, you will see a rocky bluff in the woods to your right. As soon as you cross over an (almost always) dry streambed, turn right. Within fifty feet you will come up to the base of a rocky bluff. There are two openings in the rock. If you walk up to the upper aperture and listen, you can often hear the thunderous roar of water racing through the cave below.

Clarksville Cave, 1990.

Take note that from the Clarksville Cave parking lot, you can look south directly at Bennett Hill (see chapter on "Bennett Hill Preserve").

The Hikes

Hike #1—Ward Cave Entrance Hike

In general, the area that you will be walking on contains a bedrock surface that is highly dissolved and cracked—a phenomenon that geologists refer to as karst. The walk begins from the west end of the parking area near a large sand-pit. Start off on a well-trodden trail leading northwest into the woods and follow it for over 0.1 mile. You will come to a smaller side path leading off to the left. Follow the side path uphill for several hundred feet and you will arrive at the Ward entrance to the Clarksville Cave at the bottom of a large pit. The pit, or sinkhole, is approximately fifteen feet deep and rectangular, with vertical rock walls on two of its sides and steep, earthen slopes on the other two. The cave entrance is not all that noticeable at first, being little more than a tiny hole in the earth.

Two hundred feet north-northwest from the pit entrance to the Clarksville Cave is an unusual surface feature—a huge circular wall of limestone rock slabs, approximately twenty-five feet in circumference, which was built up from an ongoing excavation dig that started in the 1970s. At its center is a wide fissure forming the top of a narrow pit that drops some twenty-five feet down to the bottom. A long ladder currently extends to the bottom of the pit. This pit should not be entered unless you have followed all of the directions given under "Special Advisement."

Leaving this peculiar surface feature behind, follow a well-worn path that leads west. This path soon crosses a main trail that extends in a north-south direction. From this point, take time to follow the various paths leading off in different directions. None of the paths go very far, and some will take you past additional karst features and more openings into the earth. At the western edge of the property is a ten- to fifteen-foot limestone cliff with deep-jointed fissures behind it.

Underground, beneath your feet, is the Ward Cave. This cave has 1,200 feet of passageway leading up to its traversable endpoint, called the Lake Room, where a small, ten-foot-deep pool of water can be found in a small chamber at the cave's terminus.

Although the name "Lake Room" suggests a sizable body of water, the chamber is quite small. It is in the tradition of cavers, however, to call such water passageways "lakes." If you visit Howe Caverns, a commercial attraction in Schoharie County, and take a trip to their lake room, called the Lake of Venus, you will understand just what cavers mean when they use the word "lake."

The tubular passageway in the main part of Ward Cave is up to forty feet wide and fifteen feet high in many places, with generally only several inches of water in the creek bed. Under conditions of heavy rainfall and flooding, however, the stream inside the cave can rise up to over two feet high.

Adventurous cave divers have traveled beyond the Lake Room, using scuba gear to negotiate a 187-foot-long sump (an underwater passageway) to emerge in a further, above-water section of the cave. There, an additional 1,000 feet of passageway has been explored.

The main chamber, called the Big Room, is directly accessible via the Ward entrance. The room is far larger than any other space in the cave and contains huge blocks of breakdown. It is spacious enough for several people.

Hike #2—Gregory Cave Entrance Hike

The Gregory Cave entrance to the Clarksville Cave is near roadside and located at the bottom of a rocky bluff, just slightly north of the parking area directly off Rt. 443. There are few hiking options at this site because you immediately come to the cliff face at whose base the cave entrance is found.

Gregory Cave is quite a bit smaller than Ward Cave, but just as interesting in every respect. It has more challenging passageways, several rimstone pools, and is divided by a short underwater passageway called Brinley's Sump—a two-foot length of passageway with a low ceiling that is generally filled with water in the springtime. During the rest of the year, the water level drops low enough to allow cavers to advance without having to hold their breath and duck under. The name of the passageway comes from a carved inscription in the wall that reads: "E. Brinley – Perth Amboy – N.J. – 1839."[4]

Geology: The Clarksville Cave is developed in beds of Onondaga limestone—a rock that formed nearly 400 million years ago from deposits of sediment that settled on the reefy bottom of a shallow sea. The cave itself was created much later, perhaps near the end of the last ice age. The passageways in the cave developed along a fault zone as water, infused with CO_2 from roots and decaying vegetable matter, produced carbonic acid, which readily dissolves limestone. Carbonic acid also created the surface features, such as sinkholes and fissures, which are so evident today.

History: The written documentation for Clarksville Cave is the oldest for any cave in New York State. Graffiti goes back as far as 1811, when the initials "G.W.L." were inscribed in the wall. The first written account of the cave is attributed to Teunis Houghtaling, who described the two sections of the cave in 1817. The following is only a partial excerpt:

> In approaching the mouth of the cave [Ward entrance] is a horizontal hole in the earth of about 20 feet in diameter and about 16 feet in depth [here, he is referring to the sinkhole entrance] then in descending the mouth of the cave is a steep descent of 20 feet which opens to a rough and massive room of 45 feet in diameter and 16 feet in height [the large chamber room, or Big Room].[5]

> When descending the mouth of the cave [Gregory entrance] we passed through a narrow passage with a steep descent of about 15 feet perpendicular; then through a chasm of 50 feet in length supported with or by solid limestone rocks.[6]

In 1820, Amos Eaton, in *Index to the Geology of the Northern States, with transverse sections extending from Susquehanna River to the Atlantic, crossing Catskill Mountains* (Second Edition), stated: "The largest of these caverns is the great cave at Bethlehem, twelve miles southwest of Albany. This is a few feet more than a fourth of a mile in length."[7,8] Although Eaton's description doesn't at first reading seem to apply to the Clarksville Cave, Thom Engel, in *A Chronicle of Selected Northeastern Caves,* sets the record straight by pointing out that in 1810 the Town of New Scotland (wherein the cave lies) was actually part of the Town of Bethlehem, and Clarksville is only twelve miles southwest of Albany as the crow flies.[9]

In 1843 the cave was mentioned in *Geology of New York* by William Mather—an early New York State geologist—who stated that breezes emanating from the cave were strong enough to cause a candle flame to flicker.[10] Mather concluded that the cave had to be fairly large to produce such a substantial wind. Mather may also have the distinction of being the first to travel the cave by boat, doing so, by his own account, in 1839.

Verplanck Colvin, who is best known for his extensive work surveying the Adirondack High Peaks, visited the Clarksville Cave several times in the latter half of the nineteenth century. Writing in *Harper's New Monthly Magazine* in 1869, Colvin stated: "These two caves are said to be respectively, one eighth and one half a mile in length. They should not be called two caves, however, for the river seems to flow from one to the other and forms a connection which a person who likes ice-water baths might explore."[11,12]

Colvin's analysis was prescient regarding the connection that was ultimately discovered between the two caves.[13] This connection, called the Ward–Gregory Link, was confirmed by four cavers—Hoyt, Kreider, Stranahan, and Porter—who dug out the interconnecting crawlway in July 1963. From that point on, Ward Cave and Gregory Cave became one long cavern that has been called the Clarksville Cave ever since.[14]

In 1906, geologist John H. Cook referred to Ward Cave as the "Big Cave" and to Gregory Cave as the "Little Cave." Cook's opinion of Ward Cave was that: "The cave presents usually a smooth, rounded arch in the harder beds, though in the thinner beds the floor is littered with fragments and presents much of the appearance of a Manlius Cave [meaning that the architecture of any cave is very dependent on the type of limestone bed in which it has formed]."[15]

The Clarksville Cave has an interesting human history that can be attributed both to its easy accessibility close to roadside and its long notoriety. In the 1880s the Big Room in Ward Cave was allegedly used as a hideout for counterfeiters. Whether they were finally apprehended is unknown. In later years the large chamber was used for the more benign purpose of growing mushrooms.[16]

In the 1930s, George Ward, a farmer, was able to save his strawberry crop from desiccation by installing a length of pipe from the Lake Room out to his fields, providing water for irrigation.[17]

In 1990 cave divers, working in the Lake Room, removed several large blocks of limestone from the bottom of the water chamber and opened up an underwater passage that led for 187 feet into a previously unknown, air-filled corridor.

The Clarksville Cave may be the premier wild cave in northeastern New York when it comes to sheer numbers of visitors (both Howe Caverns and Secret Caverns attract more visitors, but they are commercial caves). Cavers frequently refer to the Clarksville Cave as a sacrifice cave, meaning that it is offered to the public to satisfy their curiosity so that other caves may be spared undue attention.

Any cave that attracts so many visitors each year is subject to accidents and mishaps. A number of people have had to be rescued from the Clarksville Cave after becoming lodged in a tight spot. Several people have even had to be rescued between sumps after free-diving and not being able to return the same way they went in. No doubt many more mishaps have occurred than the ones that are publicly known, because injured or trapped cavers are often eventually able to affect a self-rescue or are evacuated by their group without drawing attention.

There has been one known fatal accident. On February 26, 2001, four cavers—Jonathan Allison, Robert Svensson, Michael Chu, and Joseph Baj—all in their early twenties, entered Clarksville Cave with diving equipment in order to do some preliminary exploration in the Lake Room. Although everyone in the group was an experienced caver, none were experienced cave divers. After the group had explored the Lake Room, Robert Svensson went down for one last look and never came back up. It took the concerted efforts of cavers and rescue personnel several days to retrieve the body, wedged in the entrance of the underwater passageway.[18]

Clarksville in the 1800s: As you might expect, limestone was an important commodity to Clarksville, which operated over fifty kilns for lime burning within a two-mile radius of the village. Blocks of limestone were also eminently suitable for construction. Huge blocks were quarried from Onesquethaw and hauled out in wagons pulled by teams of horses and oxen to Cohoes, where they were then used to construct some of the locks and portions of the side walls of the Erie Canal (see chapter on "Vischer Ferry Nature & Historic Preserve").

If you lived in Clarksville and weren't involved in the limestone industries, then you were most likely in the dairy or cattle business. Most farmers in the nineteenth century were fairly self-sufficient, relying primarily on their own resources to provide for their needs. Still, there were always a few items that could not be readily made at home. As a result farmers began to sell their produce in Albany and along the Hudson River in order to obtain cash for needed purchases. This trade kept growing and greatly accelerated when the Albany Delaware Turnpike was created in the early 1800s and passed through Clarksville.

In addition, because Clarksville is located halfway between Albany and Rensselaerville, it became a popular stop for wagons and travelers. A number of small businesses in the town began to flourish by catering to travelers.

Social gatherings for the community consisted of barn raisings, quilting bees, country dances, husking bees, country fairs, and church-related social events.

12   EDMUND NILES HUYCK PRESERVE

Location: Rensselaerville (Albany County)
New York State Atlas & Gazetteer: p. 65, D7

Fees: None

Hours: Year-round, dawn to dusk

Accessibility: The base of Rensselaerville Falls and the adjacent ruins of the H. Waterbury & Co. felt mill are accessible by a short, level path no more than 0.1 mile long; accessing the top of Rensselaerville Falls and Myosotis Lake involves a more substantial trek of 0.5–0.7 mile with noticeable changes in elevation; the falls downstream from the old gristmill housing the Rensselaerville Historic Society involves a 0.3-mile walk.

Degree of Difficulty: Easy to the felt mill and Rensselaerville Falls, and to the falls downstream from the Rt. 353 bridge; easy to moderate to the top of Rensselaerville Falls and Myosotis Lake

Highlights:
- Waterfalls
- Artificial lake
- Preserved Rensselaerville Gristmill and old Miller's House
- Ruins of old felt mill

Description: The Edmund Niles Huyck Preserve consists of nearly 2,000 acres of land, a biological research station, and ten miles of trails that include access to Ten Mile Creek, Rensselaerville Falls, Myosotis Lake, and Lincoln Pond. The preserve was established in 1931.[1] The main attraction is Rensselaerville Falls, which rises to over 100 feet in height. In days gone by there were a number of mills powered by several robust falls on Ten Mile Creek. You can still see old stone walls and foundations from several of these mills.

The creek runs through the picturesque town of Rensselaerville, which has many well-preserved historic homes and buildings that are privately owned. The Rensselaerville Historic Society is housed in the former Rensselaerville Gristmill and is open to the public on Wednesdays and Saturdays during the summer.

Directions: From Albany, take Rt. 85 southwest. At the junction of Rtes. 85 & 443 (northwest of Clarksville), turn left onto Rt. 85 west and drive southwest for nearly 11.0 miles until you reach the terminus of Rt. 85 at Rensselaerville. Turn right and drive west for another 0.2 mile. Just before crossing over a bridge that spans Ten Mile Creek, turn sharply right into a tiny parking area for the Edmund Niles Huyck Preserve. The main hike begins from the western end of the parking area.

Rensselaerville Falls, circa 1910.

Hikes

Hike #1—Hike to Rensselaerville Falls, "Upper Mill," and Myosotis Lake

The walk begins at the tiny parking area next to the Biological Research Station, which is the former Miller's House. From the kiosk at the end of the parking lot, follow the red-blazed trail west as it parallels the north bank of Ten Mile Creek. Within 0.1 mile you will come to a footbridge that crosses over the creek just downstream from the base of Rensselaerville Falls, a massive waterfall formed out of Devonian sandstone, siltstone, and shale—all sedimentary rocks. There are excellent views of the lower and middle sections of the falls from the footbridge.

As soon as you cross over Ten Mile Creek, you will notice to your left the old stone foundations of the H. Waterbury & Company's felt mill, built in 1870. The ruins are moss-covered and stand as silent monuments to the past. Should you desire to see the mill as it once looked, walk over to the prominent boulder next to the trail. There is a metal plaque on its face containing an outline of the mill.

As soon as you pass by the mill foundation, turn left and follow a wide path east as it parallels the south bank of the stream. You will immediately see several smaller, less obtrusive ruins to your left, just downstream from the main foundations. The path that you are following is the original road that led to the mill. This road started from the southwest end of the Rt. 353 Bridge and followed the creek upstream for 0.1 mile. The path that you initially took from the Biological Research Station is too insubstantial for wagons to have used it; furthermore, it is on the wrong side of the stream.

After exploring the historic ruins, return to the main trail. There is still more to see nearby. Another wide path heads off west, paralleling the creek ten to fifteen feet above the streambed. Although the path dead-ends within several hundred feet, it will take you to excellent views of the lower and mid-sections of Rensselaerville Falls.

After viewing the falls, return to the main path and start climbing uphill, leaving the mill foundations behind you. Within a hundred feet you will see a secondary path going off to the right. This path leads west along the upper slope of the gorge and will take you past the remains of an old earthen sluiceway on your left. This sluiceway at one time was part of an elaborate system that brought water down to the mill from a dam situated at the top of Rensselaerville Falls. The sluiceway is all that remains of this water-conveying system.

Back on the main, red-blazed trail, continue climbing uphill. Soon the trail bears sharply to the right at the edge of a pine forest on your left. You enter a large area of old farmlands and stone walls, where a second-growth forest of deciduous trees has returned to reclaim the land. In less than 0.2 mile you will

At the top of Rensselaerville Falls, circa 1910.

see a secondary trail coming in on your right. This is a continuation of the path that parallels the old sluiceway.

From here, the main trail heads downhill gradually and then comes to a trail junction. The Lake Trail leads off to the left; the Pond Hill Road Trail goes to the right.

Follow the Pond Hill Road Trail to the right, and head downhill towards the ravine. You will hear and see the stream below. Immediately, the trail divides again. Going straight ahead on an old abandoned road will take you down to the stream, where there is little to see except for an old streambed paralleling the creek. This may be a tap-off section of Ten Mile Creek that becomes active during high waters.

If you turn right at the junction and follow the main trail past a post with the number "9" on it, the trail promptly takes you down to a red-painted footbridge that spans the top of Rensselaerville Falls. Take note of the old stone abutments at both ends of the footbridge. These obviously predate the much newer looking footbridge by many years and are, in fact, the two end sections of a dam that once impounded Ten Mile Creek at the top of the falls. A gate at the west end of the dam once allowed water to be released upon demand. The water then flowed out from the dam through a pipe that led away from the top of the falls across to the opposite bank, and from there, down the sluiceway to the mill. It was quite an elaborate operation.

The dam forming Myosotis Lake is not the first one to impound Ten Mile Creek. The original dam was much smaller and considerably less substantial. It was only four feet high and was constructed out of logs. This first dam was built in the early 1800s to ensure that a reliable source of waterpower would be maintained. By that time so much deforestation had taken place that Ten Mile Creek no longer had a proper watershed, and therefore could not supply sufficient and consistent hydropower for the mills downstream. Damming up the stream ensured an adequate source of water for power.

The first dam didn't last long, however, against the power of Ten Mile Creek during torrential downpours and spring's snowmelt. It was soon swept away by floodwaters.

A second dam was immediately created. This one was much stronger and impounded a body of water that covered 100 acres of land. It was such a monumental piece of work that it took fifteen men seventy-nine days just to make repairs on it in 1836.

The lake formed by the dam was first known simply as The Pond, which explains the trail called Pond Hill Road. Later, the name changed to Myosotis Lake, a reference to the forget-me-nots—botanically known as Myosotis—that abound in the vicinity.

Walk across the bridge and look back for views of the upper section of the falls, which are block-shaped and ten feet in height, located directly below the bridge.

The large, flat, open area that you immediately come to at the east end of the footbridge is the site of two former mills. Both lasted for just a short period of time. A small dam can be seen intercepting the river just around the bend from the top of the falls.

If you wish, you can follow the road as it leads away from the footbridge. Within a couple of hundred feet the trail picks up again, going off to your left into the woods and paralleling Ten Mile Creek. This path will eventually lead you up to Myosotis Lake.

To pursue a trek with more options, cross back over the footbridge and return to the junction of the Pond Hill Road Trail and the Lake Trail. This time, take the Lake Trail (which is on your right as you approach the junction from below) and proceed west for 0.1 mile to another trail junction. The path to the left goes to Lincoln Pond, and the path to the right to Myosotis Lake.

To see Myosotis Lake, turn right and follow the trail for over 0.3 mile until you reach the lake. Staying on the trail will lead you right out onto the top of a wide dam that has created the lake. It is not possible to cross over to the other side, however, for the trail comes to a dead end at the sluiceway near the east bank of Ten Mile Creek.

Return to the junction of the Lincoln Pond and Myosotis Lake trails. If you wish to see several obscure foundations along the path to Lincoln Pond, take the Lincoln Pond trail west for 0.1 mile to a point where the main trail crosses a fairly active stream. You will also see a secondary trail paralleling the east bank of the creek off to the left. This eventually leads up to Rt. 353.

Don't cross over the stream. If you look to your right, you will notice that the creek soon flows into Myosotis Lake. Walk towards the lake, paralleling the east bank of the stream, and you will immediately come to the faint ruins of a small building. Look across the stream and you will observe a small, square-shaped column of rocks near the opposite bank. It is presumed that this foundation is the remains of a former camp. There used to be dozens of camps around the south shore.

Hike #2—Walk to the Rensselaerville Gristmill

From the parking lot, cross over to the opposite side of the road and look downstream from the top of the bridge. Just below is a six-foot-high dam intercepting Ten Mile Creek, as well as a sluiceway along the north bank that once channeled water through wooden staves to the Rensselaerville Gristmill, which stands prominently along the north bank. Directly below the dam are several small falls.

The gristmill is the third mill to occupy this spot. If you walk over to the building to look at the exterior of the mill, you can also enjoy excellent views of the falls and dam below the Rt. 353 Bridge. The mill is open for viewing on Sunday afternoons and Wednesdays during the summer.

Hike #3—Walk to "Lower Mill"

From the parking area, walk downhill on Main St. for 0.3 mile past a superb collection of old historic homes. When you get to Bennett Lane, turn right and walk south for 0.05 mile. You will come to a dirt road that parallels Ten Mile Creek. Turn right and walk up the road, going west. You will quickly see off in the distance several lower cascades, which once constituted "Lower Mill." Take note of the private homes and stay on the road. This is an area that has become residential. Old foundations have either disappeared or have been incorporated into the foundations of the present houses.

History: Rensselaerville was settled in the late 1700s by Connecticut home-steaders. The town was named after Stephen Van Rensselaer III, a Dutch patroon who offered up to 160 acres of free land to each settler willing to farm it, the only stipulation being that after seven years the homesteader would pay an annual rent (or tribute), which would be binding and perpetual not only for the original settler, but for all future owners of the land. Furthermore, it was stipulated that the patroon would retain all mineral and water rights to the land. In the years following the American Revolution and the Declaration of Independence in 1776, the concept of a feudal land baron did not sit well and led eventually to the Anti-Rent Rebellion. The rebellion lasted from 1839 to 1889 and successfully toppled the system of land barons in New York State.

Even if the Anti-Rent Rebellion had failed, however, it probably would have made little difference in Rensselaerville. The topsoil there, as it turned out, was simply too thin and infertile for anyone to make a living by farming. As a result, one by one, the farms failed, and people either turned to other enterprises to sustain themselves or left the area.

Fortunately, Rensselaerville did possess one commodity in abundance—streams of fast-moving water, most notably Ten Mile Creek. It was along Ten Mile Creek that Rensselaerville's industrial revolution began. It is said that at one time the stream was called Ten Mill Creek because of the profusion of mills on its banks.

The first mill in the village of Rensselaerville was established in 1789 at the site of the present historic gristmill now occupied by the Rensselaerville Historic Society. That mill was owned and operated by Samuel Jenkins, who came to New York State from West Stockbridge, Massachusetts. Jenkins's mill was considerably smaller than the present one and used a twenty-five-foot overshot waterwheel for power generation. In 1830 the mill was rebuilt by David Conkling. Later, a miller by the name of Steverson took occupancy of the Millers House, a building that is still in use today as the headquarters of the Edmund Niles Huyck Preserve. The mill changed ownership in 1869 when it was taken over by a man named F. Bouton. Ten years later the mill burned to the ground. Nothing was saved except for the waterwheel.

In 1880 the mill was rebuilt by Francis C. Huyck and George L. Bolton, two enterprising owners who ended up substituting a turbine in place of the waterwheel to power the mill. Except for a fire in 1897, which partially dam-aged the building, the mill has survived reasonably intact over the last 125 years. After Francis Huyck's death, the mill continued to be operated by Huyck's son, Edmund Niles, and Edmund's wife. It closed in 1945, and has remained closed since then except for special occasions. Between 1974 and 1980 considerable effort went into rehabilitating the gristmill in order to ensure its historical preservation.

In order to understand the physical locations and the timeline of the various mills that came and went along Ten Mile Creek, it is helpful to use the Rensselaerville Gristmill (now the Rensselaerville Historic Society) as a reference point. The area encompassing the gristmill and Miller's House may have been known as Middle Mill, although historical sources are not clear on this point. The section of the stream above the gristmill and up to Rensselaerville Falls was called Upper Mill. The section below the Rensselaerville Gristmill, in turn, was called Lower Mill.

We will begin with the Upper Mill section. The first mill to occupy the site next to the base of Rensselaerville Falls was built by Reuben Frisbee, John Frisbee, Samuel Hatch, and Hans Winegar between 1794 and 1795. Historians believe that the building was initially a flour mill. It later became a fulling mill, and finally the Rensselaerville Woolen Mill. Under the ownership of Henry Waterbury, the mill processed wool brought in by local farmers. The wool was carded into rolls, which were then returned to the farmers. The farmers' wives spun the rolls into yarn, and wove them into cloth. Then the cloth was returned to the factory, which fulled, fetted, and finished the product so that it was finally suitable to be made into clothing for sale.

Around 1870, Waterbury decided to branch off into an entirely different direction. He entered into partnership with Francis Conkling Huyck to manufacture papermakers' felt. The name of the company changed to H. Waterbury & Co. and produced some of the first felt ever made in America.

Erecting a mill next to a stream and a major waterfall was not without its hazards, however. In 1874 a freshet caused the dam at Myosotis Lake to rupture, resulting in significant damage to mills along the stream. The dye house at H. Waterbury & Co. was washed away. In 1878 another freshet caused the collapse of the side of the ravine where water ran from the dam to the mill. The damage was so extensive that it couldn't be repaired.

When Huyck and Waterbury dissolved their partnership in 1878, the mill closed for good. Huyck left to form Kenwood Mills, south of Albany on the Hudson River, and Waterbury departed for Oriskany, west of Utica.

Above Rensselaerville Falls and Upper Mill were two grist mills that were built between the years 1824–1839. Little is known about their history, and by 1866 neither was in operation any longer.

Just downstream from the Rensselaerville Gristmill was the section of Ten Mile Creek known as Lower Mill. In the 1790s a sawmill was erected by one of the Crocker family and H. J. & R. Frisbee (the J & R possibly stood for John and Reuben Frisbee). The mill used the same set of falls just below the Rt. 353 Bridge that furnished power to the Rensselaerville Gristmill. At some later date, the sawmill was either replaced by a new mill or underwent conversion to become a gristmill.

Around 1801, William & Uriah King established a fulling mill for dressing and dyeing cloth. It was located slightly downstream from the Rensselaerville

Gristmill and stood on the same side of Ten Mile Creek. When carding machinery was added to the mill under the new ownership of Hollister and Miner, it became known as the Machinery House.

Further downstream yet, a mill was built by Jonathan Jenkins and Asa Colvand. Below that was a sawmill established by a man named Sweet.

Rensselaerville succeeded as an industrial center for many years, then eventually began to fail as a mill town, just as it had failed earlier as a farming community. There were several reasons for this. First, the mills eventually harvested all of the trees within close proximity and found themselves having to travel in ever-widening circles from home, and at much greater expense, in order to bring back wood. Second, as the land became depleted of trees, the ground lost its ability to retain water efficiently, thus significantly diminishing the size, power, and reliability of Ten Mile Creek. This was one of the reasons why dams were established along the creek, but even that could not make up for damage that had been done to the environment. Third, the advent of railroads through the Hudson and Mohawk valleys and the inauguration of the Erie and Champlain canals resulted in Rensselaerville falling behind as an industrial center as other communities on major waterways moved into prominence.[2,3]

Part III: Berkshires Region

The history of the Berkshires is intimately connected and interwoven with that of the stately Berkshire Mountains and the rich rolling valleys bordering the Housatonic River. The early Native Americans that inhabited the region created the original pathways that were later adopted by the European colonists. Even today, highways such as Rt. 7, extending from Vermont through Connecticut, and Rt. 2 (the Mohawk Trail), extending from New York State to Boston, Massachusetts, follow these old colonial trails.

European settlers began arriving in the Berkshires in the late seventeenth century, primarily to farm the lands in the valleys. In all likelihood they enjoyed more autonomy than those settlers who lived closer to the center of British and Dutch rule in Boston and New Amsterdam, respectively. Nevertheless, when the Revolutionary War broke out, many of these farmers traded their hoes for rifles and fought valiantly along with the Continental Army.

During the nineteenth century the Berkshire region became a cultural oasis because of the beautiful but accessible mountains. It was visited by such literary luminaries as Herman Melville, Nathanial Hawthorne, Edith Wharton, William Cullen Bryant, Henry David Thoreau, William Wadsworth Longfellow, and many others. The wealthy also found it a good place to build their summer cottages.

There are many interesting areas to visit in the Berkshires where history and hiking converge:

Balanced Rocks: Visit two, distinctly different, balanced rocks that are located in separate areas of the Berkshires.

Shaker Mountain: Follow trails past old stone foundations of nineteenth-century Shaker mills and dwellings as you make your way to the summit of a mountain that once was the site of religious ceremonies for the Shaker community at Hancock Village.

No Bottom Pond: Hike to a pond that mysteriously disappears and then reappears annually.

Ice Glen & Laura's Tower: Explore a moss-covered, boulder-filled, primordial gorge that was a favorite haunt of people like Nathanial Hawthorne and Herman Melville, and then hike up to a nearby tower for an overlook of the area.

Tyringham Cobble: Climb to the top of a rocky cobble for scenic views of farmlands that were once part of an eighteenth-century Shaker community.

Ashintully Estate & McLennan Preserve: Walk to the ruins of a Gilded Age mansion where a row of thirty-foot-high Doric columns still stand, then hike through a picturesque forest on an adjacent woodland to several cascades and a dammed pond.

BALANCED ROCKS   13

Location: Lanesboro and Savoy (Berkshire County, Massachusetts)
Massachusetts Atlas & Gazetteer: p. 20, O9 & p. 21, I24

Fees: None

Hours: Savoy State Forest is open daily, with no restrictions on hours;
Balance Rock State Park is open daily, dawn to dusk.

Accessibility: Both balanced rocks are located next to dirt roads, which
allow for easy access. The road to the balanced rock in Savoy State Forest is
best negotiated by a four-wheel-drive vehicle, although during the summer
the roads are passable by any vehicle. The boulder can also be accessed by
following Ross Brook upstream from Tannery Falls, or by walking along
Tannery Falls Road, proceeding steadily uphill, and then following an
unmarked dirt road that leads left off to the boulder. Similarly, the balanced
rock at Balance Rock State Park in Lanesboro can be approached by road
or by hiking in for 0.5 mile. Keep in mind, however, that the road is gated
during the winter.

Degree of Difficulty: Easy

Highlights:
- Improbably balanced boulders, or "perched erratics," as they are
  called by some.[1]
- Other unusual rock formations

Description: There are two balanced rocks in Berkshire County—one
above North Adams and one in Lanesboro. Both are fascinating natural wonders that will surely inspire awe and amazement in both young and old.
   Balanced Rock #1: The balanced rock in the Savoy State Forest weighs
250 tons, and is ten feet by fifteen feet by eighteen feet.[2,3] It rests, seemingly
precariously, on top of a fairly flattened rock of green phyllite and is located on
the side of the same mountain whose river system has produced Tannery
Falls—one of the Berkshire's premier cascades, located only a mile away. The
boulder is formed out of quartz-feldspar gneiss and may have been transported from as far away as the Green Mountains of Vermont by glaciers during the
last ice age.

Balanced Rock #2: The 165-ton boulder at Balance Rock State Park in Lanesboro is by far the more imposing and visually stunning of the two balanced rocks.[4-9] As you walk around this massive boulder, which measures twenty-one feet by fifteen feet by ten feet, the illusion of precariousness is

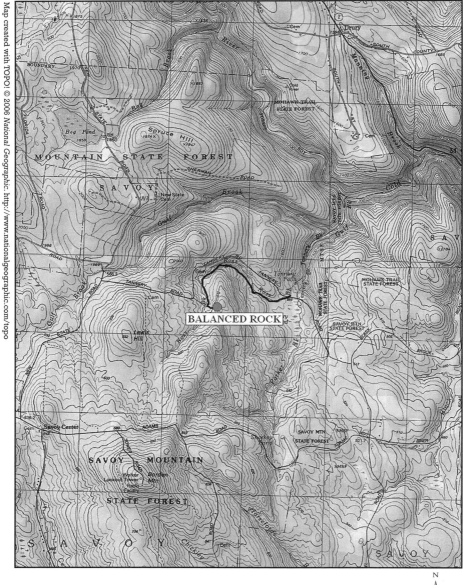

unavoidable and overwhelming. This prodigious boulder is balanced precipitously on top of a smaller, three-foot point of rock, and is seemingly ready to topple at any moment if pushed hard enough. Old postcards and photos show the rock exactly as it looks today (with the exception of the graffiti, which is more garish in modern times because of spray paints). The fact that Balance Rock has survived for centuries, despite contact with generations of humans attempting to nudge it, is sufficient testimony to the rock's improbable stability.

Directions: *Balanced Rock at Savoy State Forest.* From North Adams (junction of Rtes. 2 & 8), continue east on Rt. 2 for 11.5 miles. As soon as Rt. 2 crosses over a small bridge at the bottom of an enormous gorge, turn right onto a road that parallels Black Brook and continue uphill on Black Brook Road for 2.5 miles. Turn right onto Tannery Road and drive downhill, going northwest, for 0.7 mile. As soon as you cross over the outlet stream to the pond on the left side of the road, pull over into a parking area for Tannery Falls (on your right).

The trailhead for the Ross Brook Trail, leading toward Balanced Rock, begins across the road opposite from the parking lot, along the east side of the stream.

If you choose to drive to the balanced rock, continue on Tannery Road, proceeding uphill. Take your first left and you will reach the boulder in 0.2 mile from the turn.

Balance Rock—first view, circa 1940.

Whale Rock, 2004.

Balance Rock at Lanesboro. From Pittsfield (junction of Rtes. 7 & 20), proceed north on Rt. 7, eventually leaving the city behind. As soon as you come to Pontoosic Lake, turn left at a traffic light onto Hancock Road and drive west for 1.5 miles. Turn right onto Pecks Road and drive north for 1.4 miles. You will see the entrance to Balance Rock State Park on your left. From there, a paved road leads into the park for 0.5 mile up to a parking area where the boulder is located. From the parking area, walk less than 100 feet to the balanced rock.

Just past the huge boulder, a small trail leads through a garden of large boulders and rocks to a lower road.

To get to the other unique rocks contained in Balance Rock State Park, go back to the parking lot. You will notice a dirt road continuing out from the parking area. Follow the dirt road for several hundred feet until you reach a fork in the road. Follow the branch to the right. Within 0.05 mile you will pass by two boulders on your left. Just a short distance past these two boulders are several large boulders to your left, off in the woods and away from the road. One of these is Split Rock. If you reach a point where the road begins to curve significantly to the left, then you have gone too far.

Retrace your steps back to the fork in the road. This time, take the road to the left at the fork. Within fifty feet you will see a side path going off into the woods to the left. If you look back, you will notice Whale Rock, which is near the side of the road to your right.

Following the side path, you will quickly see Twin Rocks in the woods to your left. It is less than fifty feet away from Whale Rock.

Continue following the path for another fifty feet and you will come to a huge boulder on your right. At this point a blue-blazed trail enters from the left and does a left-angle turn, heading off on a continuation of the trail that you have been following. Follow this trail, continuing straight ahead on the blue-blazed trail, and you will arrive at Cross Rock in fifty feet, to your right.

Cross Rock, 2004.

Tannery Falls (near trailhead), 2003.

The Hikes

Hike #1—The Hike to Balanced Rock in Savoy

To start the hike to Balanced Rock, walk south from the parking area to the other side of Tannery Road and follow a small dirt road that parallels the east side of Ross Brook. You will immediately cross over a little footbridge spanning a tributary to Ross Brook. After crossing the bridge, follow the beginning of the blue-blazed Ross Brook Trail that goes off to the right.

The Ross Brook Trail parallels Ross Brook for the entire length of the trail, which is well over one mile long. The first half of the hike is over relatively flat terrain. The second half proceeds uphill in a steady fashion. There are pretty flowers and lots of flowing water to observe, but no cascades (these are all encountered on the lower part of Ross Brook). Eventually the trail leads up to a dirt road. Turn left and walk uphill for 0.1 mile. You will come to a cul-de-sac, where Balanced Rock can be seen to your left.

If you are short of time or just not feeling up to a two-mile, round-trip hike, you can drive up to Balanced Rock by going southwest on Tannery Road and then turning left onto the first dirt road you come to, which leads to Balanced Rock within less than 0.2 mile.

Balanced Rock in Savoy, 1999.

Hike # 2—The Hike to Balance Rock in Lanesboro

You can either park off Peck Road and walk up the park road for 0.5 mile to Balance Rock or, depending on the season, drive in and park several hundred feet from the rock.

History: Western Massachusetts has a number of interesting balanced rocks, including: Cradle Rock (also known as Tipping Rock and Rocking Stone) in Worcester County; Rolling Rock in Fall River; Balanced Rock (also known as Double Boulder) on Wachusetts Mountain; and two more balanced rocks in Worcester County (one of which was known in older times as Dog's Head and Old Poet). The ones closest to eastern New York are the balanced rocks in Savoy and Lanesboro.

Balanced Rock in Savoy—There is little to say historically about this enormous boulder. All of the attention and historical acclaim has gone to Balance Rock in Lanesboro.

Balance Rock in Lanesboro—One-hundred-year-old pictures of the boulder can be seen in *Berkshires: Two Hundred Years in Pictures* and in *Berkshires: The First Three Hundred Years.* What these old photographs show is Balance Rock standing alone in a wide, open field.[10,11] This is not the case today, for the huge boulder is now surrounded by a forest that has grown up around it.

Old photos also reveal another characteristic of Balance Rock—it looks completely different when viewed from different angles. In Ivan Sandrof's *Yesterday's Massachusetts* two photographs are presented—one purported to be of a balanced rock in Pittsfield, and the other claiming to be of a balanced rock in Lanesboro. Without realizing it, Sandrof had shown two images of the same rock from different perspectives.[12]

How precariously balanced is Balance Rock? Sandrof claims that the rock actually vibrated when touched, and in The Berkshires: The Purple Hills, the author seems to think that the boulder is "so perfectly balanced it can be moved with a crowbar."[13]

Considering that the rock has stood its ground for at least three centuries, with pesky humans climbing over it—like ants and with whole troops of testosterone-driven boy scouts and high school youths trying in earnest to topple the rock—it is doubtful that the balanced rock is quite so responsive that it would vibrate when touched or sway under the force of a crowbar. As Tyler Resch states in Bill Tague's *Berkshires, Vol. II,* "the behemoth has defied the efforts of most everyone to upend this famous chunk of mountain."[14]

According to Jim Moore, who has done a considerable amount of historical and field research on unusual boulders and has his own web site, the land was owned and farmed by four generations of the Squire family, with Socrates

Balance Rock—second view, circa 1920.

Squire being the last of his clan to own the land. A later owner, Grove Hulbert, was tolerant of folks coming to see the amazing rock. This tolerance, however, was sorely tested when a band of gypsies squatted on his land and began charging visitors ten cents to view the boulder. Hulbert got so angry that he roped his oxen to the huge boulder and tried to bring down the rock.[15]

In 1911 a group of concerned citizens purchased Balance Rock and surrounding lands for $2,785. In 1916, Balance Rock was turned over to the City of Pittsfield by the Balance Rock Trust to ensure its preservation. It is now part of the Pittsfield State Forest system.

At some point 45,000 Norway spruce trees were planted in the vicinity in order to return the rock to its previous, more natural setting, to the time before the cultivation of fields had denuded the land.

Herman Melville wrote about the rock in his novel *Pierre*, written in 1852.[16]

There are other, lesser-known, but notable boulders in Balance Rock State Park. Whale Rock resembles the head of a whale (or porpoise, or dolphin, or whatever your imagination favors) emerging from the water's surface. Twin Rocks consists of two parallel rocks jutting out of the ground like stone monuments. Cross Rock is a boulder whose surface has fractured in such a way that two fault lines form a cross.[17] And Split Rock is a large boulder split asunder by a tree that once grew up between its halves, but which has long since disintegrated.[18]

Geology: Balanced rocks are freakish, eye-catching natural wonders that are quite rare. In fact, an avid hiker could trek across the northeastern United States for years without encountering one. The reason why balanced rocks are so uncommon is that three conditions must occur simultaneously for them to exist.

First, a balanced rock must stand alone and not be grouped with piles of other large rocks. Talus at the base of a cliff face or at the bottom of a gorge may produce interesting formations, but not in isolation from one another. Autonomy, then, is the first condition.

Second, a balanced rock must be massive if it is to inspire awe. A fifty-pound rock delicately balanced on top of another will fail to command attention or respect. After all, one can be rightfully skeptical and wonder whether the rock was set in place by human hands. Such doubts are not generally entertained when enormous boulders are encountered. Furthermore, small balanced rocks have little weight and are easily toppled by atmospheric phenomena, earthquakes, and the ever-present intrusions of life. A balanced rock should be larger than the size of an average human being in order to be distinctive. And the larger it is, the better.

Third, a balanced rock must look like it is ready to topple at the slightest touch. Such instability is just an illusion, of course, because Balance Rock at Lanesboro, for example, has withstood tornadoes, earthquakes, endless cycles and vicissitudes of weather, and even the pesky attempts of humans to destabilize it. Such rocks may not endure for as long as cave formations (which, after all, are not subject to atmospheric conditions), but they still last for centuries, and it is their precariousness that makes them so captivating.

These, then, are the three essential conditions that must occur for balanced rocks to be crowd-pleasers—they must be autonomous, massive, and precariously poised.

But how do such massive, free-standing, precariously balanced rocks come about in the first place? Does one rock simply just land on top of another and somehow not roll off?

Is it possible, for instance, that a balanced rock could have been formed at the retreat of the glaciers 10,000 years ago? Perhaps an occasional boulder was deposited on top of another as the ice melted away? That would be the equivalent of rolling a pair of dice and having one end up on top of the other—a rare occurrence, yes, but not an impossibility, since nature figuratively rolled her dice billions of times as retreating glaciers left behind large boulders in their wakes.

On the other hand 10,000 years is a long passage of time. Crawl through a Massachusetts marble cave or hike along a deeply cut gorge, and you'll get a clear idea as to what can happen geologically in such an extended period of time. Undoubtedly, any balanced rock deposited by retreating glaciers would have toppled over long before the pyramids were built.

The likelihood is that the balanced rocks in Berkshire County formed in a slightly different manner. In all probability they were left behind to rest on top of fields of loose earth, gravel, and rocks as the glaciers retreated north. Over eons, the ground underlying these "glacial erratics" eroded away, leaving an occasional boulder perched high on top of a previously buried rock like a boat grounded on a rock when the tide goes out. When a large boulder ended up on top of a smaller one, then a balanced rock was the result.

Other balanced rocks may have started off like two sugar cubes squarely stacked, one on top of each other. Then, over the eons, they were sculpted by natural forces into more unstable configurations. The balanced rocks at the Garden of the Gods in Colorado, for example, were probably formed in this manner.

Whatever their origin, these boulders are geologically short-lived phenomena. Wind, water, snow, and ice are irresistible forces and will ultimately topple these rocks.

14 SHAKER MOUNTAIN

Location: Hancock (Berkshire County, Massachusetts)
Massachusetts Atlas & Gazetteer: p. 32, D5

Fees: None to hike Shaker Mountain; nominal fee to tour the Hancock
Shaker Village Museum

Hours: Shaker Mountain is open year-round from sunrise to sunset;
the Hancock Shaker Village Museum is open daily except Thanksgiving,
Christmas, and New Year's Day, but there is a greater variety of
exhibits and demonstrations from Memorial Day through mid-October
(www.handcockshakervillage.org).

Accessibility: Shaker Mountain—4.2-mile hike round-trip, involving an
ascent of nearly 700 feet; Holy Mountain—6.5-mile hike round-trip

Degree of Difficulty: Moderate to difficult

Highlights:
■ Mountain views
■ Small dam and waterfall
■ Ruins of former Shaker buildings

Description: The hike up to the summit of Shaker Mountain (1,845 feet),
called Mount Sinai in earlier times, involves a walk of 4.2 miles, round-trip.[1-4]
The path, an abandoned Shaker road, makes for an appealing walk as it wends
through a deciduous and pine forest, sometimes following Shaker Creek. In the
1800s the mountain was integral to the daily lives of the Shaker village, as is
evidenced by the ruins of mills and residential dwellings along the lower section of the hike. The main part of Shaker Village survives and has been incorporated into the Hancock Shaker Village Museum, located at the base of the
mountain.

If you include a hike to Holy Mount (1,927 feet)—the mountain that was
the sacred site of the New Lebanon Shakers—as part of the loop, then it
becomes a 6.5-mile trek.

The trail is maintained by the Hancock Shaker Village Museum and volunteers from the Pittsfield Boy Scout Troop. It is located in the Pittsfield State
Forest and has been designated as a National Historic Trail.

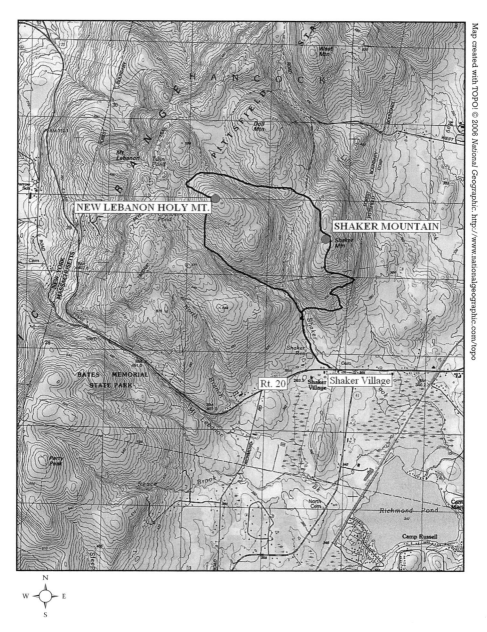

Directions: From I-90, get off at Exit 11E and drive east on Rt. 20 for 23.5 miles until you come to the Hancock Shaker Village, which will be on your left just after you have reached the bottom of Lebanon Mountain.

For those accessing the hike from Massachusetts, Shaker Village is located on Rt. 20, just west of the junction of Rtes. 20 and 41.

The trailhead begins behind the Shaker Meetinghouse on the north side of Rt. 20.

The Hikes

Hike #1—Shaker Mountain

Park in the main area for museum visitors. There is no cost to hike Shaker Mountain, but you would be remiss if you didn't pay for a tour of the museum and Shaker village while in the area. The tours are interesting and provide insight into the former Shaker community. The ticket office will provide you with a sticker for the hike and, upon request, a trail guide prepared by a local Boy Scout troop that shows the location of the various historical sites.[5]

The hike begins north of the museum village across the main highway (Rt. 20), at an elevation of 1,170 feet. Walk over to a cleared field behind the meetinghouse and pick up a trail blazed by green markers with a white triangle in the centers. The trail quickly leads into the woods and is a dirt road that formerly serviced the upper section of the Shaker community in the early nineteenth century. As you will see, the trail leads past several ruins of dams and mills, as well as the Shakers' former North Family residence. Eventually, the road goes all the way up to the top of Shaker Mountain, as well as to the New Lebanon Shakers' Holy Mount, west of Shaker Mountain.

You will begin to see traces of the early village right from the start. The beginning of the trail crosses what was once Shaker farmland. On your right before entering the woods, roughly 0.2 mile from the start, can be seen the remains of an old boiler from a Shaker textile mill. Directly to your left (looking west) are the remains of an old, raised reservoir dating back to 1790.

As soon as you enter the woods you will notice well-constructed stone walls bordering the trail, placed there when the early road was constructed. The road gradually begins to parallel Shaker Brook as it continues upward. In less than 0.3 mile you will see an old cellar hole and the outline of footings for a former bridge that once allowed Shakers to reach the North Family dwelling.

At 0.3 mile you will come to the remains of the lower dam, which was part of a well-developed system for using water productively.[6] By the 1840s the Shakers had built an underground aqueduct, conveying water from the pond created by the lower dam to the laundry, washing rooms, stables, and mills. These buildings, still standing, are across Rt. 20 on the south side, over 0.3 mile distant from the water source. Near the dam, which rests on top of a natural, three-foot-high waterfall, can be seen pipes and a cistern.

The remains of the upper, "convex" dam, built in 1810, can be reached in less than another 0.1 mile. Between the upper and lower dams are the ruins of an old sawmill that dates back to 1876.

For the sake of expediency, however, turn right at the lower dam and cross over a bridge to the east side of the stream before you reach the upper dam. There is more to see before leaving the lower grounds.

As soon as you cross the bridge, follow the trail as it turns right. Keep looking to your right as you walk south along the old road and you will see the crumbling stone ruins of a waterwheel house, woolen mill, carding mill, and sawmill. Just beyond these ruins, less than 100 feet to the south, are the remains of the North Family dwelling, built in 1821. The locations of both sites are indicated by descriptive plaques, which is fortunate since the ruins themselves are fairly overgrown and indistinct. With a little imagination, however, you can picture the once-thriving community that worked and lived here. This is an area in which you may wish to linger and explore in greater detail.

Follow the main trail as it goes northeast, to the left, at 0.7 mile and begins the ascent up Shaker Mountain. Along the way, to the left, you will pass by the remains of a charcoal pit that was used for turning logging remnants into more useful products. Unfortunately, only a shallow depression remains of the pit, which can be easily obscured by leaves in the fall.

As you continue uphill you may begin to realize that the road has changed into an old cart path. Cart paths differ from logging roads in that they were constructed by the careful placement of laid stone, though most of these stones have eroded over time.

From here the trail winds uphill, with many switchbacks, an arrangement that at one time was well suited for horse and carriage. The path is broad and lined with a variety of mature trees including oak, white pine, maple, and birch. Wildflowers abound in season.

At over 2.0 miles the trail curves to the right before heading straight to the "holy ground"—an area that is not all that easy to distinguish from the background mosaic of brush and trees. Fortunately, a plaque marks the area where horses were once tethered next to the sacred grounds. If you have picked up the map provided by the museum, you should be able to distinguish the general area where the feast ground, fountain, and altar were located, but there are no actual ruins or remains of these features.

The holy ground is shaped like a square, but is now overgrown. Fortunately, the four corners of the square are bordered by picket fences, allowing you to visualize the outline. A stone mound can be seen in the center; this, presumably, is the altar site. There are other stone remnants bordering the site but, without a proper map, attempting to identify features is virtually impossible. Take a moment to imagine the Shaker families arriving in their carriages to celebrate religious ceremonies in such a beautiful outdoor setting.

From the top of Shaker Mountain, retrace your steps. Near the bottom, cross over the bridge spanning Shaker Brook. From here, turn right and proceed to the upper dam, which is just uphill. This convex dam, built by the

Shakers in 1810, was designed to be much stronger than the lower dam and hold back more water. It was 120 feet long and may have stood as high as thirty-five feet in the center. There is still a lot of stonework evident. The dam's capstones lie in the streambed. There is a high stone wall east of the dam and an access path.

You will have hiked 4.2 miles upon your return to the trailhead.

Hike #2—Holy Mount

The trail to New Lebanon Shakers' Holy Mount begins at the top of Shaker Mountain at the northeast corner of the holy ground site. The trail goes along a ridge and then dips into the gulf between the two mountains. When you come to a fork, take the trail to the right and ascend to the top of Holy Mount. This trail is not as well traveled and is faint in places. Once you reach the top of the Mount, the remaining wall of the feast ground and the Sacred Lot are apparent. Again, the map is helpful in locating remnants of the altar, fountain, and shelter site, since these features are no longer distinguishable and have been overgrown by the woods.

The return trail is by way of a small opening in the western wall of the Sacred Lot. Shortly, you will arrive at a natural amphitheater in the southeast corner, where a spring is present. This makes for a good picnic rest stop.

The trail continues down the western side of Mt. Lebanon, veering south until it intersects and joins the Shaker Mountain Trail on the west side of Shaker Brook. Along the way, you will pass by the upper dam on Shaker Brook, part of the former water system of the Hancock Shaker family. Continue south and you will return to the Shaker Village and Museum.

The total hike is about 6.5 miles.

History: The Shakers were founded in 1778 by "Mother" Ann Lee, an English immigrant who settled in Watervliet, New York, after being jailed for her religious beliefs in England. Her followers believed her to be the female Christ. The Shakers, formally called the United Society of Believers in Christ's Second Appearing, became known as Shakers because they incorporated dance into their worship services. Their basic tenets were productive, industrious labor and chaste separation of the sexes. Men and women lived separately, though in the same building, and they were equals in every way, including economically. Sexual balance was another important Shaker tenet. They believed their communities were "heaven on earth," part of a new millennium. Though they were a spiritual community, they were very practical in developing and promoting their commercial ventures. During the sect's heyday, from 1790–1850, it grew to about 5,000 members. Most were located in the Northeast, but some lived as far away as Kentucky.[7]

The Shaker Community at Hancock, Massachusetts, was established in 1790.[8] Shakers continued living in the community until 1959, when they sold it with the stipulation that it be operated as a museum. The remaining buildings, gardens, and pastures were converted to a living museum that first opened in 1960 (see hours above).[9-11]

In the mid-1800s the Hancock Shakers were a community of six "families." Shaker families were not biological families, but rather groupings of men and boys and women and girls that might number from twenty to one hundred individuals. In the 1830s there were over 300 individuals living at the Hancock site. This community's primary industries were agriculture and the production of medicines from herbs and minerals.

The Hancock Shakers, with their cohorts in New Lebanon a few miles west of Hancock, developed the oldest pharmaceutical business in the nation. They studied and produced a wide variety of medicinal herbs for their own use that were also sold commercially as medicinal compounds until 1938. The Shakers were much respected as herbalists and botanists by the community at large, and were looked upon as experts in the field of medicinal herbs. It is said that the Samuel A. Tilden family (the Tilden of Boss Tweed Tammany Hall fame, who later ran unsuccessfully for president as the Democratic candidate) borrowed recipes and techniques from the Shakers for their pharmaceutical business.[12]

In addition to producing medicines, the Hancock community also operated several mills and a blacksmith shop, as well as a carpentry industry.[13] Thanks to their principled work ethic, the Shakers produced an abundance of simple and functional items that were appealing to the outside world—furniture, woolen garments, brooms, and wooden boxes. The Hancock Shakers were successful as a commercial venture, and by the early 1800s they were selling these items via catalogue. Grover Cleveland's wife ordered a woolen cloak from the New Lebanon Shaker community industries that she wore to her husband's presidential inauguration.[14]

Outsiders were intrigued by the concept of a celibate society and the Shaker's unique worship service, which included much music and dance. Shakers allowed outsiders to attend these services, partly as a recruitment effort, but also to dispel the rumors about devil worship. Remember, this was the mid-nineteenth century when some religions prohibited public music and dancing. You might say that the Shaker services provided some acceptable entertainment for the surrounding communities, such as Pittsfield. In fact, many notables visited the Hancock village, including Nathanial Hawthorne and Herman Melville.

The daily life of the Hancock Shakers featured quite comfortable lodgings. Each family house was furnished simply with well-designed and well-made furniture. There was indoor running water by 1830 and electricity by 1913.

Shakers wove material and made their own clothes. They grew and harvested bountiful supplies of vegetables and grain. There were herds of cows for milk and cheese and a large henhouse for eggs. There was also an apple orchard. The kitchen was well equipped with pots, utensils, dishes, and stoves for cooking and heating. The dining room was communal, but the men and women sat at separate tables.

The communal dwelling house was interesting in that it was divided in half, with men's quarters on one side of the hallway and women's on the other side. There were many windows to maximize the light. It has been recently discovered that underneath the current dark woodwork and plain white walls were original colors of bright yellow and orange, so the houses were very bright and cheery in the early 1800s. The Shakers, after all, were striving for "heaven on earth."

Membership began to decline starting in the 1880s, except for widows and orphans who needed shelter. It is conjectured that the rise of "individualism" made the Shakers' communal way of life less fashionable and appealing. As of 2006 only one very small Shaker community still exists, at Sabbathday Lake in Maine.

NO BOTTOM POND

Location: Beebe Hill State Forest (Columbia County)
New York State Atlas & Gazetteer: p. 53, AB6

Fees: None

Hours: Open continuously

Accessibility: Most of the 0.8-mile hike follows an easy road; the last 0.2 mile consists of a short downhill trail to No Bottom Pond. The pond can be explored by canoe or kayak, but you must bring your own.

Degree of Difficulty: Easy to moderate

Highlights:
- Interesting disappearing and reappearing lake
- Caves and areas of karst

Description: No Bottom Pond is a small mountain lake formed at an elevation of 1,700 feet.[1] It serves as the source for the Green River, a medium-sized stream that flows into the Housatonic River south of Great Barrington.

What makes No Bottom Pond so fascinating is that if you visit it in the spring, you will find a large body of water. If you return in late summer or fall, however, the lake may have shrunk to the size of a puddle. This phenomenon is the result of the pond's underground drainage system, part of which can be seen along its northwest shore.

Directions: From Albany, take I-90 southeast until you reach the New York State Thruway. Get on the Thruway and drive east for approximately nine miles. Get off onto the Taconic State Parkway and drive south for roughly five miles, then take the exit for Austerlitz and Chatham. The exit ramp takes you directly onto Rt. 203, going east. Drive east for 0.6 mile and turn left onto Rt. 9, which is Red Rock Road. Proceed northeast for 2.5 miles, then turn right onto Rt. 24 (Clark Road) and drive east for 3.0 miles. At this point Rt. 24 merges with Rt. 5 (Osmer Road). Continue southeast on Rt. 5 for another 1.1 miles. Turn left onto Fog Mountain Road. Within less than 0.1 mile, turn left into the parking area for Beebe Hill State Forest.

It is also possible to explore No Bottom Pond by canoe or kayak. If you do so, you may want to consider taking along a wheeled carrier to cart your canoe or kayak.

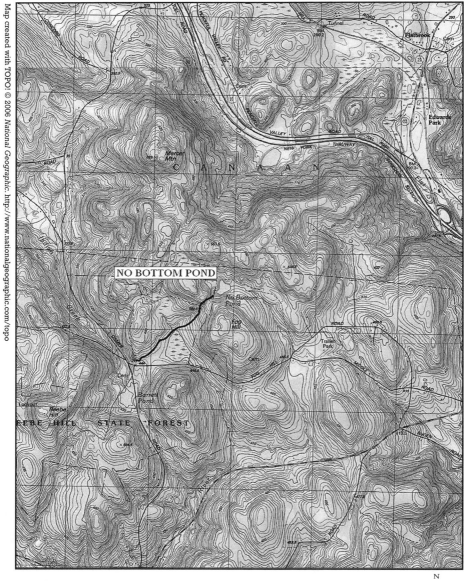

Map created with TOPO! © 2006 *National Geographic.* http://www.nationalgeographic.com/topo

No Bottom Pond—partially filled, 1995.

The Hike

The walk begins from the parking area for Beebe Hill State Forest. The forest acquired its name from nearby Beebe Hill, whose summit several miles southwest of No Bottom Pond is high enough to warrant a lookout tower.

From the back of the parking area, follow a red-blazed dirt road that leads off to the right, going northeast. The road, which is closed to motorized vehicles, proceeds uphill initially and then slowly descends until it reaches a swampy area off to your right at roughly 0.3 mile. At the inlet to the swamp, you will notice a feeder stream on your left making its way down from the highlands. A medium-sized cascade can be seen on the creek just upstream from the road.

From here, the road begins to ascend slowly. In 0.6 mile you will reach a point where the main road veers to the left, eventually intersecting the upper swamp. Instead of bearing left, follow a blue-blazed path to your right that wends its way between Fog Hill on your right and an unnamed, smaller hill to your left. The trail leads uphill momentarily and then downhill for roughly 0.2 mile to No Bottom Pond. Take note of the posted signs and remain on the trail. You will arrive at the southwest corner of the lake where a sign on a tree reads, without further fanfare, "No Bottom Pond."

From here, care must be taken to stay on state land. The more distant, northeast, part of the pond is privately owned and posted.

Following state lands, proceed to your left, going around the west shore of the lake until you reach an area of karst that contains sinkholes, crevices, and small cave openings. It is an interesting area to walk across, but pay close attention to state markers. This is clearly a patchwork of public and private lands.

During the bushwhack around the west side of the pond, look across to the opposite side and you will see the chimney of what was once an old cabin.

History: No Bottom Pond was written up by Clay Perry in his 1948 caving classic, *Underground Empire*. Perry described a strange and wonderful mountain shrouded in perpetual fog, where a lake on its upper slope would materialize and then dematerialize each year, and where underground caverns and sinkholes beckoned the brave and curious into the very bowels of the earth.

Perry included a description of No Bottom Pond by Richard F. Logan, a geologist and explorer who visited the area in 1937. To quote Logan:

> And 'twas then that I first got the creeps. ... First, it was the odor, as I approached the pond—sodden, damp, musty, as though dead things cluttered up the place. Then there was the quiet—not even a rustling of leaves on the trees or the chirp of a bird. And the toads made it worse. Thousands of them newly hatched hopped underfoot. The water was crawling with bloodsuckers.[2]

Logan's nerves finally got the better of him. He scrambled back down the mountain in a fit of trepidation, convinced that he had "found a potential setting for a murder mystery."[3] Little did he know how correct his presentiment was.

The fact that No Bottom Pond regularly fills and then empties has become a well-documented phenomenon. According to Clay Perry: "I went to No Bottom Pond some years after Geologist Logan had visited it. There was a boat on the bottom of No Bottom Pond, but it could not be used because there was no pond."[4] As it turns out, the lake frequently disappears through a natural drain at the northeast side of the pond.

While at No Bottom Pond, Perry "walked across the semi-dry bed of the pond, followed the course of a trickle of water from a brook which calmly vanished in a hole about 6 inches in diameter in the bottom of No Bottom Pond."[5] When the lake has dwindled to the size of a large puddle, you can see the opening to this underground drainage system, which is obscured when the pond is full.

Now comes the grisly story of Oscar Beckwith—the cannibal of Columbia County—and how No Bottom Pond became associated with a murder case. In 1882 a miner named Oscar Beckwith cold-bloodedly murdered his partner, Simon Vandercook, and attempted to conceal the deed by hacking up Vandercook's body and burning the parts. Beckwith did not have good luck, however. A neighbor, Harrison Calkins, happened to stop by the cabin shortly after Vandercook's murder and became suspicious of foul play when he saw what looked like pieces of a body being broiled on top of a wood-burning stove.

Calkins promptly contacted the authorities. Beckwith, realizing that the jig was up, took off and made his way up to No Bottom Pond to hide out. Within a matter of hours, a constable's party was in hot pursuit, tracking Beckwith's footprints in a light dusting of fallen snow. When they arrived at the lake, the posse suddenly came to a halt and looked out across the pond at a view that remains pretty much unchanged from what you see today. The trail had seemingly come to an end.

It was obvious to the posse that Beckwith must have hidden in one of the tiny caves near the limestone ledges, but no one felt eager to crawl in after Beckwith to engage the killer in a struggle to the death. What's more, the constable's party was already outside of their jurisdiction, having started their pursuit from Alford, Massachusetts. Convinced that nothing more could be done for the moment, the posse left No Bottom Pond and returned to the valley, leaving Beckwith to be dealt with at a later date (and he was, but not immediately and not at No Bottom Pond).[6]

No Bottom Pond has also been associated with monsters of another kind. Several Bigfoot sightings have been claimed in the Red Rock area near No Bottom Pond. No Bottom Pond just exudes mystery and intrigue.[7,8]

Waters from the underground drainage system used to issue out of Fog Hill through an opening called No Bottom Pond Cave—a minor cave, as caves go, with 200 feet of passageway, three rooms, and walls of "very hard dolomite etched with traces of pure white quartz." No Bottom Pond Cave, however, did a vanishing act of its own. In 1958, New York State obliterated the cave when it built a connection between the New York State Thruway and the Massachusetts Turnpike.[9]

16 ICE GLEN & LAURA'S TOWER

Location: Stockbridge (Berkshire County, Massachusetts)
Massachusetts Atlas & Gazetteer: p. 32, N7

Fees: None

Hours: Open year-round

Accessibility: Ice Glen, 0.2-mile scramble over and around huge boulders; Laura's Tower, 0.8-mile ascent of 485 feet.

Degree of Difficulty: Moderate for both Ice Glen and Laura's Tower

Highlights:
- Scenic gorge with huge boulders and talus caves
- Unique footbridge over Housatonic River
- Views of Stockbridge and environs from Laura's Tower

Description: *Ice Glen* is a spectacular rocky notch filled with moss-covered boulders and bordered by large white pines and hemlocks. Once inside its towering walls, you will have a sense of walking through a primordial world. You might even imagine that you have been transported in time back into a wild, nineteenth-century forest scene painted by Thomas Cole or Asher B. Durand. There is really nothing else in or near the Capital Region that is quite as awesome and sublime.[1-6]

Laura's Tower is a twenty-five-foot-high lookout that rises above the tree line atop a 1,465-foot-high mountain. From the tower there are panoramic views of Stockbridge and the surrounding mountains.[7,8] It is an ideal place to visit in mid-October when the forests are ablaze with colors, or in June when the laurel bushes are in bloom.

The trails are maintained by the Laurel Hill Association, a conservation and improvement society.

Directions: Both of these hikes begin in Stockbridge, Massachusetts. From the intersection of Rtes. 7 and 102 in Stockbridge, go south on Rt. 7 for 0.3 mile and turn left onto Park Street. There is a small parking area at the end of the street, 0.2 mile from Rt. 7. The Ice Glen and Laura's Tower can both be accessed from either Park Street or Ice Glen Road.

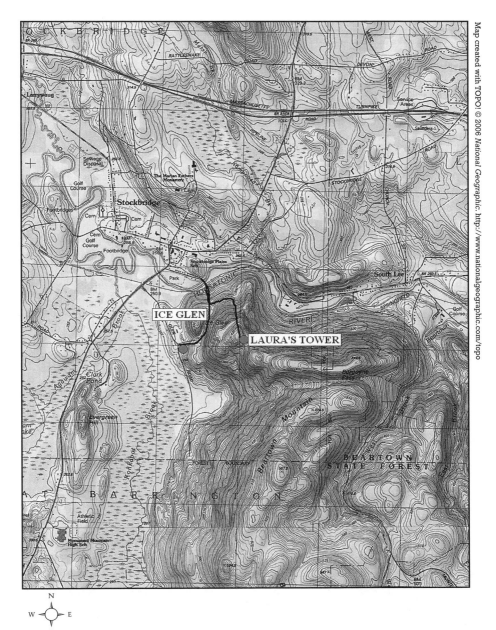

ICE GLEN

LAURA'S TOWER

N
W · E
S

The Hikes

Hike #1—Ice Glen

The hike begins from the parking area at the end of Park Street. You begin by crossing over the Housatonic River via the Memorial Footbridge. The bridge is an unusual truss design and worth pausing to inspect.[9] It is a narrow suspension bridge with stone arch trusses at both ends. From its middle there are good views of the Housatonic, named after a Native American word for "a place beyond the mountains."[10]

The clearly marked, well-worn trail crosses railroad tracks in a few hundred feet and then heads uphill through a hardwood forest consisting mostly of birch and maple. In approximately 0.2 mile you will come to a junction where the trail to the Ice Glen goes to the right, and the trail to Laura's Tower to the left.

Bear right, following the Ice Glen trail. The terrain ahead soon narrows and changes, passing through an area of swampy ferns. Fortunately, the footing is solid and reasonably dry. You may begin to have a feeling of unease as you look ahead and see the landscape turning into a steep, rocky gorge filled with boulders in disarray and overhung with giant hemlocks.[11-13]

Keep a sharp eye to the right for the engraved, moss-covered boulder dedicating the Ice Glen to David Dudley Field, who donated the gorge to Stockbridge in 1891. This marks the place where the Ice Glen begins.

The gorge can be a fascinating primeval playground for children and adults alike, but young children should be closely supervised for reasons that will become obvious as you make your way through the glen.

Across the Housatonic to Ice Glen, circa 1910.

The trail winds around and over huge boulders covered with mosses and polyphony fern. There are wooden walkways over and around some of the more difficult spots. The juxtaposition of the boulders creates numerous talus caves that can be explored for short distances.[14] For this reason one should take along a flashlight. Because the gorge is so narrow, rocky, and deep, the caves produced by jumbles of boulders harbor ice well into late spring or early summer—hence the name, Ice Glen. Whether or not there is ice still remaining when you visit, the glen generally tends to be a cool place to visit on a hot summer's day. The large, smooth boulders can make for pleasant rest or picnic spots.[15]

Walking through Ice Glen, 2002.

The white pine and hemlock along the walls of the glen are especially large and quite spectacular in their own right. They have been allowed to gain in girth and stature because nineteenth-century loggers found the terrain too difficult to harvest these trees.

The length of the gorge is approximately 0.2 mile. It is such an enchanting place to explore, however, that several hours can easily be spent climbing, peering into deep recesses, scampering about, and sitting atop rocks as you make your way through the glen.

The Ice Glen exits onto a short road where several private residences can be seen, one of which, to the left, has been erected amidst giant boulders as if defying the gorge.

Once through the gorge, you have a choice of either returning along the path you came on or continuing on the road straight ahead, which intersects Ice Glen Road in less than 0.2 mile. If you choose to proceed straight ahead, turn right when you get to Ice Glen Road and proceed west on foot to Rt. 7, a distance of about 0.6 mile. You will pass by several large estates on this road and will be afforded distant views of Monument Mountain to the southwest. Once on Rt. 7, it is about 0.3 mile to Park St., and then 0.2 mile back to the parking area.

Hike # 2—Hike to Laura's Tower

Accessing Laura's Tower, named after Laura Belden, a niece of David Dudley Field, involves an ascent of about 485 feet along a well-graded trail that abounds with mountain laurel in the late spring. The hike begins from the end

Ice Glen, circa 1920.

Laura's Tower, 2000.

of Park Street and follows the initial walk to the Ice Glen by crossing the Housatonic via the Memorial Footbridge, proceeding over railroad tracks, and then going uphill to a trail junction.

Upon reaching the junction bear left, veering away from the Ice Glen Trail, and follow the yellow-blazed trail uphill to Laura's Tower. The path is nicely graded with switchbacks and resembles a jeep road in sections. All the while, the path leads through a mostly hardwood forest of maple and birch trees, with occasional white pine and hemlocks towering over hobble bush. It is especially delightful to undertake the hike in mid June when the mountain laurels are in full bloom with pink and white flowers adorning the sides of the trail.

Even though this habitat harbors deer and coyote, you will most likely see only chipmunks and squirrels. You may be fortunate enough to spot a chickadee, blue jay, or woodpecker soaring under the forest canopy.

Shortly, the trail turns right and crosses a stream where an old springhouse is visible to the right.

At the top of the mountain, you will enter an area of brush and tall grasses. Here, the views are somewhat limited. Fortunately, a twenty-five-foot-high, steel-frame tower enables hikers to raise themselves above most of the tree line and obtain good views of Stockbridge and nearby mountains, including Mt. Greylock, Mt. Race, and Mt. Everett. Inexorably, the underbrush and trees continue to grow back each year, further limiting views, but the Laurel Hill Association periodically clears away the brush.

The top of the mountain is a superb place to picnic on a pleasant day.

From the tower, the trail continues all the way to Bear Mountain State Forest. To return to the Park Street trailhead at Stockbridge, retrace your steps, perhaps detouring to visit the Ice Glen if you have not already done so.

History: The first written description of the Ice Glen was made in 1798 by Timothy Dwight, whose journal was later published as *Travels in New England*. The glen had no name at that time, so Dwight simply referred to it as that place that had "undergone a violent convulsion at some distant period"—probably at the end of the last glaciation about 10,000–12,000 years ago.[16]

In 1829 the glen was written up in *The History of the County of Berkshire*. It was described as a chasm where "rocks of every size and form are thrown together in the wildest confusion." It was also during this period of time that the glen was given its first name—Ice Hole—presumably because the ice in its interior did not melt until middle or late summer. By 1854, however, the name of the chasm had become Ice Glen.[17]

Both the Ice Glen and Laura's Tower are especially interesting as a footnote to mid-nineteenth-century literary history. New England, and especially Massachusetts, was a Mecca for famous writers and intellectuals of the time. The *literati* sought out the peaceful Berkshires as a favorite place to write and rest—as they continue to do even today. The Ice Glen and Laura's Tower were visited by such notables as David Dudley Field, Dr. Oliver Wendell Holmes, Herman Melville, Nathaniel Hawthorne, William Cullen Bryant, Henry Sedgwick, and Catherine Sedgwick.

The original twenty-five-foot-high wooden tower was built by David Dudley Field on what he had named Laura's Retreat. It is said that Laura often climbed the mountain to find solace following the death of her husband and children.

On August 5, 1850, an illustrious group including the distinguished personages just mentioned spent a pleasant afternoon hiking in the Stockbridge area. The trek was initiated by David Dudley Field, a prominent New York attorney who had a residence in downtown Stockbridge. The party began with a hike over to and up Monument Mountain, about three miles south of Stockbridge along Rt. 7. While on top, the poem *Thanatopsis* by William Cullen Bryant was recited, presumably by Bryant himself. *Thanatopsis* was originally published in the North American Review in 1817 and is considered to be one of the first truly American poems, distinct from British poetry.[18]

After enjoying dinner at the Fields' home, the group next set out to explore the Ice Glen. It was this hike that cemented the friendship of Herman Melville and Nathaniel Hawthorne. They found this mossy, hemlock-punctuated, rocky, jumbled wonder as mysterious and fascinating as you will surely find it today.

The Ice Glen's eerie, magical quality inspired Fannie Kemble—a famous actress of her day—to inaugurate yearly evening masquerade parties in the glen, lit by torchlight.[19] It is said that the first torchlight party was arranged by Dr. S. P. Parker in 1841 for the amusement of his pupils. Parker later became the first rector of St. Paul's church at Stockbridge in the 1850s.

In the 1800s, Mary M. Chase wrote a poem about the glen that appeared in *Holden's Magazine*. Entitled "Ice Glen," the poem contained twelve stanzas, its most descriptive verse being:

> On! On! O'er our heads the fearless trunks tower,
> Watching grimly the tumult that startles the hour.
> Around lie the Titan rocks, gloomy and vast
> Fettered firmly to the earth where in wrath they were
> cast.
> Stoop! Clamber! light foot, strong hand, here we need
> Eagle eye, steady nerve, all these dangers to heed.[20]

One of the first modern accounts of the Ice Glen appeared in *New England's Buried Treasure* by Clay Perry. Perry narrated the captivating story of a mid-nineteenth-century bank robber who used the glen to hide out during the day while in the evening attempting to bore through the masonry of the Housatonic National Bank. His plan was foiled, however, when a couple of late-night strollers noticed him behind the bank, grew suspicious, and notified the authorities.[21]

Perry also described the festive, late-night processions that took place in the 1880s and 1890s, when hundreds of revelers bearing "flaming torches" and attired in "fantastic costumes" wended their way through the intricate pathways in the glen. According to Perry, once the merrymakers had gathered in sufficient numbers by the depot square, they would cross the Housatonic

River at the end of Park Street, proceed up the hill, and then through the glen, exiting at Ice Glen Road.[22]

"August 1850" commemorative picnic hikes, as well as Halloween jaunts, are still occasionally conducted through the glen, sometimes sponsored by the Stockbridge Historical Society.

Rocks abound in Ice Glen, 2003.

TYRINGHAM COBBLE

Location: Tyringham (Berkshire County, Massachusetts)
Massachusetts Atlas & Gazetteer: p. 44, A13

Fees: None

Hours: Daily, sunrise to sunset

Accessibility: 2.0-mile hike round-trip, with an elevation gain of 453 feet

Degree of Difficulty: Moderate

Highlights:
- Views of the valley
- Interesting rock formation
- Site of former Shaker community

Description: This pretty, loop hike covers a variety of terrain and vegetation as it takes you to the top of a small mountain.[1-3] The cobble is a rocky mound of earth that juts up from the surrounding, flatter land, and was created by the last glaciers about 10,000 years ago.[4] The word itself is derived from the Dutch *koble* or *kobel*.[5] The lands surrounding the cobble were Shaker community farmlands in the nineteenth century.

Tyringham Cobble is supported and maintained by the Trustees of the Reservation, a not-for-profit Massachusetts conservation organization.

Directions: From Lee (junction of Rtes. 102 and 20), take Rt. 102 west and then immediately turn left onto Tyringham Road. Follow Tyringham Road southeast for 4.2 miles to Tyringham. Turn right onto Jerusalem Road and drive southwest for 0.3 mile. You will see the parking area for Tyringham Cobble on your right.

The Hike

The hike begins from the parking lot off Jerusalem Road in the town of Tyringham. Walk through a gated entrance and follow the path through pastureland to the base of the cobble. There is an old red barn at the beginning of the trail and a kiosk with information describing the cobble, a list of regulations

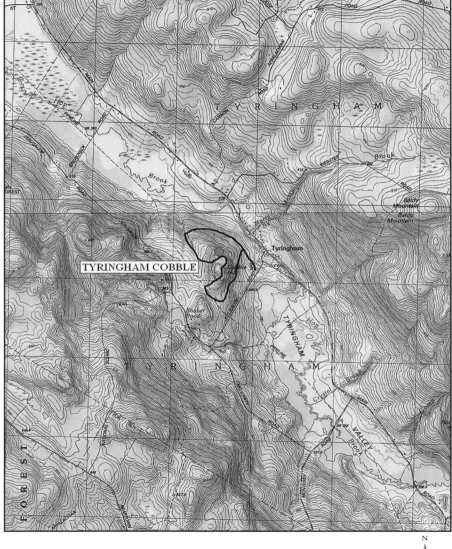

Map created with TOPO! © 2006 National Geographic. http://www.nationalgeographic.com/topo

pertinent to land owned by Trustees of the Reservation, and a donation box.

At this point you will have reached the loop trail, which goes to the right or left. We will take the trail going off to the right, which gently winds around the north side of the hill before starting its ascent. Keep an eye out for cows in the pasture. Their size and surprising speed can be intimidating to small children. There are a variety of seasonal wildflowers in the fields, including daisies in the summer and milkweed and goldenrod in the early fall.

The next 0.3 mile takes you uphill, going west through a pretty, hardwood forest. Shortly before reaching the top of the cobble, at about 0.5 mile, you will come to a grassy knoll overlooking the quaint town of Tyringham. This is a perfect stopping point for a picnic or for just enjoying the views. If you are hiking in the fall, you may observe flowering wild thyme and an assortment of wildflowers in this area. Looking down, you will see the tiny town of Tyringham with its white church and steeple surrounded by hills of splendid autumn-hued maples, bordered on the west by Hop Brook. Unfortunately, the trees and shrubbery on the lower hill reclaim more of the view each year.

Continuing gently upward, you will soon come to a rocky outcrop with additional pastoral views. You are now at the summit of the cobble, but be advised that the grassy knoll passed by earlier commands the greatest interest and has the better views.

Rabbit Rock, 1997.

Proceeding down from the summit, the hike now turns southwest at 1.0 mile, leading into a hardwood forest. Further downhill, the path overlaps a short segment of the Appalachian Trail, where sumac, juniper, and blueberries can be seen in season. If you look southeast, far off in the distance, you can sometimes see the surviving columns from the ruins of the Ashintully estate (see chapter on "Ashintully Estate & McLennan Preserve").

In less than 0.1 mile further, turn left off of the Appalachian Trail and head northeast on the lower part of the Tyringham Cobble trail loop. At 1.5 miles you will encounter an unusual rock formation that some have dubbed Rabbit Rock, for it does strikingly resemble an abstract, limestone sculpture of a rabbit—ears and all! When you get up close to it, you will notice that the limestone rock is very pitted and eroded.

From Rabbit Rock continue northeast on the trail through woods, bushy vegetation, and now-overgrown farmland evidenced by old apple trees. At roughly 2.0 miles you will be back at the pasture, having completed the loop.

History: Tyringham Cobble and the surrounding countryside contain a rich and interesting history.[6] The villages of Tyringham and Monterey (to the south) were located on a major travel route connecting the lower Housatonic Valley with Connecticut and Boston as early as 1735. Because of this traffic and trade, the settlements quickly developed. This area was known simply as Housatonic Township No. 1 until its incorporation in 1762.

By 1739 a sawmill was built in the general area by John Brewer, under a land grant inducement by the Great and General Court at Boston to encourage

Views of Tyringham, circa 1920.

settlement of the area and to accommodate the needs of the small community. Brewer carted two millstones from the east the next year, adding a gristmill to his industries.[7]

The town of Tyringham was incorporated in 1762. At that time it was primarily a farming community. The colonists coexisted with Native Americans already in residence who, it is said, had developed the process for making maple sugar before the first settlers arrived.[8]

Later, after the American Revolution when manufacturing goods were not hampered by British taxes, Tyringham had an active industrial life. Gristmills and sawmills proliferated along Hop Brook. Faint traces of dams can still be noted on the brook. In the nineteenth century a paper mill, cider mill and rake factory were erected near the town. There were also numerous crafters, such as woodworkers, smiths, and cobblers.[9] A lime kiln was located west of the pasture area on the current Tyringham Cobble lands.

Because the village was bordered to the west by the Berkshire Hills, it was somewhat protected from the fierce battles waged along the Hudson River in New York State during the Revolutionary War. The villagers were not just bystanders, however. The nearby village of Great Barrington (to the southwest) was one of the first to rebel against the taxation imposed by the British government. And although no battles were fought in Tyringham, a number of individuals from the community distinguished themselves in combat elsewhere.

In 1792 a Shaker community was established in Tyringham.[10,11] It was called Jerusalem and was located along Jerusalem Road in the vicinity of Tyringham Cobble. The lands around the cobble were used for farming by the Shakers. On the southwest side of the cobble are the remains of an old Shaker apple orchard.

Over a period of thirty-five years, the Shakers enlarged their holdings to 1,500 acres, expanding as far as West Stockbridge where they acquired an old forge mill. They had a seed packaging business that printed colored seed packets, which was notable at the time.[12] Until 1858 the community prospered, with two "families" located three-fourths of a mile apart (Shaker families were large groups of mostly unrelated acolytes).[13] At its peak the Shaker population in Tyringham consisted of about 200 individuals.

The Tyringham community finally dissolved in 1875 because the membership was sadly depleted by that time.[14] Some members had moved to Hancock and Enfield, Connecticut.[15,16]

The ministry at Mt. Lebanon had wanted to establish a Shaker community in Pennsylvania and learned of a wooded estate in Hornesdale called "The Promised Land," owned by the reverend Dr. Joseph Jones. It was decided by the Mt. Lebanon Shakers and Dr. Jones that they would exchange properties, the remaining Shakers moving to the Hornesdale property and Dr. Jones occupying the Shaker site on Jerusalem Road in Tyringham. Dr. Jones established a religious-based resort on the Tyringham Shaker site, which he called Fernside. Today there are five surviving buildings just north of Jerusalem Road in the area of Fernside. Most of them are former Shaker residences in the traditional, unadorned, salt box style. The houses appear to be in good condition and are privately owned. It is easy to imagine Shaker men and women exiting the houses and walking across the knolls and fields of Tyringham, toiling to cultivate the lands surrounding the cobble.

Shaker communities were a phenomenon primarily of the eighteenth and nineteenth centuries, though a small sect still exists today at Sabbathday Lake, Maine. The Shakers represent a communal religious group adhering to an egalitarian and chaste separation of the sexes. Shakers espouse the simple life, "heaven on earth." Initially established in Watervliet, New York, by "Mother" Ann Lee in 1778, the group has held to the tenets of a self-sufficient, monastic, agrarian life.

The men and women in the Tyringham Shaker community lived together in separate sections of dormitory-style buildings. Sexual abstinence was a necessary requirement for being admitted to and staying in a Shaker community. Thus, these were primarily adult communities, as no children were produced. They willingly accepted orphans as well as families with children, but the survival of Shaker communities depended upon the recruitment of adults. During the nineteenth century there were over 5,000 individuals in Shaker communities in this country. Today, there are none except the small community in Maine.

The beautiful Shaker furniture and implements crafted in the nineteenth century are still much sought after. The Shakers believed in simple, functional designs crafted from hardwoods, and these virtues have maintained their appeal over the years.

Though Tyringham was a small, quiet town, it attracted some famous visitors in the nineteenth century. President Grover Cleveland often stayed in the summer to enjoy his favorite occupation—fishing on Hop Brook, which borders Tyringham Cobble. Samuel Clemens (Mark Twain) stayed in Tyringham to seek solace the summer of 1904 after his wife's death.[17]

Other point of interest: Along the way from Lee to Tyringham, you will pass by one of the Berkshires' most unusual structures—the famous Santarella House. What makes this cottage so unique is that its sculpted roof, made to resemble thatch, in actuality weighs many tons. The cottage was built in the 1930s by British sculptor Henry Hudson Kitson, who intended the roof to emulate the curving hills of the Berkshires. Perhaps he was also inspired by the sight of the cobble, which is visible from the property. The cottage is currently an art gallery.

ASHINTULLY ESTATE & McLENNAN PRESERVE 18

Location: Tyringham (Berkshire County, Massachusetts)
Massachusetts Atlas & Gazetteer: p. 44, B15

Fees: None; donations to the Trustees of the Reservation are appreciated.

Hours: Ashintully Estate, open Tuesdays and Saturdays, June through October; McLennan Preserve, open year-round from dawn to dusk

Accessibility: The walks at Ashintully Estate are on garden pathways and rolling hills; the trails at McLennan Preserve are well marked and well groomed.

Degree of Difficulty: Ashintully Estate, easy; McLennan Preserve, easy to moderate

Highlights:
   Ashintully Estate
   ■ Mansion ruins, including Doric columns
   ■ Formal gardens
   ■ Music studio
   McLennan Preserve
   ■ Cascades along trail
   ■ Beaver pond
   ■ Foundations of former farms

Description: The two hikes described are both on the former properties of an early-twentieth-century Egyptologist named Robb de Peyster Tytus.[1]
   The Ashintully estate hikes consist of walks along the grounds of a once-grand mansion built on the side of a hill in 1900 by Robb de Peyster Tytus. It was a magnificent estate, in keeping with the Gilded Age mansions of the era. Unfortunately, de Peyster Tytus never lived to enjoy it. He died in Saranac Lake the year after it was completed.[2]
   The estate suffered from a number of family catastrophes, culminating in the tragic burning of the mansion in 1952. Today the striking remains—including four, huge, Doric columns—of what was once a thirty-five-room, Georgian-style manor, sit high on a hill. In addition to the intriguing ruins and views, there are lovely, landscaped, seasonal gardens. The hike is about 1.0 mile in length.

The McLennan Preserve hike is a loop of about 3.0 miles.[3] It circumnavigates Round Mountain, passing by waterfalls on Camp Brook and a pond created by beavers. The area is a natural habitat for a variety of woodland creatures and birds. There are intriguing stone walls and foundations—remnants of nineteenth-century farms long gone. The property was acquired in the early twentieth century by John McLennan, a Canadian newspaper owner.[4]

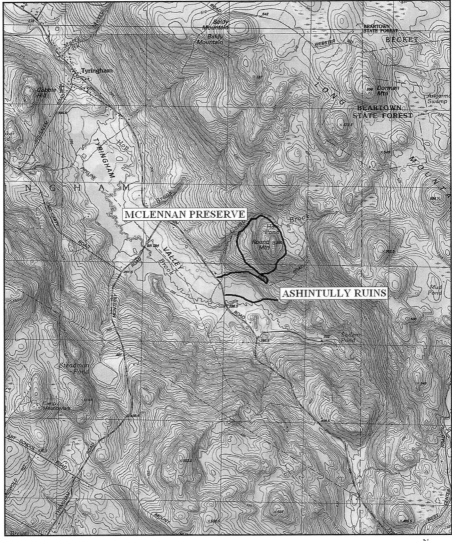

Both hikes are partially accessed through private lands and are maintained by the Trustees of the Reservation, a not-for-profit Massachusetts conservation organization.

Directions: *To Ashintully Estate.* From the McLennan Preserve, continue southeast on Tyringham Road (Sodem Road) for 0.5 mile further. Pull into the parking area at the front of the Ashintully estate, which will be on your left.

To McLennan Preserve. From Lee (junction of Rtes. 102 and 20), take Rt. 102 west and immediately turn left onto Tyringham Road. Follow Tyringham Road for 4.0 miles to Tyringham Village. At the junction of Tyringham Road and Jerusalem Road, continue southeast on Tyringham Road for another 1.9 miles. Park off to the side of the road where Fenn Road comes in on the left. Look closely as you are driving along, for Fenn Road is easy to miss. Walk east up Fenn Road for 0.5 mile to the trailhead, which will be on the left.

The Hikes

Hike #1— Ashintully Garden Hike

The hike begins at the Ashintully estate on Tyringham Road (also called Sodem Road), which is 0.5 mile south of Fenn Road.

The hike starts at the gate of a private residence. The grounds you will be walking across are rolling green lawns with lovely seasonal gardens. There are stately urns, statues, and marble terraces adorning the formal gardens. These artifacts are blended with a modern garden that is informally integrated into the beautiful natural setting.

The main hike is a loop of about 0.5 mile that begins at a gate northwest of the gardens and then wends uphill through a hardwood forest, leading you out to a startling view of the architectural remnants of the old Ashintully mansion, which was destroyed by fire in 1952. The most outstanding features of these remains are the four, huge, Doric columns that sit regally on the foundation of what was once the grand entrance to the thirty-five-room mansion. You will also find exposed stone and brick remains of the original foundation. It is truly a remarkable sight. As you look northwest from the portico and columns, you will be rewarded with magnificent views of Tyringham Cobble and the surrounding countryside.

Returning downhill through the forest, you will notice the foundation remains of the mansion outbuildings on your left. These ruins present an extensive honeycomb of stone and brick that seem to invite exploration.

Upon again reaching the decorative gate to the mansion trail, you can either visit the lovely gardens to the west or head north along a path through a natural meadow. There are delightful surprises in either direction, including a marble staircase leading whimsically to an open field, a fountain that spouts from the middle of a pond, a statue of Queen Eleanor of Aquitaine, bridges over a meandering brook, and various urns and artifacts artfully set in the rolling, sculpted landscape. Altogether, these features add close to an additional 0.5 mile of walking, making it a total walk of 1.0 mile if you take in all of the grounds.

Hike #2—McLennan Preserve

Park off to the side of Tyringham Road at the intersection of Tyringham and Fenn roads.

Walk east up Fenn Road for about 0.5 mile to the trailhead. (It is possible to drive up Fenn Road, but it is not advisable because the road is rutted and uneven, and can become muddy after a rain or thaw. It is best to enjoy the pleasant stroll up a gentle hill.) The house at the beginning of Fenn Road is referred to as the Spencer House and is pictured in Views of the Valley.[5] It is a large, white, two-story, clapboard farmhouse that was built in 1885 by the Garfield family and later modified by Robb Tytus in 1903 before he built the grand Ashintully estate. There is a profusion of maple trees bordering the road, which creates a colorful canopy in autumn. In spring you will notice

Ashintully, 2004.

pails hanging on the trees. These are used for gathering sap for maple syrup.

From the trailhead, take the path that initially wends its way north (left) through a hardwood forest, following a broad trail that once served as a road. In about 0.4 mile you will see stone pasture walls and foundations to your left, the prominent remains of old, now-obscure farms that have been reclaimed by the forest. In the fall the foundations are filled with polyphony ferns, raspberry bushes, and brushy foliage. You may also see a variety of mushrooms along the trail, including a few chanterelles. According to the trailhead sign, the preserve is habitat for wildlife, including whitetail deer, coyote, and bear.

Once past the stone foundations, the trail veers slightly left and uphill towards the sound of flowing water produced by Camp Brook. At about 0.7 mile the trail divides. Take the left branch, which leads to several pretty cascades set in a small gorge created by Camp Brook. It is a pleasant place to rest and enjoy the scenery or to have a picnic.

Once on the trail again, you will quickly arrive at a pond that beavers have created. The distance to this point from the trailhead is roughly 1.0 mile. The views of this pond are particularly stunning if you visit in the fall when the trees have turned brilliant colors.

From here, the trail parallels the west side of the pond for over 0.1 mile and then veers right, continuing south around the west side of Round Mountain. This part of the hike is fairly uneventful. By the time you return to the trailhead, you will have hiked about 2.0 miles; another 0.5 mile down Fenn Road, and you will be back at your car.

History: Both the McLennan Preserve and the Ashintully Estate are on properties once owned by Robb de Peyster Tytus, an early-twentieth-century Egyptologist who was also a Massachusetts state representative. Later, the property was acquired by John McLennan, who married Robb de Peyster Tytus' widow, Grace.

The 1,000 acres that comprise the Ashintully properties had been farmland during the nineteenth century. In fact, five separate farms had been on the lands before they were purchased by de Peyster Tytus at the turn of the twentieth century. Tytus made quite a splash in Tyringham when he bought three farms at once at the north end of town in 1905, and then shortly thereafter bought another two, combining the Garfield, Duncan, Fenn, Beach, and Clark farms.

De Peyster Tytus' plans were grandiose. He hoped to exceed the mansions of Lenox. He built large barns, and stocked cattle and horses in preparation for a commercial venture.[6] He also expanded the maple sugaring business that existed on the Fenn farm. It is the ruins of these now-obscure farms that you see on the McLennan Preserve hike. Maple sap is still collected along Fenn Road. In the spring you can see the apparatus as you walk to the trailhead for the McLennan hike.

From 1910–1912, Tytus built a magnificent, white, thirty-five-room, Georgian mansion on the side of a hill overlooking Tyringham Valley. He called it Ashintully, the Gaelic term for "on the brow of the hill." It was an estate in keeping with the finest of the Gilded Age. One can easily imagine the former grandeur of this mansion while gazing at the foundation ruins, portico, and fifty-foot Doric columns that have survived over the last half century.

Unfortunately for Tytus, he never got to enjoy the fruit of his labors. He died in 1913 at Saranac Lake, New York, barely a year after the mansion was completed. One year later, in 1914, his widow, Grace, married John McLennan, a Canadian senator and newspaper owner. In 1915 Grace gave birth to a son, John Jr., but was married barely a year before she and her new husband divorced. One wonders if Grace Tytus–McLennan somehow managed to enjoy the thirty-five rooms, ten baths, and fifteen fireplaces of the mansion during the series of marital crises she endured.

In 1937, John McLennan Jr. acquired Ashintully, after having spent all of his summers there. He was twenty-two years old at the time and a serious composer of contemporary music. At some point he moved into the farmhouse at the bottom of the hill, while maintaining the grand mansion further up on the hill. Misfortune struck again, however, and the stately mansion burned to the ground in 1952, leaving only ruins behind.

In 1966, at the age of fifty-one, John McLennan Jr. married Katherine White Bishop. It was during this happier period of time that McLennan renovated the adjacent barn, turning it into a music studio. With Katherine's inspiration and help, he also designed the beautiful gardens that are now open to the public on Wednesdays and Saturdays from mid-June through mid-

September. The property was gifted, with endowment, by McLennan in 1977, 1978, and 1991.

John McLennan Jr. died in 1996. His widow, Katherine McLennan, Ashintully curator and gracious host, is willing to talk about the history of the grand estate, take you through the music studio, and entertain you with stories about the various artifacts on display there.

Doric columns and ruins, 2004.

Part IV: Schoharie Valley Region

The Schoharie Valley lies west of the Hudson River and south of the Mohawk River. It was originally home to a number of Native American tribes, most notably the Mohawks. In 1712 the Mohawks sold some of the land abutting Onistagrawa—Corn Mountain—to Adam Vroman, an early settler who left Schenectady after his father was killed in the massacre. As the name of the mountain suggests, the land around Corn Mountain (renamed Vroman's Nose) was rich farmland. In fact, before and during the American Revolution, this flat, fertile land along the Schoharie Creek was referred to as a "breadbasket" because of its ability to grow abundant wheat, corn, oats, and hops.

Unfortunately, precisely because the land was so ideal for farming, it became a scene of contention. Eventually, even the Indians who had sold the land wanted it back. Thus it was inevitable that Vroman's Nose and the Schoharie Valley would become a battleground during the American Revolution between those who wanted the land so that crops could be harvested to feed troops, and those who wanted the land so that the crops could be destroyed, thereby starving the opposition.

Once the war was finally over, the Schoharie Creek became a center for newly emerging American industries. One of the largest and most successful industries in the early 1800s was the Pratt tannery in what was then Schoharie Kill (later Prattsville). This enterprise was a commercial success as well as a model rural community.

The following two hikes revive some of the historical legacy that the Schoharie Valley so richly has to offer:

Vroman's Nose: Hike up to a small mountain plateau with spectacular views of the Schoharie Valley.

Pratt Rock: Follow a zigzagging trail that leads up to an escarpment face that has immortalized Zadock Pratt in a series of bas-relief carvings.

19 VROMAN'S NOSE

Location: Middleburgh (Schoharie County)
New York State Atlas & Gazetteer: p. 65, D6

Fees: None

Hours: None posted

Accessibility: 600-foot ascent to summit in less than 0.8 mile
(1.6 miles round-trip)

Degree of Difficulty: Moderate

Highlights:
- Beautiful views of Schoharie Valley from the summit
- Interesting geological history

Description: Vroman's Nose (also spelled Vrooman's) is a distinctive landmark in Schoharie County, rising approximately 600 feet above the floor of Schoharie Valley up to an elevation of over 1,200 feet.[1-4] From early on, imaginative settlers, gazing at the mountain, would liken what they saw to the broad nose and forehead of a giant. It was only a matter of time before the mountain became known as Vroman's Nose, after Adam Vroman, the first farmer to settle in the area and the original owner of the land encompassing the Nose.

Anthropomorphic names involving noses for geological features are more common than you might think.[5] Near Sprakers, for instance, are The Noses—two, broad, proboscis-shaped hills that form the northern and southern portals to the Mohawk Valley. In the Shawangunks near New Paltz can be found Gertrude's Nose, a well-known and distinctive rock formation.

Vroman's Nose is a wonderful hike for those who enjoy climbing to dramatic views without having to expend a great deal of time and energy. Thanks to the concerted efforts of Vincent J. Schaefer and other dedicated nature lovers, the mountain has been incorporated into the northern section of the Long Path, which begins at the George Washington Bridge in New York City and currently ends at Thacher Park.

Directions: From Middleburgh (junction of Rtes. 145 north & 30), drive south on Rt. 30 for 0.6 mile and turn right onto Middleburgh Road. Drive west for 0.6 mile and park on the left in the area designated for Vroman's Nose.

The trail proceeds from the parking area, initially following an old wagon road uphill along the north flank of Vroman's Nose. Although the main trail goes up the west side of the mountain, take note that a path ascending along

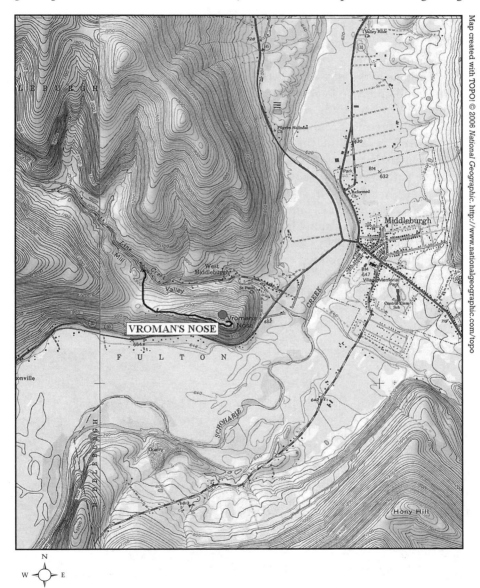

the east side of Vroman's Nose can also be taken from near the trailhead, at the top of the field above the parking area.

For a more challenging hike, the summit of Vroman's Nose can also be approached from Rt. 30 via the "Long Path." The trailhead is by roadside on Rt. 30, 1.5 miles south of the junction of Rtes. 30 & 145 north.

The Hike

The 1.6-mile trek begins at the trailhead for Vroman's Nose. Proceed uphill along a path (once a wagon road) that crosses an open field, and you will quickly come to the edge of the woods. Here the road turns right and begins its slow uphill climb, following the north shoulder of the mountain. Within a short length of time, the road turns left uphill, now going south. When the road finally turns left again, the climb becomes steeper and you will find yourself proceeding east along the edge of the escarpment with the Schoharie Valley appearing further away with each step taken.

The path eventually leads up to the flat, plateau-like summit of Vroman's Nose, roughly ten acres in size, where excellent views of the valley, the meandering Schoharie Creek, and the village of Middleburgh can be obtained. Various sections of the summit are covered by large patches of huckleberry and blueberry under a canopy of chestnuts, hickory, oaks, red cedar, and white ash. Just be sure to keep walking east along the flat bedrock so that you will get to see everything.

By continuing on the path as it descends along the northern flank of the mountain, you will eventually return to the parking area.

Vroman's Nose—Middleburgh's sky island, circa 1920.

Views from Vroman's Nose, 1997.

Another trail starts on Rt. 30 and provides a much steeper and more demanding ascent of the mountain.

History: Vroman's Nose was originally called Onistagrawa by Native Americans, meaning "Corn Mountain." Bumper crops of corn were produced on the farmlands to the north, east, and south of the mountain, thanks to the unusually fertile soil. The mountain has also been known as Sky Island because of its prominence in the skyline above Middleburgh.

The Vromans were a wealthy Dutch family who emigrated from Holland and originally settled near Schenectady. Meese Vroman was killed by Indians in the famous Schenectady Massacre of 1690. His son Adam survived. In 1712, Adam Vroman moved to the Schoharie Valley and purchased 1,200 acres of land from the Mohawks for 100 gallons of rum and some woven blankets. These lands included Onistagrawa Mountain, now called Vroman's Nose.[6]

Vroman established the first farm on these lands, but he was soon followed by a wave of German Palatine settlers and some Dutch pioneers from Schenectady. Unfortunately, the other settlers, especially the Palatines, did not think Vroman had rightfully acquired this most desirable land. They were accused of setting fire to the first house Vroman built. Vroman also had uneasy relations with some of the Native Americans in the territory. Vroman and other Dutch settlers claimed several times in correspondence to the governor of the province that the Germans "set the Indians up against them" by leading the Indians to believe that they hadn't gotten a good deal on their land. Nevertheless, there was relative peace in the valley until the American Revolution.

During the Revolution, many Native Americans fought with the Tories against the Vromans and the other American revolutionaries in the Schoharie Valley. The fighting was fierce. Sir William Johnson and Molly Brandt—Native American consort to Sir William—wielded a great deal of influence with English sympathizers and Native Americans. Their allies extended from Johnson Hall deep into the Schoharie Valley, east to Albany, and north to Canada. Molly Brant, a powerful matriarch of the Mohawk tribes, ensured political and military support for the British from the Mohawk and Iroquois tribes. Joseph Brant, her brother, fought bravely for the British and Tories.

A number of Adam Vroman's descendants were killed in the American Revolution. They had fought as commissioned officers during the French and Indian War and quickly enlisted to do battle as staunch patriots during the American Revolution. Captain Tuenis Vroman and Lieutenant Ephraim Vroman, sons of Adam, and their families were brutally attacked. Tuenis and his family and most of Ephraim's family were murdered and scalped by a British and Tory military division led by Joseph Brant. Ephraim's family tried to escape the attack by hiding in the cornfields at the base of Onistagrawa (Vroman's Nose), but Ephraim's wife became afraid and called out to her husband. This signaled her hiding place, and she and a son were promptly scalped and murdered. As the story goes, Ephraim then engaged in battle with one of the Indians while holding his infant son. The infant, not knowing he was in danger, laughed, thinking it was all a game. The Indian was either amused or took pity. He captured Ephraim, rather than killing him. Ephraim was spared and eventually returned from captivity to remain in the valley near his original homestead.

Timothy Murphy was another hero of the Revolution with ties to the Schoharie Valley. Murphy's colorful reputation became legendary, and was no doubt exaggerated. It is said that he leaped from Vroman's Nose to avoid capture by Indians during the war. Then again, it was also reported that he once fell into a hole so deep that he had to run home to get a shovel to dig himself out! What is known for certain is that Murphy was a bona fide local war hero who is buried in the cemetery in Middleburgh.

Middleburgh was originally known as Weiser's Dorf and was the oldest settlement in the valley. The original town, however, was burned to the ground in the Joseph Brant raid of 1780.

At one time the farmlands in Schoharie Valley were the richest, most fertile hop fields in the world. In the 1890s, however, the crops began to fail when a blight called blue mold (which some blamed on an excess of lime in the soil) decimated the fields. Afterwards, farmers began converting to dairying, a switch that was intensified further during the prohibition era when the market for hops plummeted.

Vroman's Nose was purchased in 1983 by the Schoharie County Historical Society in conjunction with public-minded preservationists and a number of descendants of the early valley settlers.

Geology: Vroman's Nose is part of the aftermath of a long series of ice ages that began two million years ago and came to an end as recently as 10,000 years ago. In between this enormous interval of time, at least four major glacial advances and retreats occurred as the climate underwent fluctuations during the Pleistocene era.

At the height of the last ice age, about 20,000 years ago, all of New York State was covered under a thick bed of ice except for a tiny area in the southwestern part of the state. Even Mt. Marcy (New York State's highest peak), located in the High Peaks Region of the Adirondacks, may have been overridden by the glaciers.

Schoharie Valley from Vroman's Nose, 1997.

Dr. Vincent J. Schaefer and Vroman's Nose.

Dr. Schaefer's association with Vroman's Nose is multi-faceted and endur-ing. In 1931, Schaefer conceived the idea of Vroman's Nose becoming part of a "Long Path" that would provide a continuous trail from the George Washington Bridge in New York City to Whiteface Mountain in the Adirondack High Peak Region. In 1994 part of his dream came true when Vroman's Nose was incorporated into the extended hiking trail that cur-rently stretches from New York City to the Helderbergs.[7]

During World War II, Dr. Schaefer was heavily involved in the war effort, working to create an artificial fog that could be used to conceal ships, cities, and the advancement of troops. What is particularly germane to this book is that his experiments were conducted on the flats by Vroman's Nose.

In Clay Perry's caving classic, Underground Empire, *Vincent Schaefer is described at length in the chapter entitled "High and Low in the Helderbergs." Schaefer, besides being interested in such aerial phenomena as fog and snow, was also a spelunker and explored a number of local caves in the Helderbergs, such as Bensons, Witches Cave, Gebbard (Ball's) cave, and Tory Cave. According to Perry, Schaefer's interest was prompted by the hope that he would find the remains of early man, or at least some recog-nizable traces, in the dark recesses of the caves he explored. To Schaefer's disappointment, no remains or traces were ever found.*[8]

Perry also mentions that Schaefer was the first scientist to produce arti-ficial snow, which he did by flying over Mt. Greylock in Massachusetts and releasing a quantity of dry ice.

Schaefer served as research assistant at General Electric for many years under Dr. Irving Langmuir—an eminent, Nobel Prize-winning scientist who, like Schaefer, was also an outdoor enthusiast. Langmuir is remem-bered for participating in one of the first ski ascents of Mt. Marcy from Heart Lake. General Electric, in its local heyday, shot a publicity film at Vroman's Nose depicting an incident from the Revolutionary War. Young Vincent Schaefer played the role of a soldier running from Indians in the film.

By 14,000 BC, however, the continent had warmed sufficiently to cause the glaciers to begin retreating northward from their furthest advance south. As the glaciers melted and moved north, huge volumes of water were liberated. One of the first lakes to form was Glacial Lake Grand Gorge, a substantial body of water. Five hundred years later the retreat of glaciers to as far north as Middleburgh exposed even more lands, and with increased outlets, the lake level dropped to 1,200 feet. This height is significant for it means that the tip of Vroman's Nose, previously submerged, now rose above the water line.[9,10]

Still later, as more land became exposed, a previously ice-covered gap opened up, allowing water to flow out of the lake through the Normanskill River and down into the Hudson River. At this point, Glacial Lake Delanson was created at an elevation of 900 feet. Even more of Vroman's Nose was now exposed. When the waters of Glacial Lake Delanson eventually drained out completely, Schoharie Valley became a flat, fertile area of land, and Vroman's Nose became a small mountain instead of a tiny island in a large lake.

During the ice age Vroman's Nose itself was significantly modified by the effects of glaciers. Its north side was scraped and grounded down to form a ramp-like slope. The south side of the mountain had large blocks plucked right off its side by the glaciers, leaving behind the towering cliffs that rise so dramatically above the valley floor today.

At the top of Vroman's Nose is an impressive, expansive section of flat, smooth bedrock that geologists colloquially refer to as a "dance floor." This "dance floor" was polished smooth approximately 16,000 years ago. If you look closely, you can see the scrapes and chatter marks left behind by the glaciers as rocks and stones embedded in the ice were rubbed against the bedrock's surface.[11]

The summit of Vroman's Nose is primarily Hamilton sandstone, a fairly resistant rock that formed nearly 400 million years ago. In the past, flagstone from the Nose was used for sidewalks in the Capital District.

20 PRATT ROCK

Location: Prattsville (Greene County)
New York State Atlas & Gazetteer: p. 51, B5

Fees: None

Hours: Dawn to dusk

Accessibility: 0.9-mile hike round-trip on a steep hill

Degree of Difficulty: Easy to moderate

Highlights:
- Unique rock carvings of Zadock Pratt, his family, and his favorite animals
- Views of the Schoharie Creek and environs from the rocky escarpment

Description: Pratt Rock, towering above the southeast end of Prattsville, is a rocky escarpment whose cliff face has been turned into a tapestry of carved figures and shapes.[1,2] The carvings were commissioned by Zadock Pratt, an early-nineteenth-century industrialist. It was once featured in *Ripley's Believe It or Not,* billed as "New York's own Mt. Rushmore."[3]

Directions: From the NYS Thruway (I-87), get off at Exit 21 (Catskill) and proceed west on Rt. 23 for approximately 32 miles. You will reach the intersection of Rtes. 23 & 23A. Turn right onto Rt. 23 and drive northwest for 0.4 mile. The parking area for Pratt Rock is directly on your right.

From the parking area follow a well-established path that leads up from the parking lot below a huge mound of exposed bedrock. Initially the path parallels Rt. 23, then, all at once, it begins ascending steeply, zigzagging its way to the top.

To Pratt's House: From the parking lot, drive northwest on Rt. 23 into the village of Prattsville. When you have driven 0.6 mile, look for a white colonial home with large pillars on your right. This is the house once occupied by Zadock Pratt. The home and the carriage house behind the home constitute the Pratt Museum.

160

To Pratt's grave site. From the parking lot at Pratt Rock, drive northwest for 1.0 mile (or 0.4 mile further from Pratt's house) and turn right onto Maple Lane just before a bridge on Rt. 23 that leads out of Prattsville. Continue for 0.05 mile. You will see a small cemetery on your right situated between two houses.

When you walk in through the main cemetery entrance, proceed straight ahead. Pratt's monument is the largest and tallest in the cemetery, and is located near the cemetery's center. The Pratt monument and several small gravestones are enclosed by a black fence.

The Hike

The trail up to Pratt Rock is self-evident. It starts from the pavilion next to the parking lot and zigzags up a steeply inclined slope to the base of the escarpment. The path is roughly 0.4 mile long.

At the very beginning you will pass by a huge outcropping of rock on your right, close to the pavilion. From here the path continues straight ahead, paralleling Rt. 23 for less than 0.05 mile.

Just before the trail starts its dramatic ascent, you will see a tombstone on your left, roughly twenty feet down the side of the hill. The tombstone commemorates several horses and dogs that Pratt favored.

As the trail begins upward, you will come to a rocky ledge on your right with a seat carved into it. You can sit and rest for a minute, if you wish. The

Pratt Rock, circa 1910.

Along the trail to Pratt Rock, 2001.

bas-relief of a hemlock representing Pratt's livelihood as a tanner is chiseled into the back of the rock bench. Just beyond, looking uphill as you continue your climb, will be your first clear view of the escarpment face and Pratt Rock.

In another moment you will come to a junction where a second large out-cropping of rock offers another opportunity to sit down on a carved seat and relax for a moment.

From here, if you take the path to the left, you will eventually arrive at the top of the cliffs above Pratt Rock. For the moment, take the path to the right since it leads directly to the Pratt Rock carvings. You will go up and around two horseshoe turns to finally arrive at the base of the escarpment where the rock carvings can be seen close up. The first carvings are of Pratt's horse and a hemlock, followed by an engraving of Pratt's tannery with the number "550" (which represents the length of the tannery in feet) chiseled below the sketch.

Next you will come to a tiny grotto bored into the rock face with a small seat carved inside. This small chamber was intended to be the site of Pratt's tomb, but the work was never finished. The vault was infiltrated by small amounts of water that percolated through the rocks.[4]

Above the chamber is a portrait of Pratt's son George, with a brief inscription detailing his life and death.

Beyond this are several more carvings, including one of Zadock Pratt, an arm and hammer (meant to glorify hard work), and a wreath with the names of the Pratt children. Past the last, white-colored bas-relief is one more carving, unpainted, which can be easily missed if you don't know that it's there.

From Pratt Rock there are clear views of the valley and the Schoharie Creek 250 feet below.

History: Work began on Pratt Rock in 1845 when Zadock Pratt, Prattville's founder, commissioned an itinerant stonecutter named Andrew W. Pearse to chisel out some sculptures in stone—but not just any, ordinary sculptures, and not just at any, ordinary place. The carvings were to be bas-reliefs and were to be cut into a cliff face overlooking the village of Prattsville. These carvings were meant to be a monument to Pratt's life and achievements, and it was a monumental task. In the end, a total of five stonecutters were employed over an extended period of time.

View of Schoharie Valley from Pratt Rock, 1999.

The bas-reliefs included: portraits of Pratt and his son, George; Pratt's coat of arms, featuring, not surprisingly, a hemlock as the crest; the Pratt tannery; a wreath with the names of the Pratt children; a muscled arm with rolled sleeves wielding a hammer to symbolize the need for hard work; and even Pratt's favorite dog and horse. To ensure that these figures carved into the rock face could be clearly seen from below, Pratt had them painted white (which is how they are highlighted even today).

In this fashion Pratt was able to achieve a measure of immortality, for it is by Pratt Rock that Pratt is remembered today, much more so than for his association with the town he helped found and build. Pratt's quest for immortality, however, received significant help along the way. In 1992 a "Save the Rocks" campaign was initiated to generate money so that the rock sculptures could be restored to their present condition.[5] In 1993, Pratt Rock became part of the National Register of Historic Places.

Geology: The escarpment out of which Pratt Rock was carved consists of gray sandstone, a sedimentary rock formed approximately 360 million years ago. At that time the entire area lay at the edge of an ancient sea. Flowing into this sea was a river that left behind a large delta, much like today's Mississippi River. It is this sandy delta that later became compressed and hardened to form the sandstone that you see today.

If you continue along the base of the escarpment for a short distance south beyond the carvings, you will observe just how pot-holed and contoured parts of the escarpment rock face are. At the top of the escarpment, the bedrock is exposed, forming a flat surface that geologists liken to a "dance floor." Look closely and you will observe pronounced striations along the flat surface that were caused by the movement of glaciers containing embedded stones.[6]

Before the days of Pratt Rock, the escarpment was known as High Rocks.[7]

More about Zadock Pratt: Zadock Pratt (1790–1871) lived to be eighty-one years old. He was known as the "Greene County Tanner" and is historically portrayed as an egocentric, flamboyant, highly creative, and somewhat mercurial personality. No doubt the real Pratt was all of this, and then some.[8–12]

Pratt moved to the Catskills with his family in 1802 when he was twelve years old. As was the custom in his day, Pratt worked as a boy, earning money in fur trading and as a store clerk. When he was twenty-two, Pratt decided that his days of working for others were over, and he started his own harness-making and saddle shop.

In 1824, Pratt journeyed to a tiny village that was then called Schoharie Kill. There, along Schoharie Creek less than 0.5 mile from the cliffs that would eventually become Pratt Rock, Zadock Pratt built the largest tannery in the region (and perhaps in the world at that time). The tannery was 530 feet long and two and a half stories high. At its peak it employed 200 men.

Pratt demonstrated his skills at innovation and "good old plain Yankee ingenuity" by devising not only better, more modern machinery for his plant, but presenting ideas on how to improve the town and its economy. His former home, which is now the Zadock Pratt Museum, plus many of the existing houses on Main Street, were designed and built by Pratt. He was zealous in building housing and creating a community that would be a good place for the workers in his tannery to live. Pratt became so extensively involved in the village and its activities, in fact, that Schoharie Kill was eventually renamed Prattsville in his honor.

Pratt became known on the national scene as a successful entrepreneur, as well as for achieving some notoriety for his monuments. In 1857 a newspaper account of a visit to Prattsville by journalist William Fosdick describes walking up the mountain with Pratt to view the sculptures. Fosdick states that, upon reaching the top, Pratt brought out a bottle of champagne and two leather cups so that they might quench their thirst after the climb.

Pratt's tannery closed around 1846, in part because Pratt had depleted over ten square miles of hemlock surrounding his tannery.[13] Without the tannic acid that had been harvested from the hemlocks' bark, the hides could no longer be cured into sole leather.

Pratt's vision, however, extended far beyond Prattsville, or Greene County for that matter. He served two terms in Congress and was instrumental in passing legislation that facilitated the completion of the Washington Monument.

Pratt had a very busy marital life, too. He was married five times and outlived four of his wives. Two wives were from the Dickerman family, and two were from the Watson family. Three of his wives died from consumption (tuberculosis). When he married his fifth wife, Susie Grimm, she was twenty-eight and he was seventy-nine.

Pratt had three children—a son, George W., a daughter, Julia H., and a third child who died in infancy. It's likely that Pratt had pinned his dreams and aspirations on George, his gifted son—a man who was academically accomplished and could speak several languages. George was thirteen years old when Pratt began work on Pratt Rock.

After quickly rising in rank to become a colonel in the Union Army during the Civil War, George was killed by confederate cannon fire at the battle of Manassas (Bull Run) in 1862. Zadock Pratt's perspective on life underwent a dramatic change as a result. Pratt Rock, which Pratt had intended to memorialize his accomplishments and those of his progeny, acquired a more somber, even tragic cast.

Pratt was buried in Prattsville in Benham Cemetery, where his grave can be visited today. At the time of his death, Pratt was worth over one million dollars—an enormous sum in that era. His home still stands to this day in the center of town along Route 23, and is the centerpiece of the Zadock Pratt Museum.

Benham Cemetery: Although Pratt is buried in Benham Cemetery along with common folks from the community, that was not his original intent. Pratt had planned that the chamber at Pratt Rock would serve as his mausoleum. Many have speculated that Pratt ultimately abandoned this notion when he realized that the receptacle would be unfit as a burial tomb because of the infiltration of water into the chamber. It is just as likely, however, that Pratt became distraught when his son met an untimely death and decided that he would turn Pratt Rock into a memorial for George, rather than for himself. If this was the case, then Pratt Rock was one of the first Civil War monuments.

Pratt's House/Museum: The house was constructed in 1828 and was designed in the Federal style. Columns were later added to its front, creating the popular Greek Revival style of the 1850s. When Pratt closed his bank, which was located next door, the bank building was rotated ninety degrees and then attached to the side of the mansion to form an additional room. Directly across the street was a park with fountains. It was all really quite splendid.

The structure went through many changes over the years following Pratt's death—at one time even serving as a five-room apartment dwelling. When preservationists took over the house, however, the mansion was finally restored in 1976 to its 1850s condition.[14]

The Tannery: The tannery no longer exists. Not even its foundation survives. What's more, the tannery may have been totally obliterated by as early as the mid-1850s, a supposition supported by the fact that the tannery was no longer evident on a late-nineteenth-century map of Prattsville.

Pratt's tannery was located diagonally west of his house, roughly at the end of Washington Street Extension, where the raceway can still be observed today. Fortunately, a model of the tannery can be viewed at the Pratt Museum.

Part V: Hudson Valley Region

The eight hiking areas described in this section have been selected for their unique contributions to the history of the Hudson Valley. Their history forms a patchwork of trails with tales spanning the periods from pre-Colonial times to the present. The walks will take you from Native American warfare on Rogers Island, to the early industries and grand resorts that once used the river for transport, to elegant, historic estates along the banks of the Hudson. These hikes demonstrate a rich, ever-changing history that parallels the ebb and flow of the Hudson River itself.

East Side of the Hudson River

Lindenwald & Martin Van Buren Nature Trail: Stroll along the estate grounds of the eighth president of the United States, and hike into woods where he and his eminent guests once rode horses.

Rogers Island: Paddle out to an island on the Hudson River where a famous Indian battle took place over 350 years ago.

Olana: Meander through the picturesque grounds once inhabited by Frederic Church, one of the most famous of the Hudson River School painters.

Montgomery Place: Walk through the post-Revolutionary War estate of the Livingston and Montgomery families with its waterfalls and stunning views of the Hudson River.

West Side of the Hudson River

Ravena Falls: Walk down to a waterfall that has outlasted all the mills and factories that tried to exploit its power.

Hudson River School Art Trail: Follow the picturesque scenes rendered by Thomas Cole and the Hudson River School artists from Cedar Grove and Olana to North–South Lake.

Catskill Mountain House Escarpment: Hike along an escarpment trail overlooking the Hudson Valley where Victorians once strolled on outings from the Catskill Mountain House.

Saugerties Lighthouse: Walk on a peninsula tidal preserve on the Hudson River to an historic lighthouse that was saved at the last moment by preservationists.

Overlook Mountain: Climb up to the top of Overlook Mountain where ghostly ruins of an old hotel still haunt the summit.

Sky Top & Mohonk Lake: Walk around Mohonk Lake and then up to Sky Top tower overlooking the northern Shawangunk Mountains.

EAST SIDE
OF THE
HUDSON RIVER

21 LINDENWALD and the MARTIN VAN BUREN NATURE TRAIL

Location: Kinderhook (Columbia County)
New York State Atlas & Gazetteer: p. 52, AB4

Fees: Nominal charge to enter Martin Van Buren's home; no fee to walk on grounds

Hours: Lindenwald grounds are open dawn to dusk, year-round. The Van Buren mansion and the National Park Service Visitors Center (518-758-9689) are open seven days a week from Memorial Day to the end of October, 9:00 AM–4:30 PM. The facilities are open only on weekends during November and through the first week of December. There may be an expansion of walking areas on the estate in the future. The National Park Service is considering buying adjacent land that was once part of Van Buren's farm. The Martin Van Buren Nature Trail, across the road from Lindenwald, is open dawn to dusk.

Accessibility: The walk next to Martin Van Buren's home is fairly short and on level ground; the Martin Van Buren Nature Trails, which are across the road adjacent to the historic site and maintained by Columbia County, are 3.7 miles in length, but can be hiked in sections. There is little change in elevation.

Degree of Difficulty: Easy for both the Martin Van Buren Historical Site and the Martin Van Buren Nature Trail

Highlights:
- Former president's home
- Interpretive history trail on estate grounds
- Nature preserve

Description: A short hike begins at Lindenwald, the former residence of Martin Van Buren, the eighth president of the United States. The mansion has been restored to the era of Van Buren's occupancy and is an historic site managed by the National Park Service.[1] Both the home and grounds are open to the public, but the home can be accessed by guided tour only.

A pretty, 0.5-mile trail on the estate grounds, called the Lindenwald Wayside Loop Trail, has six interpretive markers along the way describing historic events during Van Buren's tenure on the estate.

The Martin Van Buren Nature Trail, managed by Columbia County and New York State Parks, Recreation and Historic Preservation, lies diagonally across the road from the mansion. There are 3.7 miles of intertwining trails in the preserve.

Directions: From Kinderhook (junction of Rtes. 9 & 21), drive east on Rt. 21 (Hudson Street) for 0.6 mile. Turn left onto a 0.1-mile connection that takes you up to Rt. 9H. Turn right onto Rt. 9H and drive south for 1.6 miles to the nature trails, on your left. Continue for 0.1 mile further to Lindenwald, which will be on your right.

The Hikes

Hike # 1—The Lindenwald Wayside Loop Trail

This is a short trail that encircles the Van Buren estate. The six interpretive markers provide information about Martin Van Buren and life on the Lindenwald farm. The first marker is in the field west of the visitor center. The five remaining markers are either on the old post road or along the carriage path that encircles the house. The markers read as follows:

1. "... a farmer in my native town."—In these fertile fields framed by the Catskill Mountains in the background, Martin Van Buren had a daily habit of being engaged with his workmen "after breakfast ... until ... tired." He was loathe to leave his farm except to spend time fishing in nearby Kinderhook Creek. A friend said to him that he was "an amateur farmer who prides himself upon having his farm in better order than his neighbor." [note: the sign does not cite source]
2. North Gatehouse Site—Architect Richard Upjohn's renovations of Lindenwald in 1849–1850 included the construction of two gatehouses, one at each end of the carriage path. Van Buren's gardener lived in the south gatehouse. Foundation stones of the north gatehouse mark the residence of the coachman and his family.
3. North Orchard and the Lindenwald Landscape—Though this area is now shaded by tall trees, in the 1850's you could see the north orchard from this vantage which consisted of a pear orchard to the right and a larger apple orchard to the left. Van Buren's son, Martin Jr., assisted him in the management of the expanding farm and estate. Abraham, John, Smith Thompson, and their families, often gathered here to share in entertaining neighbors and friends.
4. The Farm at Lindenwald—Sites of the Lindenwald farm office, greenhouse, and family garden were south of this position. To the west, fields

Lindenwald, Kinderhook, N. Y.
Home of President Martin Van Buren 1841-62
Built in 1797 by Peter Van Ness

Lindenwald, circa 1930.

that extended to Kinderhook Creek produced potatoes, corn, oats, hay, and rye. On the other side of the cultivated field is the marker of Judge Peter Van Ness, the original builder of the house and farm.

5. Lindenwald and the Old Post Road—The Old Post Road was the main north-south land route on the east side of the Hudson River while Van Buren lived here, and actually dates back to before the American Revolution. It was regularly used by politicians and individuals with business in the state capital of Albany, 25 miles north, who could easily stop to consult with "the red fox of Kinderhook" as the ex-president, a wily politician, was known.

6. Martin Van Buren—Born in Kinderhook, Martin Van Buren studied law locally. He began his law practice and political life among neighbors. Rising rapidly by election to public office, he served in the United States Senate from 1821–1828, and became President of the United States in 1837. He is best remembered as the President who kept his country out of war, and who overhauled the nation's financial structure.

The markers contain good, succinct information that is embellished further by well-informed guides if you choose to take the guided tour. The grounds are manicured and attractive. You will walk by the mansion, a Georgian-style brick edifice that was redesigned by Van Buren to include Italianate trappings such as the four-story tower and the redoing of the bricks to a yellow ochre to emulate the stucco walls of villas in Italy. One of the two original gatehouses stands at the south driveway entrance. Only the foundation stones remain of the north gate. There are still some namesake Linden trees (thus *Linden*wald) in evidence on the property. Picnic tables are set here and there, allowing for alfresco lunching on a nice day.

Hike # 2—The Martin Van Buren Nature Trails

These trails are diagonally across the road from the Van Buren estate and provide an opportunity for more substantial hikes on land that has seen little change since Van Buren's time. These are trails that Van Buren walked and rode on, so as you walk through this preserve you will be literally following in the former president's footsteps.

This recreation area encompasses ninety acres of land owned by Columbia County. The 3.7-mile trail system winds through hardwood forest, crosses a stream, and passes a wide variety of vegetation. There are 200-year-old red oaks, sugar maples, and hemlocks. Deer and birds, including turkeys, can be seen here. This now-mature forest was growing during the time Van Buren took residence at Lindenwald.

History: Lindenwald and the village of Kinderhook are rich in early American history. Proximity to the Hudson River ensured a steady flow of population and trade from the early 1600s on. The first town records of Kinderhook were written in Dutch, and Dutch was commonly spoken well into the nineteenth century. Indeed, Dutch heritage still quietly lives on in names of places and people in the area—place names such as Kinderhook and Stuyvesant Falls, and surnames such as Van Ness, Vanderpoel and, of course, Van Buren.

Martin Van Buren was born in Kinderhook in 1782 (the first United States president to be born after independence was declared). A marker for the birth site of Van Buren can be found on County Route 21 (Hudson Street), heading west from the intersection with Route 9H, roughly 2.4 miles from Lindenwald.

Van Buren's parents were tavern keepers who also maintained a small farm outside the village. Martin was a bright, ambitious youngster who set his goals for a political life early on. He apprenticed at age fourteen with a local attorney. This was an acceptable route to becoming a lawyer at the time. Once in practice as a lawyer, Van Buren quickly rose up the political ranks: first, in local county offices; then as a United States senator; briefly as governor of New York State; then secretary of state under Andrew Jackson; then vice president of the United States; and finally, in 1837, president of the United States.

Van Buren served only one term as president, no doubt thanks to the horrendous depression that occurred during his term. He did seek the presidency in two later, colorful campaigns, but did not succeed. It is said, however, that throughout his career he was recognized as an excellent diplomat, often operating most effectively behind the scenes.

The expression "OK" is intimately associated with Martin Van Buren. "OK" stood for "Old Kinderhook," and was first used by supporters of Van Buren when he ran for the presidency in 1836.[2]

By the time he returned to Kinderhook and bought the thirty-five-room mansion he was to renovate and call Lindenwald, Van Buren was focused on becoming a gentleman farmer and sage political consultant. As a local boy of modest means who "made good," he was intent on creating a luxurious show-piece home, worthy of impressing friends, neighbors, and political cronies. He hired Richard Upjohn, a famous architect of the day, to transform the stolid country home into an Italianate villa. He was immensely pleased with the results, so much so that he often mentioned the architectural progress in his correspondence. In 1846 he wrote to a friend: "When you visit me again you shall wash off the impurities of Mammon in the bath which has been put up." He was here referring to the indoor plumbing, including a flush toilet, which had recently been installed.

Many of Van Buren's political friends visited Lindenwald. These included Thomas Jefferson, Henry Clay, and Andrew Jackson.

By all accounts Van Buren led a contented life as a sage and gentleman farmer during his twenty-one years in retirement at Lindenwald. After Van Buren died in 1862, his son John inherited the house. Unfortunately, John lost the home in a card game won by financier Lawrence Jerome. Jerome's daughter, Jenny Jerome, grew up on the estate. She later married and was the mother of Winston Churchill.[4]

The Lindenwald estate nearly disappeared into oblivion. It went through several hands and at one time was converted into a nursing home. Its last incarnation, before being recognized as a historic treasure, was as an antique shop. Lindenwald became a National Historic Landmark in 1961. In 1974 it was designated a National Historic Site maintained by the National Park Service. Since 2004 it has undergone renovation to maintain the structure, improve fire safety, and enhance the authenticity of the décor. The National Park Service is also considering the expansion of the thirty-eight-acre historic site to include most of the 226 acres that once made up the president's farm.[5]

Additional Points of Interest:

The village of Kinderhook has much Revolutionary War history associated with it. Benedict Arnold resided in a house in Kinderhook that still stands at 28 Broad Street. Arnold was brought there after he was wounded during the Battle of Bemis Heights in Saratoga. Supposedly, a cut in the door jamb that was made to accommodate the stretcher that bore him is still evident. Later, this building was used as a boardinghouse for Kinderhook Academy students. It is now a private home closed to the public.

General Henry Knox passed through Kinderhook on his way to deliver artillery and other supplies from Fort Ticonderoga to General George Washington outside Boston. The artillery were instrumental in forcing the British army to evacuate the city. Somehow, Knox and his men managed, in the winter of 1775–1776, to transport forty-four cannons, fourteen mortars, and one howitzer by sled and wagon trains pulled by horses and oxen. This arduous, 300-mile route today is called the Knox Trail.[6] It is commemorated by markers in the towns of Fort George, Fort Edward, Saratoga, Half Moon, Albany, Kinderhook, Nobletown, and Cambridge, Massachusetts.

Aaron Burr visited the house before Martin Van Buren bought it, when it was owned by Peter Van Ness. William Van Ness, son of Peter, was a close friend of Alexander Hamilton. William Van Ness, in fact, served as the second in Burr's duel with Alexander Hamilton. After Burr shot Alexander Hamilton, Van Ness gave him refuge at his home (later called Lindenwald in Van Buren's tenure). It was also at this house that the children of Van Ness were tutored by an aspiring writer named Washington Irving.[3]

22 ROGERS ISLAND

Location: Near Hudson (Columbia County)
New York State Atlas & Gazetteer: p. 52, C3

Fees: None

Hours: No restrictions

Accessibility: By boat only

Degree of Difficulty: Easy

Highlights:
- ■ Canoe or kayak trip with views of the Hudson River
- ■ An island to explore

Description: Rogers Island is a small, oblong-shaped body of land roughly 1.0 mile long and 0.5 mile across, at its widest, that is located near the east bank of the Hudson River between Catskill and Hudson. Historically it was the site of a decisive battle between the Mohawks and Mohicans in the 1600s.

At one time Rogers Island was named Vasterack Island, which comes from the Dutch *Vaste Reach*.[1,2] The name has also been spelled "Rodgers" at one time or another.

A photo-revised 1980 topographical map reveals that Rogers Island is separated from the east mainland by a shallow channel kept open by a partially submerged dike. The channel is a continuation of Hallenbeck Creek, a small stream that rises from a pond west of Mt. Merino.

Most of the land is heavily forested except for the southern end, which consists of dense, impenetrable thickets of brush. There is a reason for the disparity in forest cover. When the Rip Van Winkle Bridge was constructed in the 1930s, the southern end of the island was stripped of its trees so that workers could install the huge pillars and upper sections of the bridge. Since the 1930s, the forest has yet to return except for the brush, which took over with a vengeance.

The southern end of the island is also different in that it is split down its center by a channel of water that dead-ends about one-fifth of the way inland. The channel is canoeable, but while it may get you into the interior of the island, the surrounding land is quite marshy and hardly inviting to exploration by foot. It is a land dominated by large areas of loosestrife and pickerel weed, with towering, reedy plants.

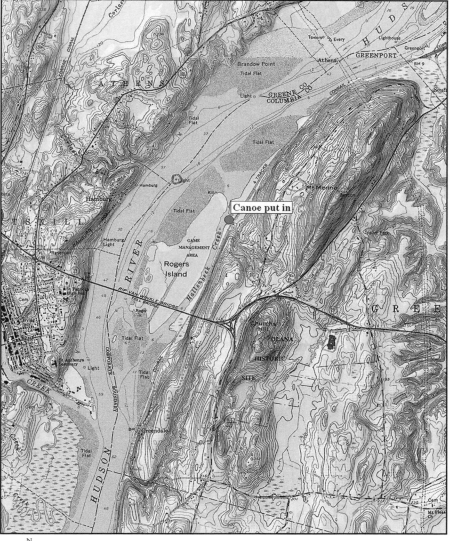

Rogers Island is mostly flat, but does have a slightly raised section along its western side and southern end. Generally, it is possible to step onto the island anywhere without difficulty, although the northern and western sides are the more inviting disembarkation points. The island as a whole, however, should be considered fairly inhospitable. It is characterized by dense underbrush, unpleasant, swampy sections, blow-down, and the ever-present smell of decay and dankness.

A campsite along the western shore occupies one of the high points of the island and is frequently visited by boaters. Several trails near the camp parallel the shoreline, but none go for any distance. The campsite itself is primitive and makeshift, with a dilapidated old stone outhouse.

The island plays host to deer, small animals, and flocks of birds. According to the *New York State Atlas & Gazetteer*, Rogers Island is a game management area. There are a number of camouflaged thatch huts along Hallenbeck Channel that are used by duck hunters.

Directions: There are two ways to get to Rogers Island. By far the easiest approach is to put in at the DEC site on the east bank of the Hudson River.

To get there from the NYS Thruway (I-87), get off at Exit 21 for Catskill and take Rt. 23 east. Drive over the Rip Van Winkle Bridge, taking note of the island to your left near the east end of the bridge—that is Rogers Island. As soon as you cross over the bridge, follow Rt. 23 as it veers to the left. Take your first left, at 0.4 mile, which is Mt. Merino Road, and follow it for 0.1 mile. Then turn left onto Hallenbeck Road and drive downhill for 0.5 mile. Turn left onto an unmarked dirt road just before the end of Hallenbeck (it is easy to miss) and follow it across railroad tracks, first making sure to watch out for high-speed trains before you attempt to cross. Once you are on the other side of the tracks, turn right and follow a stony road paralleling the tracks for 0.1 mile north. Then turn left onto a dirt road, where a DEC marker is visible, and drive to its end. A sandy gully can be found where your canoe can be effortlessly put into Hallenbeck Channel.

The other approach to the island is from the boat launch at Dutchman's Landing in Catskill. The problem here is that if you are paddling a canoe or kayak, you will have to make your way across most of the Hudson River going against the current. To make matters worse, there may be large boats, barges, tankers, and other vessels bearing down on you as they make their way up or down the Hudson River. In the old days, however, this was the favored approach to Rogers Island.

The paddle and hike: From the entry point at Hallenbeck Creek, the easiest canoe route is to paddle around the north end of Rogers Island and then let the full force of the Hudson River sweep you downstream along the west side of the island. Feel free to disembark onto the island at as many places as you desire along the way.

After paddling 0.7 mile along the west side of the island, you will come to the public campsite, which is on top of a high bank in a tiny cove roughly 0.2 mile upstream from the Rip Van Winkle Bridge. The site is distinguishable by huge wooden beams that shore up a section of its shoreline.

There are short paths that lead off north and south from the campsite, but none seem to lead to anywhere particularly special. Be prepared to bushwhack if you decide to venture into the interior of the island. If you do so, you will come to a small, fairly open field. Its only distinguishing features are a number of small holes in the loose sand, as if prospectors have been digging for ancient artifacts. There are more of these small holes on the north end of the island. As to the site described by DeLisser where the epic battle between the Mohawks and Mohicans took place over 350 years ago, no discernible traces remain, not even the row of pine trees that he mentioned.

Returning to your canoe, continue paddling along the west side of the island and then around its south end. Bisecting the south end of Rogers Island is a channel that you can follow north for a short distance, but be advised that the channel is a dead end.

Proceeding around the southeast tip of the island, turn into Hallenbeck Channel and head north until you reach your starting point. This section is a relatively easy paddle since you are not going up against the strong current of the Hudson River, as would be the case if you were heading upriver along the west shore of Rogers Island.

Rip Van Winkle Bridge and Rogers Island, circa 1930.

There is a fine variety of birds and plant life to be seen in and around the water surrounding the island. The proliferation of marsh grass, pickerel weed, marsh marigold, and loosestrife provides a habitat for great blue heron, ducks, and numerous songbirds. There are also some beaver and some very large snapping turtles. The paddle around the island can be as entertaining as the island exploration itself.

Throughout your trip it is important to remember that the Hudson is an arm of the Atlantic Ocean and, therefore, subject to tides. As a result the water level around the island fluctuates continuously, making navigation tricky at times. Consult tide tables before you embark, especially if you are using a power boat.

History: Rogers Island was first seen by Europeans in 1609 when Henry Hudson's ship, the *Half Moon,* made its epic voyage up the Hudson River in search of a passage to the west. It's unlikely that Hudson or any of his men bothered to step foot on such an ordinary, nondescript body of land as Rogers Island, for there are larger, more impressive islands along the way that would have commanded greater attention.

The island would very likely have been visited by Native Americans prior to its "discovery" by Europeans. In 1628—a scant nineteen years after Henry Hudson sailed up the river past Rogers Island—a fierce battle took place in the valley between the Mohawks and the Mohicans, which culminated in a climactic confrontation between the two tribes on Rogers Island.

The Mohawks were a fierce band of people who occupied extensive sections of the Mohawk Valley and the Hudson Valley north of Cohoes. Known as Kanyengehaga, or "people of the flint," they were highly territorial and were embroiled for many years in pushing back other tribes that were encroaching on Mohawk lands from the west, along the Mohawk Valley.

The Mohicans, a less warlike people, occupied the east side of the Hudson River from Germantown to the headwaters of the Hudson River, and the west side of the Hudson River from Catskill to Cohoes.

In 1617, however, the rules of engagement changed. The great Indian chief Hiawatha had a vision while traveling along the Susquehanna River. In his vision Hiawatha saw a single twig being easily snapped in two by a warrior, but a bundle of sticks resisted the combined efforts of the strongest. Hiawatha grasped the concept of strength in unity, and applied it to the Mohawks, Oneida, Onondaga, Cayuga, and Seneca tribes, thus forming the Iroquois Nation.

The Mohawks, no longer having to defend their western borders, suddenly had time and energy available to guard against the perceived encroachment of their territory from the south and began hostilities against the Mohicans. A number of skirmishes followed, leading up to the major battle between the Mohawks and Mohicans in 1628. According to several, differing sources, this battle began either on the hill where Olana (the former home of painter Frederic E. Church) stands, or on Wonton Island (a small island south of Catskill, along the western bank).

The battle raged on, with neither side gaining the upper hand. Finally, near dusk, the Mohawks backed off, retreating to nearby Rogers Island to camp for the night. The Mohawks, however, were under no illusions that the Mohicans would be satisfied with a partial victory. They reasoned that the Mohicans, tasting blood and believing that victory was close at hand, would surely follow closely behind and try to finish them off with a sneak attack during the night.

When the Mohawks arrived on Rogers Island, they built a campfire near the center of the island and then made it look as if they were asleep around the fire. Branches were placed under blankets to create the shape of sleeping bodies, and more sticks were propped up and covered by blankets to make them appear as sentries.

All was now in readiness. Subduing the fire to keep the flames from illuminating the fake figures too brightly, the Mohawks vanished into the woods to wait patiently. They didn't have to wait long. Suddenly, Mohican warriors came swooping in on the sleeping figures with tomahawks and knives poised; and just as suddenly, the Mohawks rushed out from the shadows and, with the element of surprise in their favor, crushed the invading war party.

From that point on the Mohicans were no longer a viable power in the region. The tribe drifted further eastward to Massachusetts and Connecticut. In 1664 the Mohicans disbanded their "council of fire" on Schodack Island (north of Rogers Island near Coeymans) and their presence in the Hudson Valley was ended.[3]

What remains of the past on Rogers Island? We know from R. Lionel DeLisser's nineteenth-century book, *Picturesque Catskills: Greene County,* that in the 1800s it was still possible for visitors to see the actual site where the battle took place—and that was 250 years after the fact. According to DeLisser, the site consisted of an "open green sward, situated near the center of the island" where "a group of enormous pines ... still mark the spot."[4]

Even in 1894, however, there were no souvenirs such as arrowheads, blades, or pottery left for curiosity seekers. The site had long since been swept clean of all traces. This should come as no surprise. By the late 1880s, Rogers Island had become a popular party destination for boaters desiring a quick jaunt from Hudson or Catskill. A huge circular pit filled with stone was fashioned on the southern end of the island and used for picnics and clam bakes. Numerous people who visited the island ultimately took away anything of historical significance.

The rustic character of the island was also changing. In 1851 the Hudson River Railroad started taking passengers along the east shore of the Hudson

River from New York City to Albany. (The track is still in use today by Amtrak.) A whistle-blowing, speeding train would pass close by the island several times a day, making the spot feel anything but secluded.

The village of Catskill also became a Mecca for tourists coming up the river and heading west from Catskill up to one of a number of mountain houses in the higher regions of the Catskill Mountains (see chapters on "Catskill Mountain House Escarpment" and the "Overlook Mountain").

In 1870, Frederic E. Church built a Persian-style home called Olana (see chapter on "Olana") on the east bank hill overlooking Rogers Island, and this gave the island an even less secluded feel.

Winter, too, brought in its share of visitors, despite the river being closed off to pleasure-boaters. Many workers were employed in the ice harvesting industry along the Hudson River, principally from Hyde Park to Castleton. Undoubtedly, Rogers Island provided wood and solid footing when fires were needed to ward off the cold during ice harvesting season.[5]

Further encroachments of civilization were inevitable. In 1935 construction was completed on the 5,040-foot-long Rip Van Winkle Bridge, which spans the Hudson River between Catskill and Hudson, thus providing a ready connection between two sides of the river that had previously been separated.[6] Because of the length and enormous height of the bridge, multiple supports were needed along its length. Rogers Island provided a convenient solid base for several of these supports, and huge piers were established on the southern end of the island. Whatever natural attributes the southern end of the island might have originally had were permanently altered or destroyed by this work project, as workers trampled over the rest of the island during their activities.

Today the island is all but forgotten, dominated by the Rip Van Winkle Bridge to its south, by Amtrak and Olana to the east, and by the village of Catskill to the southwest. Even the name of the island has fallen into obscurity, overshadowed by another strip of land on the Hudson River named Rogers Island, near Fort Edward. The Fort Edward Rogers Island is where Major Robert Rogers and his band of men, called Rogers' Rangers, encamped during the French and Indian Wars.

Location: Southwest of Hudson (Columbia County)
New York State Atlas & Gazetteer: p. 52, C3

Fees: Modest charge to enter grounds on weekends; additional fee for guided tour of mansion. One may enter grounds free of charge with an Empire Passport, or by walking or biking in.

Hours: Grounds are open year-round from dawn to dusk. Mansion tours are conducted from April to November, Tuesday through Sunday, 10:00 AM–5:00 PM; December to March, weekends, 10:00 AM–4:00 PM. Olana is owned and maintained by New York State Office of Parks, Recreation and Historic Preservation, in collaboration with the Olana Partnership, a not-for-profit organization.

Accessibility: Upper and lower parking areas provide ready access to the main walking and hiking trails. None of these trails are accessible by wheelchair, however, as they are rough shale carriage roads. The mansion tour is of the first floor only and is wheelchair accessible.

Degree of Difficulty: Easy, with moderate changes in elevation

Highlights:
- Beautifully maintained grounds
- Garden
- Mansion
- Artificially created lake
- Views of the Hudson River, the Taconic, Berkshire and Catskill mountains, Mt. Merino, and Olana

Description: Olana State Historic Site is the former estate of Frederic Edwin Church, renowned landscape painter of the nineteenth-century Hudson River School.[1] The magnificent Persian-style home set on 250 acres of scenic grounds with hiking trails is owned and managed by New York State Office of Parks, Recreation and Historic Preservation, and supported by the Olana Partnership, a not-for-profit organization. Olana is open to the public.

The trails on the site mostly follow the original carriage drives, which were designed by Church in keeping with his intent to create a picturesque landscape. The mansion is still furnished with many of Frederic Church's belongings and works of art, thanks to family members having resided in the home until 1964, when it was bought by New York State.[2,3]

Directions: From the NYS Thruway (I-87), get off at Exit 21 for Catskill/Cairo. In less than 0.2 mile after the tollbooth, you will come to a traffic light. Turn left, following a sign to Rt. 23. At 0.5 mile turn left onto Rt. 23. Drive east on Rt. 23 for over 3.0 miles, crossing over the Hudson River via the Rip Van Winkle Bridge. Take Rt. 9G south for 1.0 mile. The entrance to Olana is on your left.

The Hikes

There are over five miles of hiking trails on the property. Remarkably, each trail provides the hiker with a planned, picturesque view designed by Frederic Church to place the walker before a real-life work of art that mirrored his grand landscape paintings. This crowning achievement was his life's work, completed between 1860 and 1900, the result of forty years of thoughtful creativity. At points along the trails, you will see magnificent views of the Catskill Mountains, Hudson River, the lake, the Taconic hills, Mt. Merino, beautiful rolling landscape and, of course, the artfully displayed Persian-style mansion Olana. Church was ahead of his time in sculpting a large-scale environmental work of art.

All of the hikes begin at either the upper or lower parking areas. Practical suggestions for where you might start each of the walks are given on interpretive signs. In addition, other signs indicate special vistas or points of interest along the trails. If you begin at the upper approach road to the house, you will have the benefit of referring to a map illustrating an overview of the Olana property and hiking trails. This map is a replica of one drawn by Frederic Joseph Church, the eldest son of Frederic Edwin Church. The various hiking destinations can be divided into nine main points of interest:

1. ***House and East Lawn:*** From the upper parking area proceed to the map at the beginning of the original approach road. You will note as you start walking southeast on the approach road that you do not have a view of the Olana mansion. This is in keeping with Church's grand design. He wished to obscure the view of the house until visitors arrived at a certain vantage point, when suddenly the fantastic Moorish castle would pop into view—much like the sun peering out from behind a cloud. There are trees and shrubs on the hill along the east side of this path, and it is bordered with lovely ferns. In the latter half of the nineteenth century, ferns were all the rage.

2. *Olana Mansion:* Less than 0.2 mile from the map, the mansion appears on your right at the rise of the lower hill. It is a spectacular sight with its fanciful Arabian architecture adorned with colorful tiles and stencils. This view of the mansion on the hill is from a northwest position, the angle from which Church felt it showed to its best advantage. Looking south, there is a view of the lake and the rolling countryside beyond. As you climb slightly upward towards the house, wonderful views of the Hudson River and Catskill Mountains are displayed directly in front of you to the west. The pathway diverges: to the right you can complete a small loop of about 0.3 mile that takes you by unobstructed views of the house front; to the left is a trail to the site of Church's former studio and the lovely perennial gardens.

3. *Greenhouse Site:* At one time there was a greenhouse near this site. The greenhouse was the instigation of Mrs. Church, who loved to decorate the home with fresh flowers. At the bottom of the rise, you can still see the pipes that led to the now-defunct greenhouse.

4. *Site of Church's Studio:* The walk from the upper parking lot to the studio site and return is about 0.7 mile round-trip. The site of Church's first studio is marked by an interpretive sign. The actual studio, built in 1861, was dismantled in 1888 when Church built a studio wing to the

Olana, 2003.

main house. The original studio was built uphill from Cosy Cottage, the first Church residence, in order to take advantage of the views of the Hudson River and Catskill Mountains to the west. It was in this first studio that Church sketched and contemplated the Hudson Valley landscape before him.

5. *Ridge Road:* Church built this road somewhat later than the mansion and North Road after he acquired additional land. There are beautiful views of the Hudson River and Catskill Mountains, which Church enjoyed showing his guests from this road.

6. *North Road:* Originally this road was the main entrance to Olana. It was designed to bring guests to the house via the scenic route, wending through trees, then out into sunlight, eventually leading to a dramatic view of Olana. In the nineteenth century this road would pass the home of Church's friend Dr. Ferguson. Today it ends at a locked gate on Route 23.[4]

7. *Cosy Cottage:* The walk to Cosy Cottage and environs is about 0.1 mile from the lower parking area or roughly 1.0 mile from the upper parking area. Cosy Cottage was designed by the architect Richard Morris Hunt and built in 1861 for the newly wed Churches. They lived there until 1872, when they moved up on the hill to their new house. The structure you see today has been modified through the years, though there are plans underway to restore it to its original design. There are views of rolling farmlands and mountains to the east. There are no views of the Hudson River, however, because the cottage sits below the hill to the west of where Olana now perches.

8. *Barnyard:* The barnyard is contiguous to the lower parking area, or about 1.0 mile from the upper parking area. The five red barns are original to the time that Olana was a working farm producing corn, peaches, apples, plums, grapes, raspberries, and a variety of vegetables for household and commercial use. You will notice that trees block the view of Olana from this area. This was deliberately planned by Frederic Church. These functional buildings were meant to be discreetly hidden. Strolling around these buildings gives the sense of a once-substantial farm. Theodore Cole, son of painter Thomas Cole and a contemporary of Frederic Church, managed the farm for twenty years in the late 1800s.

9. *Kitchen Garden:* The kitchen garden is adjacent to the lower parking area, or about 1.0 mile from the upper parking lot. It is marked by a sign describing the herbs and vegetables planted for the Church family. As with the barns, the garden served a functional purpose and was therefore hidden from the main home and the landscaped views. Nevertheless, a walk on this country road is very pleasant. It looks much as it did when the Churches resided here.

10. ***The Lake:*** The far end of the lake is about 1.5 miles from the upper parking area, or about 0.3 mile from the lower parking area. The lake and surroundings are very much a part of the picturesque landscape designed by Church. The lake is man-made and bordered by trees and shrubs selected by Church. From the lake you have views of Olana sitting high on the hill. And from Olana the landscaped lake is clearly visible at the bottom of the hill. It is said that Church selected thousands of trees in designing a view, taking care to select various kinds and colors to create a particular scene. He used the variety of trees much as a painter would choose dabs of paint from his palette. Keep this in mind as you walk on paths surrounding the lake and the rest of the site. There are also a few picnic tables scattered about.

11. ***Crown Hill Road:*** The summit of Crown Hill is a round-trip walk of about 2.0 miles from the lower parking area, or about 3.0 miles from the upper lot. The trail is an old carriage road that winds in gentle switchbacks to the top of Crown Hill. On the way, the road goes through stands of pine and patches of deciduous trees. There are also lovely ferns, mosses, and berry bushes along the way. Once at the top, you reach a clearing where there are wonderful views of Olana on the neighboring hill. This particular planned vista was one of Church's last additions to his picturesque landscape. It is a great spot to stop for lunch, and there is a picnic table in the clearing.

History: Frederic Edwin Church was a painter of the Hudson River School who reached the pinnacle of his popularity between 1840 and 1860 with paintings such as: *Niagara; Above the Clouds at Sunrise; Heart of the Andes; Icebergs; Kataaden;* and *Sunset, Hudson River.* Church traveled and painted extensively in Europe, South America, and the eastern United States. His paintings are grand Romantic views of nature with dramatic cloud-strewn skies capping lush abundant greenery, very much in keeping with the style of painting of Thomas Cole, with whom Church studied for several years and with whom he maintained a close friendship until Cole's death in 1848. In fact, the Churches lived with the Coles during the building of Cosy Cottage. Later, Theodore Cole, Thomas Cole's son, managed the farm at Olana, a position he held for twenty years. Church's paintings provide clues to his intentions in the design of the Olana landscape.[5]

Frederic Edwin Church was born in 1826 in Hartford, Connecticut, and died in 1900 in New York City on his way back to Olana, his beloved estate on the Hudson River. It would seem that the forty years he spent designing, developing, and living at Olana were creative, happy years. In fact, it could be said that Olana was his grandest creative effort.

Church was at the height of his fame as a painter in 1859, living in New York City, and receiving praise and adulation at art shows. His painting *Niagara* was especially renowned and was exhibited all over the United States, as well as twice in Europe.[6] The very large (5 1/2 x 10 1/2 feet) painting *Heart of the Andes* was viewed by 12,000 people who paid twenty-five cents apiece to see it.[7] It was at this showing that he reputedly met Isabel Carnes, an admirer of his paintings, whom he married in 1860. Shortly after his marriage, he brought Isabel to the Catskills to show her the awe-inspiring landscapes that he so loved.

Evidently it was agreeable to her too, as they decided in 1861 to purchase a small farm and build a modest home in a corner of what later became the Olana estate. They commissioned the architect Richard Morris Hunt to build a house they called Cosy Cottage, which still stands on the Olana grounds. Hunt also designed a studio up the hill from the main house where Church continued to paint. They moved into Cosy Cottage and started a family, spending summers at Cosy Cottage and winters in New York City and Hartford. Tragically, their first two children, a boy and a girl, succumbed to diphtheria at Cosy Cottage.

Church continued to accrue more property until he owned all of the land to the very top of the hill, where he planned to build a larger home overlooking the Hudson River and the Catskill Mountains. This house was to be in the style of a Provençal country villa. Before those plans came to fruition, however, he was seized with a new inspiration.

The Churches took an extended trip to Europe and the Middle East that deeply influenced their concept for a new home. The Middle Eastern, Moorish-style of architecture especially impressed Church and inspired a new creative vision. When he returned from his travels, toting Persian rugs and beautiful Arabian artifacts, he discarded plans for the Provençal villa and hired a new architect, Calvert Vaux, to begin the design of the house that would grace the highest point on Church's estate.[8] Calvert Vaux, along with noted landscape architect Frederick Law Olmsted, had been one of the principal architects of Central Park in New York City. Church had an ongoing friendship with both of these men. He also remained well connected to the art world of New York, which provided him with opportunities for a dynamic exchange of ideas.

It is said that Calvert Vaux did not so much design, as consult, on the project. Olana was primarily the project of Church. It was an immense creative vision that happily occupied him for forty years. He did color sketches of the house plans and the landscape design. He made stencils for the house walls and ordered specific kinds of trees to complement his landscape vision. Church is quoted as saying, "About one hour this side of Albany is the center of the world ... I own it."[9]

Olana is all of one piece—a unified artistic vision. When you enter the property, you step into the "landscape painting" that Church created. When you walk the paths, you see the curve of a hill or a view of the Hudson River as Church intended for you to see it, right down to the type of ferns at a path border or the kinds of trees in the distance by the lake. Sometimes there are views of the mansion from a path, but only from vantage points and angles from which Church wished it displayed. The textures, swatches of color, and vistas created by the various plantings may have changed slightly with the growth of nature, but remain true to his creative concept. That is what makes hiking on these trails today so exciting and intriguing—you actually enter an enormous, three-dimensional landscape painting.[10]

It is thanks to the sensitive and collaborative efforts of The Olana Partnership and the New York State Office of Parks, Recreation and Historic Preservation that Olana is faithfully maintained.

24 MONTGOMERY PLACE

Location: Annandale-on-Hudson (Dutchess County)
New York State Atlas & Gazetteer: p. 52, D2

Fees: Modest charge for using the grounds; additional fee for admission to the mansion

Hours: Open daily except Tuesdays, 10:00 AM–5:00 PM, April through October, plus some weekends in November and December. Montgomery Place is owned and managed by Historic Hudson Valley.

Accessibility: The trails to the mansion, gardens, and views of the Hudson River are on rolling terrain with minimal elevation changes. The trails to the bottom of the falls, the powerhouse, and lake follow dirt roads downhill through the woods.

Degree of Difficulty: Easy to moderate

Highlights:
- Historic mansion and gardens
- Hiking trails
- Waterfalls
- Ruins
- Scenic views of Hudson River

Description: Montgomery Place is one of the original grand estates on the east side of the Hudson River, with history dating back to the American Revolution. It is owned and managed by Historic Hudson Valley.

The house and grounds were established by Janet Livingston Montgomery in 1802 after the death of her husband, General Richard Montgomery, a Revolutionary War hero. The estate essentially stayed in the hands of the Livingston family for nearly 200 years before becoming a National Historic Landmark and park. During the Livingstons' tenure, the property was well maintained and beautifully landscaped, evolving into one of the most notable of the great estates on the Hudson River. Though some of the earlier architectural and landscape features no longer remain, there are still hiking trails, waterfalls, beautiful gardens, and scenic views surrounding the lovely federal-style mansion, all carefully maintained by Historic Hudson Valley.[1]

Montgomery Place, 2002.

Directions: From the east end of the Kingston–Rhinecliff Bridge, travel east on Rt. 199 for 0.6 mile, then turn left at a traffic light onto Rt. 103 (River Road). Drive north on Rt. 103 for 2.9 miles. Turn left onto a road leading into Montgomery Place and drive 0.4 mile to the parking area by the Visitors' Center.

The Hikes

There are two interesting short hikes at this historic site. Hike #1, the Saw Kill Trail, is 0.8 mile long, and Hike #2, the West Lawn Trail, is 0.5 mile long.

Hike #1—Saw Kill Trail

The Saw Kill Trail has two points of entry: one near the Visitors Center and one near the north side of the Montgomery Place mansion. Both take you down to a pretty set of cascades on the Saw Kill that are a featured showpiece of the estate.

The trail near the Visitors Center begins at roadside between the site of the former conservatory and the arboretum. It is clearly marked and follows a carriage road that leads off into the woods in a northwest direction. After you have walked for slightly over 0.1 mile, you will come to a junction. If you take the Lake Trail, which goes off to the right, you will arrive at views of a tiny pond and a small dam that spans the Saw Kill. If you continue straight ahead for less than 0.2 mile, you will reach the Saw Kill and lower cascades.

To explore the area in its entirety, take the Lake Trail first. Very quickly you will begin to hear the roaring of the Saw Kill in the distance as the carriage road takes you downhill and around the top of a basin containing a pond. The sound of cascading waters is produced by an upper cascade on the Saw Kill next to the hulking ruins of an old swimming pool and bathhouses on the north side of the Saw Kill. The ruins belong to Bard College and were abandoned several decades ago. Sadly, they are now covered with graffiti and garish Day-Glo paint. The cascade, derelict pool, and bathhouses are not readily visible from the Lake Trail unless you follow an informal path that leads off to your right around the east side of the pond to the Saw Kill gorge.

Back on the Lake Trail, the small body of water that you see below is called "The Lake"—a quaint Victorian hyperbole, since "The Lake" in actual fact is a tiny pond. The Lake is contained in a semicircular basin that was likely formed during an earlier epoch when greater torrents of water flowed through the gorge. The Lake Trail quickly brings you to the Saw Kill.

As soon as you arrive at the south bank of the Saw Kill, take note of the small dam that intercepts the river. It is the dam that has created the "lake" by causing water to back up and fill what was probably a flat, marshy area initially. Were it not for the dam, there would be no "lake."

You will also notice, looking at the south end of the dam, the presence of a gate that once permitted water to be released upon demand. There is still old

The Saw Kill is a medium-sized stream that rises in the hills southeast of Red Hook and flows into the Hudson River at South Bay. Like many of the tributaries to the Hudson River, the Saw Kill has seen its share of past industrialization. The stream has powered mills since the mid-1700s, assisting in the production of flour and woolen goods. The Saw Kill has also created several pretty cascades that have been popular for the last three centuries.

The Saw Kill's location directly between Montgomery Place and Bard College has ensured that its waters will neither be forgotten nor neglected by nature lovers.

Falls on Saw Kill, 2004.

machinery in place that facilitated this operation, although it is rusted from years of disuse. You might be wondering what happened to the water when it was released. If you look down the south bank, you will notice that a large pipe leads away from the dam. The pipe descends gradually, ultimately arriving at an old powerhouse less than 0.1 mile away.

From the dam there are two possible ways to proceed. You can take the Lake Trail back up to the Saw Kill Trail, and then follow the Saw Kill Trail downhill to the powerhouse. Or you can take a footpath from the dam. The footpath parallels the Saw Kill and leads you quickly down to the powerhouse and the lower section of the Saw Kill Trail.

We recommend that you take the footpath. That will allow you to follow the pipe all the way down as it goes through and between several hills. Eventually you will come to the cement ruins of the old powerhouse. The powerhouse was built in the 1920s by General John Ross Delafield to furnish electricity to Montgomery Place. At the time there was simply no other way to bring power to the estate. The powerhouse operated until 1964, when it became convenient to access power from main lines in town.

You cannot enter the ruins; they are posted and fenced off. It is still possible to get a good look into the interior of the structure, however, where old rusted machinery is visible. You can observe where water was ushered in via the large pipe coming down from the dam and then released back out to the Saw Kill through a sluiceway. You can still see the outline of the sluiceway leading out from the base of the powerhouse, if you look closely.[2]

In all probability, however, it is not the powerhouse that will capture your attention, but the Saw Kill and its magnificence. Less than a hundred feet north of the powerhouse ruins is a viewing area that allows you to look upstream at two cascades that from a distance merge into one huge torrent of cascading water. It is a pretty sight to behold.

If you look downstream, you will be surprised at how close you are to South Bay, which is formed at the confluence of the Saw Kill and Hudson River. During high tide the waters of the bay are nearly backed up to the base of the cascades.

Don't be surprised if you should see a number of younger people walking along the opposite side of the stream. Bard College abuts the north bank of the Saw Kill, and the area is very popular with students, who use a trail on their side for hiking and exploration. South Bay is also a popular area for canoeing and kayaking.

Follow the Saw Kill Trail (which becomes a path at this point) southwest as it leads away from the powerhouse and ascends towards the Montgomery Place mansion, approximately 0.2 mile away.

This hike can also be done in the reverse order, starting at the trailhead next to the mansion and ending up near the Visitors Center.

Hike #2—The West Lawn Trail

The trail begins near the north side of the mansion and leads into the woods, paralleling the rim of the west lawn. Very quickly you will reach a high embankment where views of the Hudson River can be obtained. From this vantage point you can see, over 0.2 mile away, the narrow causeway that was created for the Hudson River Railroad and which is now used by Amtrak. The finger-like projection of land continues for a surprising distance as it parallels the east bank of the Hudson River. Although you can't tell just by looking down from the top of the escarpment, the water is extraordinarily shallow between the causeway and the shoreline, being only two to three feet deep in most places.[3]

The path eventually leads you out onto the west lawn directly behind the mansion, and over to a small pond.[4] The pond is dam-created, with no noticeable creek entering it. It is undoubtedly fed from underground sources further uphill. A couple of benches suggest the wisdom of sitting down for a moment

Janet Livingston Montgomery's brother, Robert, was a distinguished patriot and founding father of the United States. In 1789, Robert Livingston administered the oath of office to the first president of the United States, General George Washington. In 1802, as Minister to France, Robert negotiated the Louisiana Purchase with France.

or two to enjoy the peaceful surroundings and views. It was in this area, back in 1818, that Janet Montgomery stood to watch the boat carrying the remains of her husband, General Richard Montgomery, in a funeral cortège making its way downriver from Albany to New York City. You can imagine her standing here as the boat stopped to play a somber funeral march in her honor before continuing its journey down the Hudson.[5]

Continue around the pond to its south side and you will see a small, informal path that leads back into the woods and immediately down to the top of the escarpment, from where further views of the Hudson River can be obtained. From this vantage point you will see not only more of the causeway and, if you are lucky, perhaps catch a glimpse of an Amtrak train shooting by, but also a tiny, rather singular island between the causeway and the east shore. This small island of rock is called Skillpot Island, after the Old Dutch name for a "large turtle."[6] Far across on the opposite side of the river, slightly south, can be seen Turkey Point.

Retrace your steps back up to the pond. From there, walk across the lawn to the south side of the mansion. You are now on your own, free to enjoy the various other sections of Montgomery Place, including its magnificent twentieth-century gardens.

History: Montgomery Place is historically significant as an example of one of the great, early estates on the Hudson River and as the home of distinguished members of the Livingston, Montgomery, and Delafield families.

The known history dates to before the Revolutionary War, when the land was farmed by the Van Benthuysen family. The Van Benthuysens were Dutch farmers who immigrated to the American colonies in order to take advantage of the plentiful, rich farmlands along the Hudson River.[7]

In 1802 the property was purchased by Janet Livingston Montgomery, widow of General Richard Montgomery, Revolutionary War hero. She built a grand, federal-style mansion on the property and named it Chateau de

Montgomery. Prior to her husband's death in 1775, Janet had resided at their home in Rhinebeck.[8]

Chateau de Montgomery, right from the start, was meant to be a spectacular estate. Egged on by her esteemed nephew, William Jones, from General Montgomery's side of the family, she spared no expense. Even the mild disapproval of her brother, Robert Livingston, then Minister to France, didn't dampen her enthusiasm for the extravagant project.[9]

Janet Livingston Montgomery was sixty-one years of age when she moved into the mansion. The building had walls two feet thick, high ceilings, and great windows. It was set on a high embankment with magnificent views of the Hudson River. Janet contentedly reigned and entertained at Chateau de Montgomery for another twenty-five years. You can visit this mansion and see the splendid rooms and furnishings, some dating back to Janet Montgomery's era. There are also furnishings and artworks that belonged to later generations who inhabited the mansion.

Janet indulged an interest in gardening at Chateau de Montgomery that she had begun cultivating as a young woman at Clermont, her family home. She also maintained the existing farm on the property as a small commercial venture, hiring James McWilliams to manage it. In fact, Montgomery Place still maintains an active farm that sells produce and jams at a roadside stand on Route 103 south of the estate.[10]

There is a poignant account of Janet's last encounter with her long-deceased husband while she resided at Chateau de Montgomery.[11] In 1818, forty-three years after General Montgomery's death in 1775 at the Battle of Quebec, his remains were disinterred to be reburied in New York City and were transported with much ceremony from Quebec via Lake Champlain, the Champlain Canal, and the Hudson River. General Montgomery was one of the major heroes of the American Revolution and he was greatly honored in his funeral journey. In Albany, where the general had lain in state for a week, the black-draped coffin was transferred to the ship *Richmond*. As the solemn procession continued down the river, towns along the way honored Montgomery with gun salutes. Janet was notified by Governor Clinton of the hour when the *Richmond* would pass Chateau de Montgomery. As was her wish, she stood alone on the Chateau de Montgomery embankment as the *Richmond* anchored. The military band played The Dead March, fired a salute, and moved on. She was evidently overwhelmed by this emotionally charged experience. When her companions came to join her, they found that she had fainted.[12]

Though Janet enjoyed having gardens to enhance the landscape, it wasn't until Edward Livingston, Janet's youngest brother, inherited the estate in 1828 and renamed it Montgomery Place that attention to horticulture and landscape design reached new heights.[13] It was to his good fortune that a neighbor and esteemed horticulturist, Andrew Jackson (A. J.) Downing, took an interest in assisting Edward, his wife Louise, and daughter Cora in developing the gardens. Though A. J. Downing acted more as a friend than a paid consultant, he was a strong influence in the design and choice of plants selected for Montgomery Place.[14]

Downing was an arbiter of good garden tastes of the time. He was a writer on horticultural subjects and selected Montgomery Place as an illustration of best practices in estate gardening. In the October 1847 issue of *The Horticulturist*, Downing took his readers on an extended tour of Montgomery Place.[15] In this article, Downing described the setting, and then explored the morning walk along the Hudson, the wilderness to the north of the mansion, the cataract, and the lake. The article was illustrated by his long-time collaborator, Alexander Jackson Davis, a famous architect of the day whom Edward had commissioned to design expansions to the mansion.

Needless to say, the depictions of Downing and Davis highlighted the best features of Montgomery Place. It was during this period that many of the secondary structures such as the conservatory, gazebos and potting shed were added to the estate. Unfortunately, they are long gone, but the gardens and landscape features initiated by Edward's wife Louise and influenced by A. J. Downing remain and are well maintained. In 1985, J. Dennis Delafield, the last of the family to inhabit Montgomery Place, gave the property to New York State. Today, the estate still enthralls us with the grandeur of that earlier time.

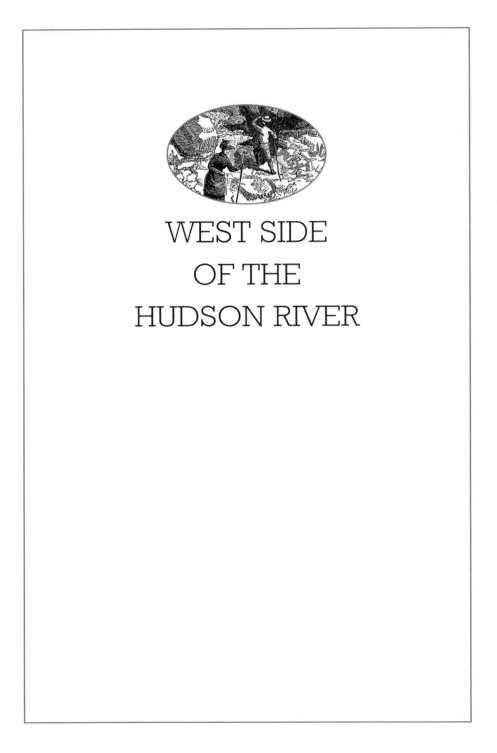

WEST SIDE
OF THE
HUDSON RIVER

Location: Coeymans (Albany/Greene counties)
New York State Atlas & Gazetteer: p. 52, A3

Fees: None

Hours: Every day, dawn to dusk

Accessibility: Hike # 1—0.5-mile walk to the waterfall on descending, old town road, now a hiking trail, with moderate change in elevation; Hike # 2—0.3-mile walk down to the Hudson River

Degree of Difficulty: Easy

Highlights:
- Waterfall
- Ruins of old mills
- Views of Hudson River
- Unique milk-carton bridge

Description: Ravena Falls is located in the Hannacroix Creek Preserve, owned by the Open Space Institute and managed by the New Baltimore Conservancy. The fall is formed on Hannacroix Creek, a medium-sized stream that rises in the hills west of Clarksville and flows into the Hudson River just south of Coeymans. The fall is nearly fifteen feet high and block-shaped, spanning a fairly wide section of the creek. The main trail, roughly 0.5 mile in length, comes out onto a promontory overlooking the cascade. Other trails in this section of the preserve lead to stone foundations from early-nineteenth-century mills and buildings.[1]

The milk-carton bridge is located in the lower section of the preserve near the Hudson River, and juxtaposes the geological antiquity of Ravena Falls with modern techno-ecological awareness.

Directions: From Albany, take Rt. 9W south to Ravena, a drive of approximately twelve miles. Turn sharply left onto Rt. 143 (Main Street) and proceed east through the village of Coeymans for 1.4 miles. As you approach the Hudson River, turn right onto Rt. 144 and drive south for 0.9 mile. Then turn right onto a dirt road where a green and white sign indicates that you are at the Hannacroix Creek Preserve, and park in the designated parking area.

The Lavern E. Irving Trail leads west, then south to the falls and old foundations. The Interpretive Trail leading due south crosses Rt. 144 and takes you east down to the Hudson River.

The Hikes

The preserve contains two completely different hikes: one to an old, industrialized waterfall; and one to the Hudson River via a unique bridge made of recycled plastic.

Hike #1

The hike to Ravena Falls begins at the northwest end of the parking area for the Hannacroix Preserve. The trail is a moderate climb uphill for about 0.2 mile following an old, grass-covered road. Originally this was a village road that led to several mills, the town poorhouse, and a number of other buildings.

Along the road, depending upon the season, a nice variety of wildflowers can be seen, including daisies, chicory, Queen Anne's lace, loosestrife, and lilies. At the top of the hill, the road veers to the left, narrowing as it heads downhill into deeper woods.

Ravena Falls, 2001.

At the bottom of the hill, the road comes out to Hannacroix Creek. Within another 0.1 mile, the road passes by the crumbling stone remains of the former Croswell Mill on your right. Look closely and you will see the outline of two of the main buildings. On the opposite side of the road, adjacent to the old mill ruins, are the remnants of another stone foundation, also part of the mill.

There is clear evidence of an old sluiceway south of the foundations. You can follow the trough of this sluiceway—where water once coursed—from the site of the mill ruins to the top of the fall, where a wooden dam once impounded the stream.[2]

When you reach the fifteen-foot-high waterfall, you will find yourself standing on a stony overlook. The hollow to your left that looks like a natural formation is part of the old sluiceway. The waterfall, now unobstructed, at one time was dammed to create a mill pond. The rocky overlook makes a charming place to rest or picnic.

From the top of the fall, head back for several hundred feet to the main trail, turn right, and then follow the road uphill for 0.2 mile until you reach the ruins of the former county poorhouse on your right. Stone foundation remnants clearly outline what was once the building.[3] Just further south are the stone remains of another building, directly to your left. The blocks of this foundation are notable for being exceptionally wide, up to three feet in sections. Local historians are not quite sure what industry, if any, previously occupied this site. The unusual thickness of the walls, however, has led to speculation that a large building, perhaps for cold storage for ice or produce, may have rested on the foundation.

Although you can continue even further south along this road, which eventually comes out onto another road that leads back to Rt. 144, the shortest and most interesting course is to return to the parking area along the same route you came. Once you have returned to the parking area, take note of the stone foundations visible at the southeast corner of the parking lot. These are remnants of a building that existed at a time when the road continued south and proceeded uphill past a number of other buildings, which have all been reduced to crumbling foundations over the years.

Hike #2

From the southwest end of the parking lot, follow the path that leads "To Hudson River Interpretive Trail." The trail takes you downhill to Rt. 144. From there, walk cautiously along the shoulder of Rt. 144, going south for a couple of hundred feet, and then turn left onto the Hudson River Interpretive Trail, going east.

Soon you will notice a brick tower on a tiny hill to your right. The tower is what remains of an old kiln that was associated with a former icehouse. Stay on the trail, for the lands by the kiln are on posted, private property.

Continuing southeast you will quickly come to an unusual bowstring truss bridge that crosses over a tiny stream. According to an informational sign, this is the world's first bridge made out of high-strength recycled plastic. The plastic was formed from 68,000 recycled one-gallon milk cartons, and has a load-bearing capacity of fifteen tons. The project was designed and built in 2000 by McLaren Engineers Inc., with the help of the engineering school at Union College, the New Baltimore Conservancy, and volunteers.[4]

The lagoon-like pond next to the bridge is home to herons, osprey, and kingfishers, plus some feisty beavers.

The trail ends at the Hudson River, where another beautiful view is afforded.

History: The land encompassing Ravena Falls and the towns of Coeymans and New Baltimore was originally settled in the late 1600s by both Catskill Mountain and Mohawk Valley Native Americans.

Shortly after the American Revolution, Ravena Falls was used to generate power for a gristmill that was erected near the waterfall. By 1826 the mill was acquired by Nathanial Bruce, who proceeded to convert it into a paper mill. It suffered fire damage on several different occasions over the next few years. The mill went through four or more different owners until it was purchased in the mid-1800s by a man named James Croswell, who operated it for many years as a paper mill. Different varieties of paper were made, including wrapping paper and wallpaper. Accounts from the 1950s quote old-timers as recalling seeing bales of rags coming up the river by boat or overland by train to the mill. It is said that the mill also used straw in the manufacture of paper. The Croswell mill closed about 1897.[5]

Another mill, run by Rob Carroll and established in the early 1800s, was located lower downstream on Hannacroix Creek.

The former county poorhouse was located on land that is now part of the preserve. Foundation stones can still be seen close to the old dirt road leading up from the mill. The town "poor master" was overseer to the poorhouse. The poorhouse was a one-room structure covering a floor space of about fifteen by thirty feet. The tenants of the poorhouse were generally the elderly, young orphaned children, the mentally ill, and other individuals with significant infirmities.[6] They were provided basic food and water, as well as a mattress for sleep. Looking at the remains of this old foundation, you may well wonder what conditions must have been like for its inhabitants.

The tall, brick, kiln-like chimney that is visible from trailside on the way down to the Hudson River was part of a now-obliterated icehouse complex. There is little information available about the icehouse. We do know, however, that ice harvesting and delivery was a prime industry of the New Baltimore area in the 1870s. Men from neighboring villages who worked as "ice harvesters" lived away from home in boardinghouses during the winter season. They were paid two dollars a day for their labor, and paid sixty cents a day for their lodging.[7]

New Baltimore was an active port town shortly after the Revolutionary War and remained a thriving mill community until the early 1900s. Boat building became an important industry for New Baltimore because of its proximity to the Hudson River and the port of Albany, beginning in 1797 when a ship was commissioned by four merchants from New Haven, Connecticut. The first boat of record, named *Venus*, was a one-deck, two-masted, seventy-five-foot-long, twenty-three-foot-wide vessel.[8]

Many minorities settled in the New Baltimore area. Most were originally West Indian slaves of seventeenth-century settlers. Many of their descendants remained in the area because work was available and, all in all, they were comfortable residing in the community.

26 HUDSON RIVER SCHOOL ART TRAIL

Locations: There are eight sites on the Art Trail:
Thomas Cole National Historic Site, Cedar Grove
(Catskill, Greene County)
Olana State Historic Site (near Hudson, Columbia County)
Mount Merino (near Hudson, Columbia County)
View on Catskill Creek (Catskill, Greene County)
Kaaterskill Clove (between Palenville and Haines Falls,
Greene County)
Kaaterskill Falls (near Haines Falls, Greene County)
North–South Lake, Site of Thomas Cole's painting *Lake with*
Dead Trees (North–South Lake Campground, Greene County)
Sunset Rock (also known as Bear's Den) and Artist's Rock
(North–South Lake Campground, Greene County)

Fees: Fees are charged for touring Cedar Grove and Olana; there are seasonal park entrance fees to North–South Lake Campground.

Hours: See individual site tours below.

Accessibility: All sites are open to the public; see individual site tours below for details.

Degree of Difficulty: Easy to moderate

Highlights:
■ Cedar Grove, former home of Thomas Cole
■ Olana, former home of Frederic E. Church
■ Waterfalls
■ Lakes
■ Mountain vistas
■ Views of Hudson River Valley

Description: The Hudson River School Art Trail is a series of wonderful treks to sites and vistas popularized in the nineteenth century by the Hudson River School of landscape painters.[1] The trail also includes, as starting points, the former homes of Thomas Cole and Frederic Edwin Church—the two most famous members of this art movement. Although the tour of the homes/

museums and the series of walks could be completed in one full day, you might better enjoy the Art Trail at a more leisurely, two-day pace, especially if you combine it with the Olana or the Catskill Mountain House Escarpment hikes (see chapters on "Olana" and "Catskill Mountain House Escarpment").

It is interesting to compare the relatively modest Cedar Grove, the Federal-style home of Thomas Cole, with Olana, the opulent, Persian-style mansion of Frederic E. Church. These two men were close friends and illustrious painters who formed the backbone of the Hudson River School.

The Trail: The Hudson River School Art Trail begins in the village of Catskill at the former home of Thomas Cole, who is credited as being the first of the Hudson River School painters. The Art Trail then crosses over the Hudson River to Olana, the mansion where Frederic Church, a student of Thomas Cole, resided. Following the visit to Olana, the trail continues to Promenade Hill Park in Hudson for views of Mount Merino. The trail then crosses the river again, back to the west side and to several sites of the picturesque scenes depicted by the Hudson River School painters. Some may want to begin the trail at Olana so as to obviate the need of crossing the Hudson River twice.

Site #1. Thomas Cole National Historic Site, Cedar Grove:

Cedar Grove is the former home of Thomas Cole and has been a registered National Historic Landmark since 1965. Located in the village of Catskill, it is

Thomas Cole's studio, circa 1910.

James Cramer painting the Thomas Cole House, 2002.

here that Cole and his wife Maria raised their family. Cole built a studio on the grounds, in which he painted many of his scenes of the Hudson Valley. The house was built by John Thompson, Maria's uncle, in 1815 on property that had been in Thompson's family since 1684. At one time there were 110 acres of farmland attached to Cedar Grove. Today the property occupies five and a half acres. The house was situated to capture views of the Catskill Mountains from the front porch, a fact that must have been very appealing to Cole. Located on the porch today is a plaque displaying an outline of the horizon and identifying each mountain by name.

Visitors are encouraged to stroll around the property. In between the house and the studio is a tiny yellow building that was once a privy. It is the only surviving structure that Cole actually designed himself.[2] A beautiful Italianate studio built by Cole just south of the house was demolished in the 1970s.[3] Cole's first studio on the property has survived, however, and is now open to the public.

The nicely restored Federal-style home and studio contain numerous Cole artifacts, period furnishings, and original sketches and paintings. During regular hours of operation, there are docents on hand to provide information about Cedar Grove and the Hudson River School of painters. Cedar Grove distributes a pamphlet on the Hudson River School Art Trail and often hosts activities and special events pertinent to Hudson River Valley history and culture. The Art Trail pamphlet and other relevant information can be accessed at *www.thomascole.org*.

Directions: From the NYS Thruway (I-87), get off at Exit 21 for Catskill/Cairo. At the stoplight beyond the tollbooth, turn left, following a sign to the Rip Van Winkle Bridge. At 0.5 mile turn left onto Rt. 23, proceeding east. Continue east on Rt. 23 for 1.6 miles. Shortly before reaching the Rip Van Winkle Bridge, which spans the Hudson River, you will come to a stoplight. Turn right onto Spring Street (Rt. 385). Immediately, you will see Cedar Grove on your left. Park in the designated area directly north of Cole's estate.

From Olana, drive west across the Rip Van Winkle Bridge and turn left at your first stoplight. Cedar Grove is immediately on your left.

From the parking lot, follow a path that leads to the Visitors Center on your left, where tickets can be purchased. The main house and studio are open from the first Saturday in May to the last Sunday in October each Friday, Saturday, and Sunday, from 10 AM to 4 PM. This includes a guided tour. The estate is also open on Memorial Day, Labor Day, Columbus Day, and Independence Day from 1 PM to 4 PM.

Site #2. Olana State Historic Site:

The site encompasses the Persian-style mansion where Frederic Edwin Church resided and worked, and includes five miles of walking trails, a man-made lake, Cosy Cottage (an earlier home of the Church family), and preserved farm buildings. (See the chapter on "Olana" for information and a description of the walks around the grounds.) The Olana website (*www.olana.org*) offers further information about Frederic Church, Olana, and current exhibits and activities.

Directions: From the NYS Thruway (I-87), get off at Exit 21 for Catskill/Cairo. When you come to the traffic light after the tollbooth, turn left, following a sign to the Rip Van Winkle Bridge. At 0.5 mile turn left onto Rt. 23 east. Continue east on Rt. 23 for over 3.0 miles. As soon as you cross over the Rip Van Winkle Bridge, which spans the Hudson River, bear right onto Rt. 9G and drive south for less than 1.0 mile. Turn left into the entrance for Olana, and follow the road uphill until you reach the main parking area for Church's estate.

Upstream view from Catskill Creek, circa 1930.

Site #3. Mount Merino:

Mount Merino is notable for its place in the history of Columbia County and the city of Hudson, and for its close proximity to both Olana and Cedar Grove—landmarks of the Hudson River School of painters.

Mount Merino was originally called Rorabuch, for reasons that remain obscure.[4,5] This small hill, rising less than 546 feet above the Hudson River, was once crowned by a little fort that served as an observation post.[6–8] In 1810 Daniel Penfield sold the property to Samuel Jenkins, who then established a population of Merino sheep—the mount's namesake—on his 400-acre farm. The slopes of Mount Merino thus became one of the first habitats in America for Merino sheep.

In the nineteenth century Mount Merino and South Bay were popular subjects for the Hudson River School painters. Most of the scenes depict South Bay and Mount Merino in the foreground, with the majestic Catskills looming beyond. One of the earlier paintings, *View near Hudson Looking Southwest to Mount Merino and the Catskills* by William Guy Wall, was so popular that it was reproduced on Staffordshire China from 1829–1836. Frederic Church painted *South Bay and Hudson Iron Works* in 1852. Perhaps the most famous painting of Mount Merino, however, is *Mount Merino and the City of Hudson in Autumn* (1851) by Sanford Robinson Gifford. Henry Ary, a friend and contemporary of Gifford and a native of Hudson, was the most prolific painter of Mount Merino and its environs.

Promenade Hill became a park in 1795 when it was granted to Hudson's Common Council by the "proprietors"—the founders of the city of Hudson.[9] Soon thereafter, an octagonal-shaped building was erected with "a saloon on the lower floor and a covered balcony around the upper part."[10] These accommodations ensured that tourists were afforded not only superb views of the Hudson River and Mount Merino, but refreshments as well. The building came to be known as the Round House because of its unusual shape, and the park, in turn, gradually became known as Round House Hill. Some also called it the Flag House because of its tall flagpole.[11] In 1834 the park was re-named Parade Hill,[12] but informally the name Promenade Hill Park endured as well.[13] The bronze statue in the center of the park is of St. Winifred. It was created by George Bissell in Paris in 1896, commissioned by General John Watts DePeyster.[14]

Promenade Park, Hudson, N. Y.

Promenade Park provided Hudson River School painters with unparalleled views of Mount Merino. Photograph, circa 1910.

These nineteenth-century paintings show a pastoral scene similar to what you will see today. The most striking difference—beyond the obvious intrusion of civilization—is that the mountain is now more tree-covered than it was 150 years ago when sheep were grazing on its slopes.

These artists would set up their easels at the southern end of Promenade Hill Park facing Mt. Merino. Sometimes they painted beautiful views of the city of Hudson from across the river, looking east from the Athens waterfront. Even after the landscape had become blighted by railroads and industry, artists continued to depict Mount Merino and the South Bay, often either ignoring or diminishing the encroachments of industry on the scene.

Directions: Mount Merino can best be seen from two vantage points: Promenade Hill Park/Parade Hill, in downtown Hudson, or Athens Riverfront Park, across the Hudson River in the village of Athens.

To Promenade Hill Park/Parade Hill: From the NYS Thruway (I-87), get off at Exit 21 for Catskill/Cairo. At 0.2 mile from the tollbooth, turn left at the traffic light and drive east for 0.5 mile. Turn left onto Rt. 23 and continue driving east for over 3.0 miles. As soon as you cross over the Rip Van Winkle Bridge, bear left, continuing on Rt. 23 for 0.7 mile. At the junction of Rtes. 23 & 23B/9G, go left and follow Rt. 23B/96 northeast for 2.8 miles (along the way Rt. 23B/9G turns into Third Street as you enter the city of Hudson). When you come to the traffic light at the corner of Third Street and Warren Street, turn left onto Warren Street and drive northwest for over 0.3 mile. Promenade Hill Park will be directly in front of you. Turn either right onto North Front Street or left onto South Front Street and park immediately along the side of the road.

The elegant Victorian manor of Dr. Gustavus A. Sabine is closely associated with the history of Olana. Sabine was Frederic E. Church's friend and physician. The manor was built in 1870 and was in close enough proximity to Church's estate to allow Sabine to make medical visits as often as needed. The mansion has since been converted into the Mount Merino Bed & Breakfast. The entrance to this historic building (now a B&B) is off Rt. 23, 0.2 miles east of the junction of Rtes. 23 & 23B/9G.

The entrance to the park is directly in front of Warren Street's terminus. Walk slightly uphill to the promenade, which is a long walkway that follows the top of a high escarpment overlooking the Hudson River. A good view of Mount Merino can be had from the southern end of the park escarpment.

To Riverfront Park, Athens: Mount Merino can also be viewed from the west side of the Hudson River at Athens's Riverfront Park. From the junction of Rtes. 23 & 385 by Cedar Grove (home of Thomas Cole), take Rt. 385 north for approximately 4.0 miles and turn right (east) onto Second Street in Athens. You will immediately come to Riverfront Park at the road's terminus, from where views of Mount Merino can be obtained.

Site #4. View on Catskill Creek:

This view, from which Thomas Cole painted *View on Catskill Creek* (ca. 1833), is only a short distance southeast of Cole's Cedar Grove home. One can easily imagine Cole setting out on foot with his sketchbook, bound for this quiet, bucolic site. Today the site is within the village of Catskill, next to a bridge and surrounded by buildings. Nevertheless, it is still possible to get the impression of what Cole must have seen as he gazed at the distant mountains. Frederic Church painted this same scene when he was a student of Cole's.

Directions: From Cedar Grove, drive north on Spring Street (Rt. 385) to Rt. 23, a distance of a hundred feet or so. Turn left onto Rt. 23 and drive west for 0.4 mile. Turn left at a sign pointing the way to Rt. 9W south (crossing over the eastbound lane of Rt. 23) and follow a ramp downhill for 0.3 mile to Rt. 9W. Proceed south on Rt. 9W for just over 0.3 mile. Park by the Rt. 9W bridge spanning Catskill Creek. From the bridge—or from the property of Tatiana's Restaurant at the north side of the bridge—you can revisit the scene of Thomas Cole's painting *View on Catskill Creek*.

Site #5. Kaaterskill Clove:

Kaaterskill Clove can be viewed most easily from the parking area for Kaaterskill Falls on Route 23A. There are now a number of homes dotting the mountainside to the southwest, but you can still appreciate the picturesque beauty of this awesome clove (mountain gorge). The parking area was once occupied by a souvenir shop and snack bar in the 1950s.[15] At one time it was called Lookout Point. Take note of the plaque commemorating Frank D. Layman, a local fireman who died while fighting a blaze on a nearby hill in 1900.

The clove was the site of a tannery village that was abandoned in the late 1800s. There are a number of ravines entering the clove from the south wall. During heavy rainfall or snow- melt, these ravines produce high-altitude

"Lookout Point" above horseshoe turn, circa 1920.

waterfalls that can be seen as you drive through the clove between Moore's Bridge and the horseshoe turn.

Directions: If you are continuing from Site #3 at the bridge over Catskill Creek, drive south on Rt. 9W for 1.3 miles to the junction of Rtes. 9W & 23A. Drive west on Rt. 23A for 8.5 miles until you reach the village of Palenville. From Palenville (junction of Rtes. 32A & 23A), continue west on Rt. 23A, driving through Kaaterskill Clove as you wend your way uphill following Kaaterskill Creek. After 3.4 miles from the junction of Rtes 32A & 23A, you will come to a horseshoe turn with Bastion Falls visible on your right. Continue uphill for another 0.2 mile past the falls and park in a large area on your left.

Site #6. Kaaterskill Falls:

The Catskills' most famous and exciting waterfall was frequently visited and painted by Thomas Cole, Sanford Robinson Gifford, Jacob Ward, Asher Durand, and other artists of the Hudson River School. The waterfall is 231 feet high and consists of two huge drops. The upper fall is 167 feet high, and the lower fall is 64 feet in height.

At one time a sizeable mountain hotel named the Laurel House stood near the top of Kaaterskill Falls. Catwalks and stairways allowed guests of the hotel to

Kaaterskill Falls—the Catskills' most spectacular waterfall, circa 1930.

South Lake, circa 1900.

descend midway to the huge amphitheater at the base of the upper falls. From there, guests would be treated to spectacular views of Kaaterskill Falls as the dammed waters of Lake Creek were suddenly released to put on a show. Remnants of the dam still exist, but the hotel, catwalks, and stairways are all long gone.

Directions: From the parking area for Kaaterskill Falls (see directions for Site #4, Kaaterskill Clove, above), walk back downhill on Rt. 23A for 0.2 mile, carefully staying as far to the side of the road as possible, until you reach Bastion Falls. From the east side of Bastion Falls, follow the yellow-blazed trail upstream, paralleling Lake Creek, for 0.5 mile until you reach the base of Kaaterskill Falls. This is a moderate hike with some elevation gain.

Site #7. North–South Lake, Site of Thomas Cole's painting *Lake with Dead Trees:*

Although the campgrounds and environs may seem relatively tame now, in Thomas Cole's day this area was wilderness. It only takes a little imagination to visualize the wild scene depicted in the Cole painting entitled *Lake with Dead Trees* (1825). You can follow in the artist's footsteps and stand at nearly the very spot where Cole set his easel.

At one time railroad tracks crossed over a causeway that ran between North and South lakes, right by the site of Cole's painting.[16] The mountain that you see off in the distance, and which was framed by Cole's painting, is Round Top.

Directions: From the parking area for Kaaterskill Falls, drive west, going uphill on Rt. 23A, for another 1.4 miles. In the hamlet of Haines Falls, turn right onto Mountain Lake Road (Rt. 18) and drive east for 2.3 miles until you reach the entrance to the North–South Lake Campgrounds. At the gatehouse ask for a trail map and then continue straight ahead, heading towards North Lake. In roughly 0.5 mile you will come to a stop sign. Turn right and follow the road downhill until you reach the level of the lake, where a cottage-like building can be seen. Park in this general area.

Across the road from the park cottage is an abandoned railroad bed. Follow it east for 0.05 mile and turn right through a clearing in the trees to the shore of the lake. It was here, looking southwest, that the sketches for *Lake with Dead Trees* were made. This is a short, easy walk.

Site #8. Sunset Rock (also known as Bear's Den) and Artist's Rock:

As Robert Gildersleeve illustrates in his book *Catskill Mountain House Trail Guide*, some of the place names in the North–South Lake area have changed over the years. Today's Artist's Rock was formerly called Prospect Rock or Prospect Ledge. The original Artist's Rock is located nearby on the escarpment and was named in honor of Thomas Cole.[17] On occasion Cole would invite friends to the overlook so that he could point out the precise location of his home about twelve miles away.[18] On a clear day you can see the Hudson River and the mountains beyond.

Artist's Rock, circa 1900.

Trail below Sunset Rock, 1997.

Sunset Rock is further up the escarpment trail. It was named for its magnificent westward views of the setting sun. Nineteenth-century hikers knew this vantage point as Bear's Den. It was from this overlook with its magnificent views of the Hudson River Valley that Thomas Cole and other painters—including William H. Bartlett, Asher Durand, Johm Kensett, and Sanford Gifford—made sketches for their enduring paintings. There is even a Currier & Ives print featuring this view. [19]

From Sunset Rock one can get wonderful views of North and South lakes, Pine Orchard, South Mountain, and Kaaterskill High Peak. There were also great views of the Catskill Mountain House before it fell into decline and was razed in 1963 (see chapter on "Catskill Mountain House Escarpment").

While enjoying the mountain views that Thomas Cole made world-famous, it is satisfying to know that a Catskill mountain was later named after him. Although you cannot see this peak from Artist's Rock, or even higher up at Sunset Rock, in the Blackhead Range near Windham stands Thomas Cole Mountain at an elevation of 3,940 feet.

Kaaterskill Lakes from Bears Den, Catskill Mts.
(Kaaterskill House, High Peak and Round Top in distance.)

North–South Lake from Sunset Rock, circa 1900.

Directions: From the gatehouse entrance to North–South Lake Campgrounds (see directions to Site #6 above and be sure to ask for a trail map at the gatehouse), continue straight ahead until you come to a stop sign at roughly 0.5 mile. Continue straight, wending your way slowly around to the back of North Lake. You will eventually reach a huge parking area near the road's terminus and the beach.

Park here and walk back up the road for 100 feet. The trailhead is clearly marked. Follow the blue-blazed trail for 0.4 mile to Artist's Rock. The hike ascends 500 feet. Sunset Rock is nearly 0.5 mile further up the escarpment trail from Artist's Rock and involves taking a short, yellow-blazed spur trail to reach the overlook.

Don't be confused by the fact that there is another Sunset Rock—on the blue-blazed trail at South Mountain. That is also a hike worth taking, but it is in the opposite direction from Artist's Rock and the Sunset Rock on North Mountain.

History: The Hudson River School Art Trail is an idea conceived by the Thomas Cole National Historic Site and inspired by the proximity of the homes of Thomas Cole and Frederic E. Church to the sites of some of the most famous paintings of Catskill Mountain scenery.

Thomas Cole is credited with inspiring the Hudson River School of landscape painting when three of his paintings based on sketches of Catskill Mountain scenery were unveiled to critical acclaim in 1825.[20] Cole paintings such as *Falls of the Kaaterskill* and *Cascade in the Catskill Mountains* caught the eyes of patrons and artists alike. Lumen Reed, a successful New York City art gallery owner and former Kingston merchant, became his staunch patron. It was not long before Cole was recognized as a major figure in the early-nineteenth-century art world.

Asher Durand, a like-minded painter of picturesque Hudson River landscapes, was Cole's close friend. Frederic E. Church, who was tutored by Cole in 1844, remained a close friend and colleague until Cole's death in 1848. Cole's son Theodore managed the farm on Church's Olana estate, a post he maintained for twenty years.

Cole, Durand, Church, and other artists were irresistibly drawn to the splendid scenery along the Hudson River. They also wrote about their philosophy of art and held in common a romantic vision of nature. They believed that venturing into the mountain forests to sketch straight from nature would produce art that faithfully represented their ideals for landscape painting. Most of these artists actually created their paintings back in their studios, but based them on sketches made from nature. Some, like Asher Durand, also hiked into the mountains with their canvas and easel to paint outdoors.

In the first quarter of the nineteenth century, the time was ripe for lush, wild landscape paintings. It was a period of relative peace and prosperity and the beginning of the growth of industrialization, leading to improved transportation and the steady transit of goods and passengers. People who were wealthy enough to travel to the hinterlands of the Catskills enjoyed displaying paintings in their homes of this almost mythical place. Galleries exhibiting paintings of these romantic and primeval scenes were guaranteed a successful showing. It was against this backdrop in 1825 that artists and other travelers made their way up the Hudson River by steamboat and then took carriages to the mountains. The Erie Canal also opened in 1825, beckoning more travelers up the Hudson River and then west on canal boat. By the 1830s there was rail transit as well.

More about Thomas Cole: Thomas Cole and his family immigrated to America from Lancashire, England, in 1818 when Thomas was seventeen years old. Thomas had worked as a calico designer and engraver's assistant before coming to America. In Philadelphia he worked as a wood engraver, art teacher, itinerant portraitist, and wallpaper designer.[21] His father operated a small wallpaper factory in Pennsylvania. Cole was always interested in drawing and painting. Though largely self-taught, he befriended local artists and studied the paintings exhibited at the Philadelphia Art Academy.

Cole made his first sketching trip up the Hudson River to the Catskills in 1825. He was enamored of the mountain scenery and spent that summer toting his pencils and sketchbook to the vistas described along the Art Trail. He moved to New York City by 1826 and began to create paintings based on his Catskill Mountain sketches. No doubt influenced by romantic literature describing the awesome, untamed wilderness, Cole developed a singular vision of picturesque American scenery. His paintings were an immediate success and Cole quickly became America's foremost landscape artist.

Not content to be known only as an American landscapist, in 1829 Cole traveled to Europe where he studied the works of the old masters. He also became interested in depicting lofty themes and allegories. Paintings such as the series *The Course of Empire* (1836) and *Voyage of Life* (1839) were a result of these studies. These allegorical works, though critically acclaimed, were never as popular as his American landscapes.

In 1832 Cole rented a small outbuilding on the Cedar Grove property in Catskill to be used as a studio. Cedar Grove was owned by John Thompson, a bachelor who shared his residence with four spinster nieces—Maria, Emily, Harriet, and Frances Bartow. While at Cedar Grove, Thomas Cole's friendship with Maria Bartow blossomed into a courtship. They were married in 1836 and moved to the west wing of the main house, though Cole still painted in his studio. Their son Theodore was born in 1838.

The Cedar Grove estate began with a 1684 land grant, followed by a land subdivision in 1773. From the beginning Cedar Grove was always a farm and had always belonged to the Thompson family. In John Thompson's day a variety of kitchen garden crops were grown. Oxen, horses, cows, cattle, and chickens were kept. Orchards and vineyards provided a full variety of fruits that were considered Thompson's specialty.

By 1815, John Thompson had become a gentleman farmer prosperous enough to build the grand, Federal-style house that remains today.[22] Though the 110 acres of farmland at that time extended to the river, the home was oriented to face the Catskill Mountains. The wonderful views of the "Wall of Manitou" were especially pleasing to Cole.[23] When Cole traveled to Europe, he wrote home that neither the "Alps nor the Apennines ... dimmed in my eyes the beauty of the Catskills."[24]

In 1844, now an accomplished and famous painter, Cole accepted Frederic E. Church as a student. Unlike Cole, Church was from a very wealthy family. He could well afford to board with the Coles while apprenticing for the year with the painter. Cole and Church remained colleagues and friends for the duration of Cole's life.

In 1848, at the age of forty-seven, Cole died unexpectedly after a short illness. It was a shock to his friends and to the art world in general. Frederic Church and his family remained close friends with Maria Bartow Cole after Cole's death, and even stayed at Cedar Grove while their first home, Cosy Cottage, was being built on a hill across the Hudson River (see "Olana" chapter for further details).

Poet William Cullen Bryant was especially saddened by Cole's untimely demise. Jonathan Sturgis—partner to the then-deceased influential art gallery owner, Lumen Reed—commissioned Asher Durand to paint *Kindred Spirits*. In this famous painting, completed in1849, Bryant and Cole stand on a rocky precipice overlooking a waterfall and a deep, tree-filled ravine that is believed to be Kaaterskill Clove, Site #4 on the Hudson River School Art Trail.[25] The painting is a fitting tribute to all three men—Thomas Cole, William Cullen Bryant, and Asher Durand. The 44-inch-by-36-inch painting hung in the New York Public Library for many years, but was recently sold to a private collector.

The Hudson River School continued to flourish after Cole's death. Artists such as Asher Durand, Frederic Church, Jasper Cropsey, Sanford Robinson Gifford, Charles Moore, and John Kensett remained true to his landscape painting ideals. The popularity of this style of art plummeted in the late nineteenth century and remained at ebb tide for most of the twentieth century, but has suddenly and dramatically risen in recent years. Today the works of the Hudson River School painters are again as revered and valued as they were in the early and mid-1800s.

CATSKILL MOUNTAIN HOUSE ESCARPMENT · 27

Location: North–South Lake Campgrounds
(Haines Falls, Greene County)
New York State Atlas & Gazetteer: p. 52, C1

Fees: Entrance fee charged seasonally when the state park's campgrounds are open; no fee charged when the campgrounds are closed

Hours: Hiking trails open continuously; campgrounds open seasonally

Accessibility: Both Alligator Rock and the site of the former Catskill Mountain House are accessible by carriage road; Boot Jack Rock, Boulder Rock, and Split Rock are accessed by a 0.7-mile trail hike.

Degree of Difficulty: Easy to moderate

Highlights:
- Fascinating rock formations
- Site of the famous Catskill Mountain House
- Spectacular views of the Hudson River Valley

Description: This 2.0-mile, round-trip hike starts near the site of the former Catskill Mountain House and leads you past a series of natural rock formations including Alligator Rock, Boot Jack Rock, Boulder Rock (also called Rip Van Winkle Boulder, and The Boulder), and Split Rock. What adds to the hike's enjoyment is that most of it takes place along an escarpment ridge that provides incredible views of the Hudson River Valley far below.[1]

Directions: From Catskill (junction of Rtes. 9W & 23A), drive 8.5 miles west to Palenville. From Palenville (junction of Rtes. 32A & 23A), drive northwest on Rt. 23A for 5.0 miles to the hamlet of Haines Falls. Turn right onto North Lake Road (Rt. 18) and drive east for 2.3 miles. As soon as you pass through the entrance gate to North–South Lake Campgrounds, turn right and drive downhill. At 0.5 mile you will pass by the end of South Lake. At 1.2 miles you will reach a fork in the road. Stay to the right, where a sign directs you to "Catskill Mountain House & Historic Site." Drive over 0.1 mile further to the north end of the parking lot.

To get to **Alligator Rock,** follow an orange-blazed carriage road going off to your left, northwest. This eventually leads to the lake. Along the way, at just over 0.1 mile, you will come to Alligator Rock, which will be on your left, directly by roadside.

To reach the **Catskill Mountain House site,** return to where you parked and follow the carriage road at the north end of the lot. This leads to the Pine Orchard (the former mountain house site). The hike up to the Pine Orchard is slightly over 0.2 mile.

From the site of the former Catskill Mountain House, follow the blue-blazed trail south for approximately 0.4 mile. You will see **Boot Jack Rock** on your right, opposite an escarpment overlook to your left.

From Boot Jack Rock continue south on the blue-blazed trail for another 0.2 mile until you come to **Boulder Rock.**

Split Rock can be reached by hiking 0.05 mile further along the blue-blazed trail.

Retrace your steps to return to the parking lot.

Alligator Rock, circa 1940.

Catskill Mountain House and the escarpment, circa 1900.

The Hike

The walk begins at the east end of South Lake. A short detour from the main carriage road takes you to Alligator Rock—an enormous boulder whose front end has fractured horizontally, producing the appearance of the head and gaping mouth of a dinosaur-sized predator. Jagged rocks have been placed in the hinged jaw for teeth, and a rounded rock has been placed in the "eye socket," further heightening the appearance of a dagger-toothed, gleaming-eyed monster. This tradition of enhancing the appearance of Alligator Rock dates back to the 1800s when Victorian hikers and tourists would pass the boulder as they traveled between the Catskill Mountain House and the lakes.[2,3,4] The boulder has also been called the Whales Mouth, but Alligator Rock is much more fitting.

Backtracking for several hundred yards, the hike continues on the main carriage road that leads up to the site of the former Catskill Mountain House—an area of flat bedrock with stupendous views of the Hudson Valley out to a distance of fifty miles.[5] This site is known as the Pine Orchard, and at one time it was the most famous place in the Catskills. As you approach this site, you will see several small foundations where ancillary structures once stood, but nothing remains of the mountain house itself. A large sign provides historical information about the Catskill Mountain House and its days of glory.

History: The Catskill Mountain House

In 1823, James Powers and several associates began work on a mountain house that would look out across the Hudson Valley from an area called Pine Orchard, near North and South Lakes. Townsfolk were initially skeptical, calling it the "Yankee Palace," because like so many other Yankee projects that were started, it was likely never to amount to anything. This time, however, the townsfolk were proven wrong, for the initial, primitive, ten-room hotel complete with ballroom and male and female dormitories soon blossomed into a magnificent and stately mountain house.

Powers intentionally built the hotel as close to the edge of the cliff as possible. That way, guests would have a magnificent view looking down into the valley; while those gazing up from below would be so inspired that they would journey up to the top of the escarpment to see the hotel and perhaps even patronize the establishment.

The hotel was built during an era when natural wonders were just starting to be exploited as tourist attractions. Already, Niagara Falls had a piazza, Lake George had a coffee house, and Trenton Falls had a hotel. The Catskill Mountain House offered what other resorts could not—high altitude and lots of fresh, balmy air. In addition the hotel was able to provide guests with access to a variety of natural wonders including Kaaterskill Falls, an escarpment trail that led to a variety of interesting destinations and wonderful views, and two mountain lakes that seemed to defy gravity by virtue of their height and position relative to the escarpment's edge.

The Mountain House received a huge promotional boost when James Fenimore Cooper wrote *The Pioneers* in 1823—a work of fiction that used the magnificent area around Pine Orchard as a background setting.

The hotel opened in 1824, but after its initial success it began to struggle to make ends meet. In 1846 the mountain house was purchased by Charles L. Beach, and under his management the hotel once again began to flourish. A Greek Revival facade was added to the front of the hotel, giving the Mountain House the look that would be immortalized in Hudson River School paintings. Business was good for several decades as Victorians came in great numbers to benefit from the rarefied air, stunning views, and plethora of natural wonders.

By 1883, however, the hotel-building mania in the Catskill Mountains had subsided, and the Catskill Mountain House—now just one of many grand hotels—failed to make a profit as the economy spiraled downward. The hotel continued to be run by the Beach family until the 1930s; then it was run as a Kosher resort by an operator named Andron. By 1942 the hotel had run its course and permanently closed at the end of the season.

For many years, the hotel sat on the flat bedrock of Pine Orchard, abandoned and desolate, visited only by hikers making their way along the escarpment trails or by campers from the shores of North and South lakes. The land was ultimately acquired by New York State, which deemed the building unsafe and burned it to the ground in 1963. The fire could be seen from as far away as Albany.[6]

From this point the hike follows a well-worn, blue-blazed path that leads south along the top of the escarpment ridge. During the walk you will come to several overlooks where wonderful views of the valley can be obtained.

The first interesting feature that you will reach is Boot Jack Rock,[7] which undoubtedly has been known by other names depending upon the imagination of the onlooker. The rock is shaped like an enormous lever resting on a fulcrum and pointing upwards. You can scamper up its back and perch well over six feet above the ground.

In another 0.2 mile you will reach Boulder Rock (also known as Rip Van Winkle Rock, and The Boulder). Long ago Boulder Rock had rustic stairs with railings leading up to it and even a gazebo on top, but these makeshift structures no longer exist, and Boulder Rock has returned to its natural state.[8]

Besides being a natural hiking destination for Victorian strollers, this huge glacial rock also served as an approximate boundary line delineating the property of the Catskill Mountain House from its main competitor, the Hotel Kaaterskill, located 0.8 mile southwest of the rock.[9] Both of these hotels are long gone and have left little to show of their former elegance.

Boulder Rock (with Hotel Kaaterskill in background), circa 1900.

The Fried Chicken War

Legend has it that rivalry between the Catskill Mountain House and Hotel Kaaterskill began even before the Hotel Kaaterskill was built, at a time when there was only one hotel on the North and South Lake escarpment— the prestigious Catskill Mountain House.

The story goes that in 1880, George Harding, Esq., a wealthy and prominent lawyer who was a frequent guest at the Catskill Mountain House, had taken his ill wife and ailing daughter to the hotel for a vacation and quite possibly to benefit from the supposed curative powers of the fresh mountain air. Harding's daughter was on a strict diet that excluded red meat, but not chicken. She especially liked fried chicken.

Harding was aware of the hotel's rule stipulating that guests would be served only what was on the menu of the day. No substitution would be made under any circumstances. Guests were also expected to accept this unconditional rule without complaint. Still, Harding felt that the hotel management would make an exception in his case because of his substantial patronage of the hotel and his high social status.

He was wrong. Charles L. Beach, the rather obstinate hotel owner at that time, was unwavering. There would be no substitution of fried chicken for the beef entrée. The two men got into a heated argument, during which Beach told Harding that if he didn't like the service and thought that he could do better, then he should build his own hotel.

And that is exactly what Harding did. Within several years Harding had constructed an enormous hotel four stories tall and 324 feet long, close to the Catskill Mountain House but high above it on the summit of South Mountain. It was Harding's daughter, Emily, who came up with the name—Hotel Kaaterskill.

The rivalry between Beach and Harding lasted for many years and came to be known as the Fried Chicken War.[10]

Is the legend of the Fried Chicken War historically accurate, or apocryphal? There is no way to know with certainty. What the story does illustrate with accuracy is our volatile human nature and how a small slight can have far-reaching consequences.

During the nineteenth century there were considerably more boulders resting along the edge of the escarpment than there are now. All but a few, like massive Boulder Rock, are now gone. Victorians considered it good sport to roll rocks off the edge of the cliffs and listen to them thunder into the valley below.

The only other large rock of distinction in the general area is at Sunset Rock, which is on the escarpment trail but in the opposite direction, 1.0 mile north from the site of the Catskill Mountain House.

The last attraction is Split Rock, which is a section of the cliff edge that has split off from the main part, forming a chasm.

28 SAUGERTIES LIGHTHOUSE

Location: Saugerties (Ulster County)
New York State Atlas & Gazetteer: p. 52, D2

Fees: No fee for accessing the preserve; small fee to enter the lighthouse museum

Hours: Ruth Reynolds Glunt Nature Preserve open continuously; lighthouse museum open on weekends from 2:00–5:00 PM, Memorial Day to Labor Day

Accessibility: Short, level, 1.0-mile hike round-trip

Degree of Difficulty: Easy

Highlights:
- Lighthouse
- River views
- Protected marshland nature sanctuary
- Canoeing on the Hudson River and Esopus Creek
- Lighthouse accommodations as a B&B (The Lighthouse Conservancy: 845-246-4380)

Description: The hike begins at the Ruth Reynolds Glunt Nature Preserve, named after a historian and preservationist, and ends at the Saugerties Lighthouse, which was saved from the brink of destruction and totally renovated in the 1980s. The lighthouse now serves as a Bed & Breakfast and contains a museum, a caretaker's apartment, two guest bedrooms, and a living room. The living quarters are in the style of the 1920s when the lighthouse was last inhabited and fully operational.

Overnight Bed & Breakfast accommodations are available to guests by advance reservation *www.saugertieslighthouse.com.*[1,2]

Directions:
Land Approach: From the middle of Saugerties at the intersection of Rtes. 32 and 9W (Partition Street and Main Street, respectively), go 0.4 mile north on Rt. 9W (Main Street). Turn right onto Mynderse Street and proceed downhill for 0.4 mile. Turn left onto Lighthouse Road and drive east

for 0.7 mile. You will see the parking area on your right, just past the U.S. Coast Guard station.

Except for two hours during high tide, when part of the path is submerged, the lighthouse can be easily reached by a 0.5-mile-long footpath over a wooded sandbar. If you wish to stay dry, check tide tables or contact the lighthouse before setting out.

Water Approach: The lighthouse can also be reached by boat. Water transport is available from the south side of the Esopus Creek.

From the center of Saugerties, follow Rt. 9W south. You will quickly cross over a bridge spanning Esopus Creek. Immediately turn left onto East Bridge Street and drive downhill for 0.2 mile. You will see the parking area on your left for the Saugerties Waterfront Park.

From there, put in your canoe or kayak and paddle downstream for roughly 0.5 mile. The Saugerties Lighthouse is impossible to miss. It is directly on your left at the Esopus Creek's confluence with the Hudson River, where a dock allows easy boat access.

Saugerties Lighthouse, 2000.

The Hike

The walk takes you along a 0.5-mile trail that leads through the Ruth Reynolds Glunt Nature Preserve. The trail begins from a parking area next to the U.S. Coast Guard station and ends at the lighthouse. Along the way the path wends through marshy woodland where two small footbridges help to facilitate crossings at particularly wet spots.

The trail near the lighthouse is partially flooded at high tide, which generally lasts for about two hours. The water usually rises only to an inconvenient couple of inches, which doesn't pose any problem if you wear water shoes. Storms and cycles of the moon can cause infrequent higher tides, however, so it's always good to check tide tables or call the lighthouse before a visit.

The preserve encompasses seventeen acres and contains a variety of marsh flora indigenous to wetlands—purple loosestrife, yellow iris, phragmites reed, narrow leaf cattail, big burr reed, sedges, joe-pye weed, aster, and marsh marigold, to name a few. The flora changes with the seasons. The trees rising above this lush carpet of colors and shapes are mostly black willows, with a smattering of red maples and elms.[3] The preserve is also excellent for bird watching. A variety of birds including great blue herons, kingfishers, ospreys, and bald eagles can be observed.[4]

At low tide you may wish to walk along the shoreline beach to the north of the trail. At 0.2 mile into the hike, you will see a side path leading north to the beach. If you turn west at the beach and proceed for about 0.1 mile, you may see remnants of the pond, or weir, used in the old days by commercial fishermen to store their catch. The pond today looks mostly like a marsh.

According to archaeological evidence from land digs around the confluence of the Hudson River and Esopus Creek, the area was previously used by Native American inhabitants dating back as far as 4,000 years ago.

At the end of this pretty marshland walk you will approach the lighthouse, which is positioned on the Hudson River at the mouth of the Esopus Creek. There is a tiny island behind the lighthouse, connected to the property by a footbridge. This small island is actually the stone foundation of an earlier lighthouse.[5]

At one time the mouth of the Esopus next to the lighthouse was a major port for a fleet of fast riverboats and steamers, which included the famous *Mary Powell*.

Lighthouse History: The Saugerties Lighthouse, dating back to 1869, is an imposing, Italianate-style, yellow-colored brick structure with a forty-six-foot tower. It sits on a massive circular stone and wood piling base sixty feet in diameter and twelve feet deep at the end of a half-mile, man-made peninsula. The tower light was originally a kerosene-powered, sixth-order Fresnel lens.

The current light is operational and has a solar-powered Fresnel lens that was installed in 1990.

In 1834, Congress appropriated $5,000 for a lighthouse to be built at the mouth of the Esopus Creek. This early lighthouse was completed in 1838 and consisted of a stone building built on a forty-by-fifty-foot pier, with enclosed whale-oil lamps. The lamplight was amplified by parabolic reflectors. The foundation of this early lighthouse remains as part of the island base to the east of the present lighthouse.

The early lighthouse apparently developed structural problems. In 1867 funds were provided for a new lighthouse, which was built just west of the original one. The current lighthouse that you see today harkens back to this period. The 1869 lighthouse was a marvel of construction. Its stone base, twelve feet deep, rests on three rows of fifty-six pilings topped with three layers of six-inch planking. The twenty-inch-thick brick cavity walls were constructed on stone fill within the circular pier. Originally, a fourth-order Fresnel lens, fueled by kerosene, provided the light. In 1909 a weight-driven fog bell was installed. It operated like the mechanism in a grandfather clock.

Both the 1834 and 1869 lighthouses were surrounded by water, requiring the lighthouse keeper to row ashore for provisions unless there was a hard freeze that allowed for walking or skating to shore. In 1888 the Saugerties harbor at the mouth of the Esopus was enlarged by dredging, and jetties were built to accommodate the large boats of the prospering shipping industry. The dredging process required the building of reinforced bulkheads that held back the dredged mud and sand, resulting in a man-made sandbar that connected the lighthouse to the mainland. By 1889 a small road was constructed on the peninsula connecting the lighthouse to the town of Saugerties.[6]

The original tower light, fueled by kerosene, was labor intensive and had to be carefully maintained by a keeper. The first lighthouse keeper, Daniel Crowley, came aboard in 1869. His daughter took over the lighthouse in 1873 and stayed at the job until 1885. After that a series of other lighthouse keepers (their names are listed on the fence surrounding the lighthouse today) kept the lighthouse going until 1954. Early on, there was a gas stove for cooking and an icebox for keeping food. Amenities such as electricity, steam heat, and telephone were not added until the 1940s.

In 1954 the light was automated by the U.S. Coast Guard, and the lighthouse was sealed up because the services of a caretaker were no longer required. Over the next thirty-six years the empty building deteriorated through neglect and disuse until demolition seemed inevitable. In the late 1970s the crumbling lighthouse only whispered fleetingly of its past glory days.[7] Thanks to the concerted efforts of Ruth Glunt, a local historian, a movement began to save the lighthouse. Glunt rallied other concerned townspeople, and the lighthouse was listed on the National Register of Historic Places in

The Mary Powell, *a steamer-style day boat, was called the "Queen of the Hudson" because of the amenities it offered and its elegant fittings. The vessel served full meals in a ladies' saloon on the main deck and had another saloon on the promenade deck. Advertisements of the day touted the wondrous Hudson River scenery you could see from its open decks. It was in operation from 1884–1902 and named after the widow of Thomas Powell, founder of the Hudson River Day Line.*

1976, which gave the structure national attention even while it continued to deteriorate. After a massive renovation project, however, the lighthouse was restored to full operation on August 4, 1990.[8]

If it weren't for the persistent efforts of Ruth Glunt and the Saugerties Lighthouse Conservancy, this wonderful historic edifice would have crumbled into the sandy river bottom by now.[9]

Life as a Lighthouse Keeper: What was it like to live in the Saugerties Lighthouse when it first opened in 1869? We can only conjecture, as there are few recorded details, but the daily life of Mr. Crowley, the first lighthouse keeper, couldn't have been easy. His primary task was to keep the kerosene tower lamps lit and in good working order. In addition he was kept busy closely monitoring the weather, sounding the fog bell when necessary, and maintaining the grounds and boat. Just maintaining the home and securing adequate supplies of food, clothing, and household goods must have absorbed the rest of the day for the Crowley family and subsequent lighthouse keepers.

Food and household goods were delivered by boat to the lighthouse keeper. Candles and kerosene lanterns provided light, and wood fueled the fireplaces and cookstove. A fireplace in the kitchen provided heat for cooking, and fireplaces in other rooms provided warmth to the household. A cistern to collect rainwater for drinking was kept under the floor in a corner of the building. There was no indoor toilet, and drinking water was limited to the contents of the cistern. Like most middle-class folk, clothing was restricted to two or three changes of summer wear and a few warm garments for winter. Mending and washing of these garments and linens was a constant chore. Much of the day, depending on the season, was occupied with keeping the fire and preparing the food, canning fruits and vegetables, and maintaining the upkeep of the home. The children were probably schooled at home, as it would have been difficult for them to travel to and from school because of the lighthouse's isolation from the community.

Meanwhile, as the communities along the river prospered, the country and the world kept moving at a faster pace towards a more mechanized era. Less than one hundred years after the lighthouse's construction, manual labor was no longer needed to keep the light burning or to sound the foghorn. Furthermore, much of the town's industry and the port's activity had diminished. The lighthouse began to fade away with the passage of time.

Hudson River Lighthouses: The system of lighthouses along the Hudson River began in 1825, following the opening of the Erie Canal. The first lighthouse on the Hudson River was established at Stony Point. By the beginning of the twentieth century, there were fourteen lighthouses along the river, including the Saugerties light. The lighthouses kept the river safe for navigation and the transport of manufactured goods and passengers, providing reassuring beacons of light on dark, foggy, and stormy nights.[10]

The village of Saugerties was a dynamic and prosperous commercial and industrial center in the nineteenth century, thanks to its port on the Hudson River. At one time Saugerties had the largest collection of hydropower machinery in the country. White lead and bluestone were mined and quarried in the area and shipped out on the river. Water from Cantine Falls on the Esopus Creek generated power for an iron works, a glass factory, a gunpowder factory, and a paper mill. These products were transported down the Esopus to the deepwater port in Saugerties, and then out onto the Hudson.[11]

Ice harvesting and iceboats also flourished on the river and creek. Commercial travel was important as well. Travelers could access daily boats from the Saugerties port to Manhattan and Albany, as well as take ferries across the river to Tivoli.

The lighthouse was once apart from the mainland. Photograph circa 1910.

29   OVERLOOK MOUNTAIN

Location: Near Woodstock (Ulster County)
New York State Atlas & Gazetteer: p. 52, D1

Fees: None

Hours: No restrictions; interpreters staff the fire tower and cabin during fair weather from the first weekend in June through Columbus Day. Their hours are from 11:00 AM–4:00 PM.

Accessibility: The trail follows an old carriage road, which is eroded in places, but which still provides a serviceable means of reaching the summit. The ascent requires a moderate, sustained effort. Care must be taken when cold weather arrives, for sheets of ice frequently stretch across the carriage road. Alternative route: Overlook Mountain can also be accessed from Platte Clove (to the north) via the old Overlook Road trail. This is a much longer (4.8-mile) hike up to the mountain house ruins, with another 0.5-mile hike to get to the summit and fire tower, for a total distance of 5.3 miles one-way.

Degree of Difficulty: Moderate to difficult

Highlights:
- Scenic views
- Ruins
- Lake
- Fire tower

Description: Overlook Mountain stands at an elevation of 3,140 feet and forms the southern terminus of the Wall of Manitou—the magnificent eastern escarpment of the Catskill Mountains that faces the Hudson River.[1-4] It is a grand hike.

One of the unusual and appealing features of this hike is the ruins of the last incarnation of the Overlook Mountain House. Beginning in the early 1800s, a succession of hotels was built near the summit of Overlook Mountain. Each hotel, in succession, burned to the ground and was replaced by a new hotel. In their heyday these mountain houses were a major attraction. Travelers came from far away to enjoy Overlook's sweeping views of the Catskill Mountains and the Hudson Valley, to hike the mountainous regions around

Woodstock, and to plumb the awesome depths of Platte Clove. The ruins visible today are of a hotel that never opened to the public. It was near completion in 1929 when it was abandoned. The ghostly ruins whisper of times gone by.

Directions: From the center of Woodstock at the junction of Rtes. 212 & 33 (Rock City Road), go north on Rt. 33. At 0.6 mile, Rt. 33 crosses Glasco Turnpike and turns into Meads Mountain Road. When you reach the Buddhist temple, after a drive of 2.5 miles from Rt. 212, turn into the designated parking area on your right. The trailhead begins from the parking lot.

A fascinating little church, the Western Rite Orthodox Church of the Holy Transfiguration, can be visited just 0.1 miles south of the Overlook Mountain parking area.

The Hike

The walk begins from the parking area across the road from what at one time was Meads Mountain House, but which is now a Tibetan Buddhist conference center. The red-blazed trail follows an old carriage road that leads up to the fire tower at the summit of Overlook Mountain—a distance of 2.6 miles. It is a steady uphill climb, taking one to two hours to complete depending upon your ability and stamina. Along the way, during the late summer, you can stop and pick raspberries that grow abundantly near the trail. You can also observe interesting flora. There are hemlocks, striped maple, mountain laurel, mosses, ferns, and a variety of seasonal wildflowers. When you reach the top, you will notice that the few conifers are smaller than those at the bottom because of the harsh wind and cold during the winter months. In season, blueberries thrive in these higher regions.

Deer, bear, turkey, grouse, eagles, porcupines, and rattlesnakes inhabit Overlook Mountain, but there is enough traffic on the mountain to keep most wildlife wary and hidden.

The hike up to the mountain house ruins is approximately 1.8 miles from the trailhead. Just before you reach the main building, look to the woods at your left and you will see the remains of a fireplace, chimney, and stone foundation. This building may have been the living quarters for staff, perhaps even the grounds caretaker. When you reach the ruins of the main building, you will want to linger for a while and explore the foundation walls, which are still standing. There has been some discussion about bringing down the remainder of the structure because its deteriorating condition poses a hazard to incautious hikers, but so far no action has been taken.

The skeletal structure of the ill-fated mountain house can be entered and explored. Keep on the lookout for bits of glass and miscellaneous obstacles. Don't try to climb up to what was the second floor of the mountain house; there are no floor boards for support.

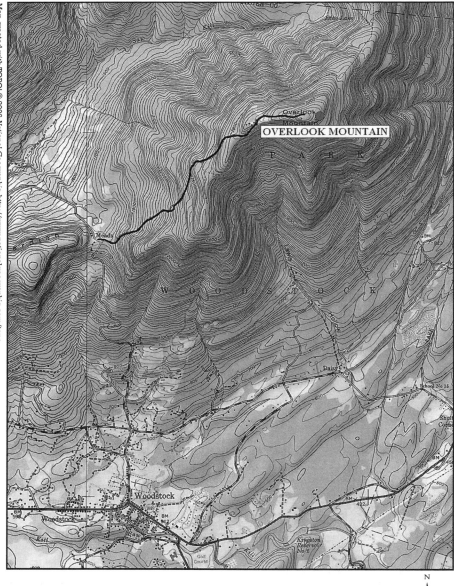

OVERLOOK MOUNTAIN

There are a number of additional ruins, presumed to be hotel outbuildings, in the vicinity of the large cement structure.

About twenty feet diagonally behind the main hotel ruins is a smaller cement structure, called the "1928 House" because the year 1928, etched into cement, is still clearly visible over the main entrance. This building was used to house the family and guests of Morris Newgold, the owner of the Overlook Mountain House. By 1935 this structure, unlike the hotel itself, was completed and fully operational with its own light, heat, power, and water.

Northeast of the 1928 House are other ruins, sometimes partially obscured by brush and blending into the natural rocky areas. One ruin is at a slight rise about eighty feet from the 1928 House. This area consists of a man-made foundation built on natural rocks. Since its location would have afforded views of the mountains to the north, it might at one time have been the site of a gazebo or other open-air picnic structure.

In the woods off the trail to the right is a stone cistern and, south of that, the overgrown foundations of a medium-sized structure.

As you continue on the path 0.8 mile to the fire tower, there are more intriguing ruins to your left. One ruin consists of a chimney or vent and a stone foundation surrounding a series of rectangular brick structures about four feet by six feet in size.

Overlook Mountain House ruins, 1996.

Echo Lake Trail: Proceeding east from the Overlook Mountain House ruins, you will quickly arrive at a blue-blazed trail that bears left and leads to Echo Lake, 2.0 miles away. Echo Lake is a shallow, muddy body of water. In the glorious days of the mountain houses, it was a picnic site for hotel guests, who were brought there in carriages. In its heyday there was even a refreshment stand. It was a destination not only for guests of the Overlook Mountain House, but also for hikers from establishments overlooking Platte Clove and Kaaterskill Clove. Today it continues to be a popular hiking and camping destination. Unfortunately, the area is sometimes littered by the thoughtless leavings of partying hikers.

Fire Tower Trail: The fire tower is uphill on the red-blazed trail 0.6 mile from the junction of the red-blazed trail with the trail to Echo Lake. At about 0.2 mile north from the junction sign, you will see several paths going off to the right that ultimately lead to wonderful overlooks of the Ashokan Reservoir to the southwest and the Hudson River to the east.[5]

By following the main trail you will eventually come to a point where the mountain summit and fire tower are clearly visible, towering above you on your left. Soon after, you will pass by the ranger's cabin. The cabin is now open to the public as a museum during the summer season or when staffed by a volunteer fire tower steward or interpreter. The weekend volunteers can be identified by the New York State volunteer shoulder patches on their shirts. Pictorial posters at the cabin describe the rich history of Overlook Mountain.[6]

At the top of the mountain is an eighty-foot-high, metal-framed fire tower in an open area that is surrounded by hardwoods, particularly red oaks. From the rocky summit and top of the tower, there are views of the Hudson Valley including, on a clear day, Albany approximately fifty-five miles to the north. Weather permitting, you may be able to see as far as the Massachusetts and Connecticut borders to the east (a distance of about thirty miles), the Shawangunk Mountains to the south, Slide Mountain and its neighboring peaks to the west, and the Ashokan Reservoir to the south. Some of the best views to the east are obtained by going back down to the Ranger's Cabin—just below the summit— and following an unmarked path that descends 200 feet from the cabin to a rocky ledge overlooking the Hudson Valley, less than 0.1 mile away.

History: The area around Overlook Mountain is rich in history and harkens back to a period in American history when the public's perception of the wilderness was changing from the prior view of nature as foreboding and inhospitable, to a new vision of nature as a peaceful retreat from the excesses and evils of daily city life. In 1833, James Booth erected what was described as a "rough little house" on the Overlook plateau and named it the Woodstock Blue Mountain House.

The original Overlook Mountain House—not the one whose ruins you see today—was a wooden structure built by John E. Lasher in 1870 at an elevation of 2,978 feet. The exterior of this hotel was simple in design, with broad porches.[7] It was a white, T-shaped structure, two stories high and accommodating up to 300 guests. Though Spartan on the outside, the interior had splendid rooms with flowered carpets and gilt-framed pictures. The hotel provided an orchestra for dance music and a caged bear for the guests' entertainment. Other diversions were bowling, billiards, picnics, concerts, and masquerade balls. President Ulysses S. Grant was a visitor in 1873. Tourists typically reached the Overlook Mountain House by horse-drawn carriages that picked them up at the railroad station in West Hurley and brought them up the long, winding road from Woodstock.[8]

Hiking to the top of Overlook Mountain, 2001.

Guests would hike from the hotel and visit such intriguing-sounding places as the Minister's Face, Indian Head, Turtle Rock, Poet's Glen, Lover's Retreat, Platte Clove, Shue's Lake (now Echo Lake), and the upper Sawkill Valley.[9] One of the favorite pastimes was boulder pushing, in which a large boulder would be pushed over the edge of cliffs for no other purpose than the amusement of the onlookers. Obviously, this was a time-limited activity, for the number of available boulders was soon exhausted.

Five years after opening, in 1875, the hotel was destroyed by fire. The fire occurred on April 1 (April Fool's Day), and hotel personnel initially thought that one of Lasher's children, who reported seeing black smoke issuing from a chimney, was trying to fool them. The delay in responding to the outbreak of fire was enough to doom the building.

Like a phoenix rising from its own ashes, however, the hotel was rebuilt in 1878 by the Kiersted brothers of Saugerties. This structure was also built of wood. It stood three stories high, was 200 feet in length, and was firmly anchored to the mountain by steel cables to prevent high winds from hitting the hotel broadside and toppling it. It could accommodate up to 150 guests.

The Overlook Mountain House was in competition with the Catskill Mountain House at Pine Orchard to the north. The Catskill Mountain House was bigger and had more natural wonders in closer proximity (see chapter on "Catskill Mountain House Escarpment"). The Overlook Mountain House, however, was significantly higher in elevation. In fact, the Overlook was the highest mountain hotel in New York State. This fact was very significant to tourists of that era, because they believed that mountaintop air and fresh balsam scents were remedies for many ailments, including tuberculosis and hay fever. It was believed that the higher up you went, the purer and more rehabilitating was the air. One newspaperman even proposed bottling the air on Overlook Mountain and selling it as Overlook Oxy Gin (an obvious pun on the word "oxygen").[10]

The Overlook Mountain House, however, was never able to develop a comparable system of trails through and around Platte Clove, which it overlooked, to match the Catskill Mountain House's symbiotic attachment to Kaaterskill Clove and the scenic wonders surrounding North and South lakes. As a result the Overlook Mountain House forever played second fiddle to the Catskill Mountain House, as well as to the Hotel Kaaterskill and Laurel House—two other famous mountain houses in close proximity to Kaaterskill Clove.

In 1917, Morris Newgold, a successful entrepreneur, inventor, and hotel owner, bought the property. In 1926 the second Overlook Mountain House burned to the ground.

Mr. Newgold had learned an important lesson from the fire-ravaged history of mountain house hotels. In 1929 construction on a new Overlook Mountain House began. This time, however, the material used was not wood,

An earlier hotel on Overlook Mountain, circa 1900.

but fireproof poured cement. Mr. Newgold and his architect, Frank Amato, envisioned a building sturdy enough to withstand wind, ice, snow, and most of all, fire. In addition Newgold also planned to build a funicular railroad (consisting of counterbalanced rail cars pulled along two tracks by a cable) and a landing field for planes to make the hotel even more accessible.[11]

Unfortunately, bad luck struck again, though this time it wasn't fire. According to William Newgold, the grandson of Morris Newgold, the demise of the hotel came about because of his grandfather's illness and death in 1944, coupled with the lack of interest of other family members in continuing the building project. Other sources commonly attribute the demise of the mountain house to the stock market going up in flames in 1929. It was said that following the stock market crash, all work on the hotel was immediately halted because of a lack of financial backing, and construction was never resumed. It may be that both the lack of family interest and finances played a role. The new hotel, though nearly completed, never opened to guests. To this day, only the foundation stands—a ghostly reminder of the grand dreams of earlier times.

The Overlook Mountain Fire Tower: The fire tower is sixty feet high and affords great panoramic views. Placed on top of Overlook Mountain in 1950, this is the newest of the five remaining fire towers in the Catskill Park.

The actual fire tower pre-dates 1950, however, as it was constructed in 1927 on Gallis Hill just west of Kingston. In 1950 the Gallis Hill fire tower was dismantled and trucked up to the top of Overlook Mountain, where it was reassembled. In 1988 the tower ceased to function as a fire tower and was closed to the public. Thanks to the work of a committee of Overlook Fire Tower Stewards, however, it was repaired and reopened to the public in the spring of 1999. Now, once again, hikers can enjoy its bird's-eye view of the region.

The tower has been recognized as an historic treasure and is on the National Historic Lookout Register. The ranger's cabin has been converted into a museum that interprets the history of Overlook Mountain. Volunteer Overlook Fire Tower interpreters are on hand weekends between Memorial Day and Columbus Day to provide information about the mountain and its surroundings.[13]

Echo Lake: Echo Lake is worth a visit on the way up or down Overlook Mountain. The lake is formed at an elevation of roughly 2,000 feet and is the source for the Saw Kill River, which runs directly through Woodstock. Supposedly, Echo Lake acquired its name from the sounds hikers would hear as they called out from different parts of the lake. Previously, the lake was known as Shue's Pond.

During the tenure of Col. James Smith as the manager of the Overlook Mountain House, the lake was stocked with trout and had a boathouse on the perimeter, as well as a refreshment saloon made of logs. Today, the lake still has a reputation as a party spot, but without the refreshment stand.

Meads Mountain House

Meads Mountain House, built in 1863 by George Mead, was initially merely a way station for guests wishing to pause for refreshment and rest on their way up to the Overlook Mountain House. In time, however, Mead's Mountain House became a destination in its own right. The views from Mead's were reputed to be even better than the ones from the Overlook Mountain House, although today this seems hard to imagine, since it is at a lower elevation and dense forest blocks the view.

After Mead, the mountain house was owned by Captain Mike, a Yugoslavian-born architect and aviator. Today, Mead's inn is a Tibetan Buddhist conference center, which lends an international feel to the Overlook Mountain hike.[12]

Previous names of Overlook Mountain

Back in the 1700s, Overlook Mountain was known by a variety of names depending on where you stood in relation to the mountain. To people in the village of Woodstock, it was known as Woodstock Mountain because of its proximity to the town. To people in Catskill, it was known as South Peak because it was the southernmost mountain facing out towards the Hudson River. Dutch-speaking farmers called it Kortof, which, roughly translated, means "abrupt or curt." Undoubtedly the Dutch name referred to the fact that the mountain posed as a natural barrier to an easy passage to the west. By 1853 the mountain appeared on maps as Overlook Mountain, and it has been known by that name ever since.

Glass Factories

There were glass factories on the side of Overlook Mountain from the late 1700s until the mid-1800s. One factory, referred to as the Old Glass factory, was located on the plains northwest of the Overlook fire tower. The Bristol Glass house was located in the Town of Shady, and the Woodstock Glass Factory was located in Keefe Hollow, about 0.5 mile beyond the Overlook parking area. These factories produced window glass and glass bottles for household items.[14]

Bluestone Quarrying

The Catskill region was heavily quarried for bluestone from the mid-1800s into the 1900s, and there were quarries around the southern and eastern base of Overlook Mountain.15 You can still see the overgrown, shallow depressions in the landscape left by these quarries. At one time bluestone was the material of choice for sidewalks, steps, and curbs. With the invention of cement, however, bluestone quarrying became less profitable and soon the demand for the product ceased.

30 SKY TOP & MOHONK LAKE

Location: Mohonk Lake (Ulster County)
New York State Atlas & Gazetteer: p. 36, BC2

Fee: Modest day-use fee; no charge if you are a guest staying or dining at the Mohonk Mountain House

Hours: None posted

Accessibility: Sky Top—0.4-mile hike involving an elevation change of 300 feet; Mohonk Lake—1.0-mile trek around perimeter of lake. Several short trails off the Lake Shore Carriage Road and Spring Path invite further exploration. The Sky Top Path, Labyrinth Path, Lake Shore Path, and Undercliff Path are closed during the winter.

Degree of Difficulty: Sky Top—moderate; Mohonk Lake—easy along east shore trail, easy to moderate along west shore trail; side trails off east shore trail—easy to moderate, depending upon the amount of rock scrambling you do

Highlights:
- Scenic views
- Mountain lake
- Rustic summerhouses (gazebos)
- Enormous fields of talus

Description: The two primary hiking destinations, Sky Top and Mohonk Lake, are formed in the higher reaches of the Shawangunk Mountains in a unique, craggy, nineteenth-century fairyland located on the Mohonk Mountain House grounds. The hikes are punctuated with "summerhouses" (also known as gazebos) that provide extraordinary views of the landscape. The folded rocks of the Shawangunk cliffs, comprised of quartzite conglomerate, are visible at many vantage points. Huge blocks of talus can be seen at the base of steeply formed cliffs.

Directions: From the NYS Thruway (I-87) get off at Exit 18 for New Paltz and Poughkeepsie. Drive 0.2 mile to the traffic light. Turn left on Rt. 299 and drive west for 1.5 miles until you reach the junction of Rtes. 299 & 32 North in New Paltz.

To Mohonk Mountain House: From the junction of Rtes. 299 & 32 North (New Paltz), continue west on Rt. 299 for 0.3 mile. Turn right onto Springtown Road and drive west for 0.5 mile. Turn left onto Mt. Rest Road and drive uphill for 3.5 miles (continuing straight ahead when you come to a stop sign at 1.2 miles). At 3.5 miles turn left and drive up to the gate entrance to the Mohonk Mountain House.

For those with reservations at the hotel, drive 2.0 miles to the mountain house (or 2.2 miles to the valet parking entrance). For those without hotel or dining reservations, bear in mind that access to the Mohonk Mountain House is reserved for guests only.

For those hiking in on foot, pay a day-use fee at the entrance gate and park in the lot to the right. From the parking area follow a footpath that will eventually take you to the mountain house area. Take note that the mountain house issues only as many day passes as there are parking spaces, so be sure to arrive early in the day if you plan an approach to Sky Top from the gatehouse.

Seasonally, a shuttle runs between the gatehouse and the mountain house. Be prepared to pay a modest fee for transportation.

The Trapps Approach: From the junction of Rtes. 299 & 32 North in New Paltz, continue west on Rt. 299 for 6.1 miles. Turn right onto Rt. 44/55 and drive northwest for 1.8 miles to the parking area on your right for West Trapps. Along the way, at 1.5 mile, you will pass under the Trapps Bridge.

From the parking area, proceed on foot to the Trapps Bridge and follow the Undercliff Carriage Road for 2.3 miles. This is a very exciting hike because the trail leads along the base of the towering Trapps escarpment. Cross over the Rhododendron Bridge, turn left, and continue on the Old Minnewaska Road for just over 1.0 mile. You will come to a junction where Forest Road goes to the right and Lake Shore Road continues ahead. There are gorgeous views of Sky Top from the carriage road here. Continue straight on Lake Shore Drive, which takes you to Mohonk Lake in less than 0.2 mile. Stay on the road until you reach the northeast end of the lake, across from where the mountain house is situated.

Alternate Approach: When you come to the junction of Old Minnewaska Road and Forest Road, turn right onto Forest Road and walk east for a hundred feet. You will see the Spring House to your left. From there follow the Spring Path for 0.4 mile, which will bring you out next to Sentinel Rock, just down from the Mohonk Mountain House.

The Hikes

Hike #1—Sky Top

Description: The trek starts at Mohonk Lake and takes you up to the top of the towering cliffs at Sky Top. It is a relatively short hike, but long in history. From the top of the Albert K. Smiley Memorial Tower, which rests on top of the bluff, panoramic views can be obtained of Lake Mohonk, the Catskills, the valleys below in the distance, and the faint profile of distant mountains in adjacent states. The tower memorializes the founder of Mohonk.

The Hike: The path up to Sky Top is clearly marked and proceeds steadily uphill. The walk begins from the northeast end of Mohonk Lake near the Council House. It passes by the Council House to your left, quickly followed by the new Ice Skating Pavilion built in 2001, which is also on your left. Opposite the pavilion is Glacier Rock, a summerhouse that provides the first of many overlooks from the trail.

Just uphill from Glacier Rock, to your right, are several little footbridges that lead over to enormous, free-standing blocks of rock that have split off from the cliff face. Each massif has a summerhouse on it to allow for lingering views of the lake and the mountain house. One can look down into the gulf below and watch hikers make their way along the intricate Labyrinth Path.

Uphill from the Skating Pavilion, to the left, is the trailhead for Reservoir Path, which leads 0.2 mile uphill to an artificially created body of water called the Lily Pond. This more secluded destination is a lovely small pond with several summer houses perched along its perimeter. There is a small island in the pond with a footbridge leading to it.

The hike up to Sky Top can be divided into two segments. The first segment leads along the escarpment's edge and treats you with awesome views of Mohonk Lake, the Mountain House, and of the enormous gulfs and chasms below. The second segment begins after a switchback takes you away from the escarpment, increases your height by another hundred feet or so, and then brings you back to the edge of the escarpment at a noticeably higher altitude.

You will immediately come out to Hayes Overlook, named after President Rutherford B. Hayes. Hayes appointed Albert Smiley to the Board of Indian Commissioners and attended four "Friends of the Indians" conferences that were conducted at Mohonk over a span of thirty-three years.[4] From this site superb views of Mohonk Lake and the Mountain House can be obtained.

Before climbing any higher, proceed across a short trail that follows the escarpment's edge and leads down within a hundred feet to Thurston Rock, a summerhouse named after Edward Thurston's father, a former guest at Mohonk.[5] From there, looking south, you will have commanding views of

Sky Top, circa 1920.

All of the gazebos at Mohonk are called "summerhouses," a tradition that has endured since the 1870s when the structures were first erected.[1] The word "summerhouse" normally conjures up a mental image of a house or cottage, but in the nineteenth century it meant a rustic, open-air structure. The staff at Mohonk is valiantly trying to keep the term "summerhouse" current, but newcomers invariably refer to the quaint structures as gazebos.

There are no other resorts in existence today that dot their landscapes with summerhouses in the manner that Mohonk does. At one time there were as many as 125 summerhouses on the property. Today the number is considerably less, in part because some of the once-scenic views have been obscured by a regenerated forest, thus making it pointless to replace a gazebo that no longer serves a function.[2]

The original summerhouses had thatched roofs, but yearly maintenance proved to be so labor-intensive that today all summerhouses needing roof replacements are covered with cedar shakes. The only formally designed structure was the ornate, two-storied garden summerhouse copied from a design by A. J. Downing in the nineteenth century.

Mohonk Mountain House and Mohonk Lake, 2002.

Lily Pond was named for its abundance of lily pads. It was built in 1895 as a reservoir for firefighting. It has not been used for that purpose since 1926, when the Sky Top Reservoir was completed.[3]

Close at hand, overlooking the gardens below, is the Cleveland Seat (gazebo), named after President Grover Cleveland.

The Trapps and Millbrook Mountain and also, looking straight down, of the enormous field of talus slabs and boulders that have calved off from the rock face of Sky Top.

Return to Hayes Overlook and begin climbing again. The path immediately comes up to the Sky Top Carriage Road. Cross over the road and continue following the path up to the Memorial Tower, which is now just above you.

When you reach the summit, climb up the eighty-foot-high Albert K. Smiley Memorial Tower. From the top of the tower, on a clear day, you can see five states—Connecticut, Massachusetts, New Jersey, Pennsylvania, and Vermont—in addition to New York. To the northeast are the distant Green Mountains of Vermont. Closer to home, to the east, are views of the Wallkill Valley and its checkerboard pattern of farmlands. To the west is the Rondout Valley. To the north and west are the Catskill Mountains, and to the south are the Hudson Highlands and West Point. To the southeast is an enormous gap where the Hudson River has cut its way through the Hudson Highlands. Finally, dominating the immediate horizon to the southwest, are The Trapps and Millbrook Mountain. Eagle Cliff, at an elevation of 1,434 feet, can be seen directly west across the lake. At one time a slender, wooden observation tower, built in 1880, stood on its rocky bluff.[6] Until 1963, when rangers burned the unsafe, deteriorated structure to the ground, it was possible to see the Catskill Mountain House on the eastern wall of the northern Catskills from this vantage.[7]

Sky Top Path is not the only route to Sky Top. The Sky Top Carriage Road also leads to the top of the mountain, albeit in a more circuitous fashion. The road has been rebuilt several times—the last time being in 1895—and is used by both hikers and cross-country skiers because of its gentle grade.

History of Sky Top: The Albert K. Smiley Memorial is the last of four towers that have been erected atop the 1,542-foot-high summit of Sky Top over the last 150 years.[8] The first tower, made of wood, was established in 1870. One month later it was destroyed by high winds. The second tower was a rectangular edifice made of matched pine. It was built in 1872,[9] rose up to a height of over twenty-five feet, and contained an observation deck on top with a 360-degree view. Five years later the tower burned down. A third tower, also made of wood, was completed in 1878. It, too, was destroyed by fire, in 1909.

After the loss of these first three towers, it became evident that a wooden structure atop Sky Top was impractical. In 1921 work was begun on an eighty-foot tower made of stone. The tower was completed in 1923, and in August of the same year was dedicated to Albert K. Smiley who, with his twin brother Alfred, founded Mohonk.

From a distance the tower appears to be part of the mountain, and in a sense it is, for the rocks used to build the memorial were quarried from the Shawangunk conglomerate bedrock next to the base of the tower. The hole left behind was lined with cement and decorated with boulders around its perimeter, and it is now used as a reflecting pool for the tower as well as for providing a 1.2-million-gallon water reservoir in the event that a fire should erupt at the mountain house below. A larger reservoir (Lily Pond) was created further down the mountainside, next to the Sky Top Carriage Road between the Memorial Tower and Huguenot Drive.[10]

The Albert K. Smiley Memorial Tower was constructed by two architects from Philadelphia—Allen and Collins—who were known for their Gothic Revival work. Originally the tower also served as a fire tower and was manned by observers with binoculars that scanned the horizon for forest fires. The tower was abandoned in 1971 as more sophisticated fire detecting systems became available.

During the seventeenth and eighteenth centuries, Sky Top was known as Paltz Point because of the bluff's nearness to the village of New Paltz.[11] Mohonk Lake at that time was known as Paltz Pond.[12] The name "Paltz" arose from the first settlers to the area—twelve French Huguenots who fled the religious persecution of King Louis XIV of France. After first journeying to Die Pfalz in Germany, they migrated to America and named their new home New Pfalz.[13]

One might wonder why the tower was dedicated to Albert Smiley and not to both of the brothers. In 1879 Alfred Smiley's focus had changed from Mohonk to Lake Minnewaska, where he established two large hotels. When it came time to establish the memorial tower, most guests that donated money for the tower's completion only knew Albert, and it was in his name that their donations were made.

View of Mohonk from Albert K. Smiley Memorial Tower, 2004.

Hike #2—Mohonk Lake

Description: The walk around Mohonk Lake takes you on a carriage road and path next to the east shore, and then returns you to the starting point via a walking path along the west shore. During the first half of the walk, the mountain house is constantly in view, looming near the edge of the northwest end of the lake. On the west shore walk, Sky Top dominates the scenery. It is a thrilling walk with cliffs rising up from the shore all around. One feels as though one is at the bottom of an enormous basin.

Mohonk Lake is one of five small bodies of water in the Shawangunks. It sits at an elevation of 1,247 feet and encompasses seventeen acres of land. Mohonk Lake is often poetically referred to as a "sky lake," meaning that it was formed as a glacial lake and is filled by precipitation from the sky, rather than by subterranean springs.

The Hike: The walk begins from the putting green next to the Mohonk Mountain House and initially follows the Lake Shore Carriage Road. As soon as you begin the trek, you will come to a wooden footbridge to your right that leads to a tiny island, called Sentinel Rock, with a gazebo on it. This is a wonderful place for quiet meditation, surrounded on all sides by the lake.

Opposite Sentinel Rock are two trailheads. One is for Labyrinth Path and the other, just a few yards beyond, is for Spring Path.

Sky Top and Mohonk Lake were favorite subjects for a number of nineteenth-century artists who ventured into the Shawangunks. Sanford Robinson Gifford painted Shawangunk Mountains at Sky Top *in 1854.[14] In 1872, Daniel Huntington painted Lake Mohonk. Huntington's painting appears to have been done just before the installation of the second tower on Sky Top, for no tower is evident on the canvass. In 1881, J. R. Lambdin rendered* Shawangunk Mountains: From Sky Top, Lake Mohonk, *showing* The Trapps and Millbrook Mountain in the distance. *Lambdin ended up being friends with the Smileys, and even had a ravine near the Mountain House named after him.*

Despite these efforts the Shawangunks never achieved the artistic recognition that was given to the nearby Catskills, and even today the region is not as heavily visited as the Catskills or the Adirondacks to the north.

The Labyrinth Path: This route, roughly 0.4 mile in length, is a one-way traverse over and around mammoth boulders (some the sizes of automobiles and houses), through crevices and talus caves, and up wooden ladders. It finally comes out about forty feet below the Sky Top tower. The route was first blazed in 1871 and has been a favorite of mountain house guests since then.[15] What makes the ascent via Labyrinth Path possible is the strategic placement of wooden ladders throughout the trek. Otherwise, only rock climbers would be able to negotiate the climb.

The Spring Path: This route begins just a few feet beyond Labyrinth Path trailhead and ultimately leads to the Mohonk Spring House, which is a circular stone structure with a wooden roof built in 1904.[16] In days past, the spring was a favorite stopping point for travelers as they made their way up to the mountain house by carriage. Waters still issue from the spring, but visitors today are warned to drink at their own risk.

Spring Path is a marvelous trek, taking you through a sloping field of enormous boulders and talus caves. Above you loom the vertical cliffs of Sky Top, which grow more perilous and pronounced as you continue your walk. To your right is Mohonk Lake, which begins to recede the further in you walk. Near the start of the walk, under an overhanging rock ledge, is the last surviving bench from the early days of Mohonk.

After exploring Labyrinth Path and Spring Path, continue southeast along the Lake Carriage Road for less than 0.2 mile. You will quickly come to a point where the Lake Shore Carriage Road goes straight ahead (eventually turning into the Old Minnewaska Road) and the Lake Shore Path veers off to the right towards the lake. Bear right and follow the Lake Shore Path, which will take you to the southeast end of the lake.

Once you have cleared the end of the lake, bear right at a junction and follow the Undercliff Path. The path goes up and down a bit, but it is easy to traverse. In less than 0.3 mile you will come out to the beach area, where a flight of stone stairs takes you back up to the top of the west escarpment and the mountain house.

The hike is not over yet, however. After you have come up the stone stairway from the beach and turned right to go towards the mountain house, look for a path on your right for Pine Bluff and Washington's Profile. It leads immediately up to a bluff overlooking the lake from where (with a lot of imagination) you can see a profile of George Washington's face in the cliffs below Sky Top.

History: The Lake Shore Carriage Road was constructed in 1870. It follows the east shore of the lake and, not surprisingly, was the first well-constructed carriage road to be built at Mohonk.

All of Mohonk's roads were constructed from the late 1800s to about 1921. They were truly roads built to last, with a construction cost in 1903 at $1.00 per linear foot.[17] Workers went out with pickaxes and other hand implements of the time and toiled for endless hours to build the roads that endure today and still defy erosion.

Sky Top and Mohonk Lake, circa 1920.

Spring House, 2005.

The Mohonk Preserve: The Mohonk Mountain House and its grounds are virtually surrounded by the Mohonk Preserve—the largest private not-for-profit nature preserve in New York State. The preserve encompasses 6,500 acres of land that include secluded glens, waterfalls, soaring cliffs, mountain lakes, rock outcroppings, old-growth hemlocks, and rare and unusual plant and wildlife. The preserve contains over sixty-five miles of carriage roads and foot trails.[18]

The Mohonk Mountain House and adjacent land is separate from the preserve and remains a private, for-profit business. A strong interrelationship between the preserve and the mountain house continues to endure, however.

History of Mohonk: The enchanting land surrounding Mohonk Mountain House was known to early Native Americans, who arrived after the period of glaciations 10,000–12,000 years ago. They established footpaths across the ridges and through the valleys that were used later in the seventeenth century by European settlers in the New Paltz area.

Though the rocky terrain was not particularly well suited for farming, early settlers nevertheless ventured from the Rondout Valley into the Shawangunks to establish small communities and eke out a living.[19] By 1859, John F. Stokes opened a ten-room tavern on the banks of Mohonk Lake. The tavern became a hub of activity for young people in the area, as it provided music, dancing, shooting matches, and skating parties.

The Spring Path has side trails of it own. After roughly 0.3 mile from the trailhead near Sentinel Rock, you will encounter "Rock Scramble to Crevice," which leads you immediately into the maze of boulders near the base of Sky Top. Just beyond, at the point where Spring Path veers sharply right, is "Staircliff Path & Birchen Trail," other trails that take you into the talus field for further exploration.

Alfred Smiley made the trip from Poughkeepsie to Stokes Tavern and was immediately captivated by the scenery before him. He was so taken by the lake and mountains that he wrote excitedly to his twin brother, Albert, suggesting that he purchase the land and tavern from Mr. Stokes. In November 1869, Albert (a former educator) became proprietor of the inn. From that day forward began the history of Mohonk as we know it today. Albert began the Mohonk project with an eye on both comfort and appearances. First came its fairyland castle and carriage roads. Over the intervening years the mountain house and hiking trails have evolved significantly, but the early intent to preserve and beautify the natural landscape has remained a cornerstone of the Smiley family philosophy.

The vision set out by Albert included developing carriage roads not only around the lake, but also up to overlooking ridges and through the mountainous forest. Some of the most winsome architectural features that he took great pleasure in creating were the summerhouses (gazebos) that remain prominent features of Mohonk today. (Summerhouse architecture had been popularized by noted nineteenth-century Hudson Valley landscape architect Andrew Jackson Downing.) Each of the rustic, open-air shelters at Mohonk differed from one another, the design being limited only by the imagination of the carpenter.

The main building phase and landscaping of the grounds occurred at the end of the nineteenth century. Even today the impression made by the Mohonk Mountain House and its grounds is distinctly Victorian. This is not by accident, as the Smiley family (continuous operators of the resort from 1869 to the present) has carefully retained all of the original resort features while adding renovations or new additions.

Albert, a Quaker, upheld temperance principles in the operation of his resort. He held daily religious services, which were optional for guests, and served no alcoholic beverages. (Later generations of the Smiley family felt the need to keep pace with the times and now offer a full service bar at mealtimes.) Albert concentrated on creating a delightful system of hiking and carriage trails, beautifully landscaped grounds, boats for recreation and fishing, and fine dining. In the resort's earliest days it is alleged that only the men were allowed to swim in Lake Mohonk. Bathing costumes for women were considered immodest.

By 1892 Albert Smiley's half brother, Daniel, had assumed charge of Mohonk. He remained proprietor until his death in 1930, and all of the current members of the Smiley family operating the mountain house are his direct descendants. It was during Daniel's tenure that the final mountain house additions were completed. Today the exterior of the sprawling main building looks as it did in 1902 under Daniel's direction.

In 1986 the Mohonk Mountain House, along with eighty-three other structures on the property, was recognized as a National Historic Landmark.[20]

Throughout its 136 years of continuous operation of the mountain house, the Smiley family has been adept at changing with the times, but always within the context of the original mission to preserve nature while providing Victorian elegance for its guests. Some of the newest additions include a winter skating rink, an indoor heated pool, and a spa center that offers a variety of massage and spa treatments. It is a popular venue for banquets and special occasions. The grounds were even used in the 1992 movie *The Road to Wellville*.[21]

The Mohonk Preserve Visitor Center: The center provides much geological and natural history on the Shawangunks and offers exhibits, a nature shop, and short trails. The center's most interesting feature is its relief map of the Shawangunks, which occupies center stage in the building. The visitor center is located 0.5 mile northwest of the junction of Rtes. 299 & 44/55.

About the Authors

Russell Dunn is the author of an ongoing series of guidebooks to the waterfalls of eastern New York State, including *Adirondack Waterfall Guide: New York's Cool Cascades* (Black Dome Press Corp., 2003), *Catskill Region Waterfall Guide: Cool Cascades of the Catskills & Shawangunks* (Black Dome Press Corp., 2004), and *Hudson Valley Waterfall Guide: From Saratoga and the Capital Region to the Highlands and Palisades* (Black Dome Press Corp., 2005). He is also the author of *Adventures Around the Great Sacandaga Lake* (Nicholas K. Burns Publishing, 2002) and has written articles for *Adirondack Life, Kaatskill Life, Adirondac, Hudson Valley, Adirondack Explorer, Northeastern Caver, Catskill Mountain Region Guide, Glens Falls Magazine, Voice of the Valley, the National Speleological Society,* and *Sacandaga Times.*

Barbara Delaney is a New York State Licensed Guide and keen outdoorswoman. She has written pieces for *Mohawk Valley Heritage* and has been the cartographer for Russell's guidebooks. Barbara is currently writing a work of historical fiction on the Sacandaga Valley and the lost village of Griffin.

Russell and Barbara have been conducting weekend waterfall hikes at Trails End Inn in Keene Valley (in the Adirondacks) since 2002.

Notes

Part I: Saratoga Region

Starks Knob & Schuylerville Champlain Canal Towpath

1. *www.nysm.nysed.gov* provides history and facts about Starks Knob.

2. H.P. Cushing and R. Ruedemann, *Geology of Saratoga Springs and Vicinity, Museum Bulletin # 169* (Albany, N.Y.: The University of the State of New York, 1914). Pictures of Starks Knob can be seen between pages 116 and 117. On page 15 the authors write: "Woodworth proposed the name of Stark's Knob for this hill." [The Woodworth they refer to is J.B. Woodworth.] Schuylerville residents simply referred to the Knob as "The Volcano."

3. James H. Stoller, *Geological Excursions: A Guide to Localities in the Region of Schenectady and the Mohawk Valley and the Vicinity of Saratoga Springs* (Schenectady, N.Y.: Union Book Co., 1931), pages 54–58. What's interesting to note is that a roadside sign north of the village of Schuylerville once incorrectly read: "Stark's Knob. Extinct Volcano. State Property. Public Welcome." We know today that Starks Knob is not the remnant of an extinct volcano.

4. *www.virtualvermont.com* provides historical information and facts about General John Stark.

5. Tim Holmes, Schuylerville Town Historian and founder of the Friends of Stark's Knob Association.

6. Cushing, op cit. Geological information is provided about the Knob on pages 115–135.

7. Stephen Williams, "Stark's Knob Takes Tourists to Hudson River Overlook," The *Sunday Gazette*, section B10, February 25, 2001, provides information on the Knob's unique geology and contains a picture of a man standing on top of the hill.

8. Van Diver, *Upstate New York,* op cit., 175. "Stark's Knob is a mass of basalt about 50 feet high surrounded by Middle Ordovician Normanskill (Trenton) shales."

9. Mylod, *Biography of a River,* op cit. A fairly lengthy description of the Saratoga Battle Monument in Schuylerville is provided on page 32.

10. Stone, 25 *Bicycle Tours in the Hudson Valley,* op cit. A picture of the Saratoga Battle Monument is displayed on page 20.

11. *www.vitessepress.com* provides background information on the Champlain Canal, including an account of what it was like to ride on it.

Additional Sources of Information:

J.B. VanDerwerker, *Early Days in Saratoga County* (Interlaken, N.Y.: Empire State Books, 1994). Text includes a section on Starks Knob written by Thomas Hanrahan pages 68, 69, 71.

Claire K. Schmitt and Judith S. Wolk, *Natural Areas of Saratoga County* (Niskayuna, N.Y.: The Environmental Clearinghouse of Schenectady, 1998), 14.

Saratoga National Historic Park

1. Michael A. Schuman, *New York State's Special Places: day trips, weekends, and outings in the Empire State* (Woodstock, Vt.: The Countryman Press, 1988). The author points out that a 21-minute film called "Checkmate on the Hudson" can be viewed at the visitor center.

Notes

2. Baroness Friederike von Riedesel, *Letters and Journals Relating to the War of the Revolution* (1867; reprint, Gansevoort, N. Y.: Corner House Historical Publications, 2001). The baroness describes her experiences during the battles of Saratoga on pages 115, 116, 122.

Additional Sources of Information:

The Saratoga National Historical Park web site *(www.nps.gov/sara/f-sara)* describes Saratoga National Historical Park, provides background and history of the battles of Saratoga, and a map and information about the significant sites located in the battlefield.

Raymond C. Houghton, *A Revolutionary Day along Historic US Route 9* (Delmar, N. Y.: Cyber Haus Computer Learning Centers). Historical events of the battles of Saratoga are noted on pages 81, 83, 88, 89, 91, 92.

John Henry Brandow, *The Story of Old Saratoga and New York's Share in the Revolution*, 2nd edition (Albany, N.Y.: The Brandow Printing Company, 1919).

Charles W. Snell and Francis F. Wilson, *Saratoga National Historical Park, New York* (1950; reprint, Washington, D.C.: United States Department of the Interior, 1961). A 36-page history and guide to the park is provided.

Geyser Park

1. Robert Joki, *Saratoga Lost: Images of Victorian America* (Hensonville, N.Y.: Black Dome Press Corp., 1998), 167–168. A short chapter contains information on the Geyser region.

2. Schmitt, *Natural Areas of Saratoga County*, op cit., 12–13. A small chapter is devoted to the park.

3. Van Diver, *Upstate New York,* op cit. Van Diver includes a picture of Orenda Spring on page 175. On page 174 he writes that the tufa accumulates "at the astounding rate of 2 tons per million gallons of water!"

4. Grace Maguire Swanner, S*aratoga Queen of Spas: a history of the Saratoga Spa and the mineral springs of the Saratoga and Ballston areas* (Utica, N.Y.: North Country Books, 1988), 79.

5. Van Diver, op cit. Information on the geology of Saratoga Springs is provided on pages 173–175.

6. Joki, op cit., 54. A picture of Coesa Lake (Geyser Lake) with Vichy Spring in the background is provided.

7. Ibid., 20. A picture of the dam at Coesa Lake can be seen, plus a picture of Geyser Springs (one of the brick buildings around the edge of the lake).

8. Ibid., 131. A footbridge below Geyser Lake can be seen clearly in this photograph.

9. Violet B. Dunn, ed., *Saratoga County Heritage* (Saratoga, NY: Saratoga County, 1974), 18.

10. Nathaniel Bartlett Sylvester, *History of Saratoga County, New York* (Philadelphia, Pa.: Everts & Ensign, 1878). On page 149 Sylvester mentions that High Rock Spring was visited by such famous men as Sir William Johnson, General Phillip Schuyler, and General George Washington.

11. William L. Stone, *Reminiscences of Saratoga and Ballston* (Virtue & Yorston, 1875), 439.

12. Ibid., 436.

13. Ibid., 178–179.

14. Swanner, *Saratoga Queen of Spas,* op cit., 46–88. This book is a goldmine of information on Saratoga Spa, particularly the mineral springs, replete with illustrations.

Additional Source of Information:
Roseann Doyle, "The Queen of the Spas," Mohawk Valley USA, Vol. 2, no. 5 (summer 1981), 23–30.

Part II: Capital Region

Vischer Ferry Nature & Historic Preserve
1. Schmitt, *Natural Areas of Saratoga County*, op cit., 26–31. A map and information about hiking options are provided.

2. William R. Washington and Patricia S. Smith, *Crossroads and Canals: The History of Clifton Park, Saratoga County, New York* (n.d.; reprint, Albany, N.Y.: Fort Orange Press, 1985). An entire chapter is devoted to Vischer Ferry, pages 56–62.

3. Leland R. Palmer, "Vischer Ferry. Nature and Historic Preserve," Mohawk Valley USA, Vol. 4, no. 2 (Summer 1983), 4–6. The article contains pertinent information about the preserve.

4. Washington, *Crossroads and Canals*, op cit. On page 61 can be seen a picture of Clute's Dry Dock prior to the creation of the Barge Canal, and on page 59 "before and after" pictures of the lock.

5. John L. Scherer, *Images of America: Clifton Park* (Dover, N.H.: Arcadia Publishing, 1996). Photos of Clutes Dry Dock circa 1890 can be seen on page 90.

6. Ibid. A photo of Lock 19 is shown on page 73.

7. Ibid. An old photo of the bridge spanning the canal at the end of Ferry Drive can be seen on page 72; in addition, photos of Vischers Mill circa 1900 are presented on page 91.

8. Francis P. Kimball, *The Capital Region of New York State*, Vol. II (New York: Lewis Historical Publishing Company, Inc., 1942), 233. "From the Hudson River to the level of the canal above Vischer Ferry canal boats are lifted a total of 196 feet, equivalent to a height of about twenty stories."

9. Scherer, op cit. A photo of the ferry scows at Vischer Ferry and Forts Ferry are presented on page 70.

A small book entitled Enjoy Saratoga County (1974), by the Bicentennial Commission, mentions that Vischer Ferry was originally called "Amity."

Peebles Island State Park
1. Claire K. Schmitt and Mary S. Brennan, *Natural Areas of Albany County*, 4th edition (Schenectady, N.Y.: Environmental Clearinghouse of Schenectady, 2004). Background information on Peebles Island is provided on page 33, and there is a map on page 32.

2. Thomas Phelan and P. Thomas Carroll, *Hudson Mohawk Gateway: An Illustrated History* (Sun Valley, Calif.: American Historical Press, 2001), 14. Van Rensselaer wrote, "the territory of the Mahicans ... being not only fat, clayey soil of itself, but yearly enriched by the overflow of high water."

3. Howell and Tenney, *History of the County of Albany, NY: From 1609 to 1886 with Portraits, Biographies and Illustrations* (1886; reprint, Salem Mass.: Higginson Book Company, n.d.), 13. "Near the junction of the Mohawk and Hudson is Haver Island, on which tradition tells us, was Moenemines Castle, once an important Mohawk Village."

4. Phelen, op cit., 17. The fortifications built by Thaddeus Kosciusko were never used in battle.

5. Chuck Porter, former Hudson Valley Community College geology professor.

6. Ibid.

7. Phelen, op cit., 13. Kiliaen Van Rensselaer purchased large tracts of land from Native Americans in 1630, including the area later known as Peebles Island.

8. Paul Huey, from a lecture presented during the May 17, 2003, Peebles Island State Park and Resource Center annual open house.

9. Francis P. Kimball, *The Capital Region of New York State,* Vol. II (New York: Lewis Historical Publishing Company, Inc., 1942), 202. "At Haver Island could be seen the remains of an old fort thrown up during the Revolution." Kimball points out that the bridge from Van Schaick to Haver Island was 202 feet long.

10. Ibid. On page 268 references are made to "Haver or Oat Island (Poebles)"— other names by which the island has been known.

11. Arthur G. Adams, *The Hudson River Guidebook* (New York: Fordham University Press, 1996), 279. Adam's mentions that the island was earlier known as Van Hover's Island.

12. Chris W. Brown III, *Guide to New York Waterways and Lake Champlain* (Gretna, La.: Pelican Publishing Company, Inc., 1998), 267. The author provides background information on the Thaddeus Kosciusko Bridge.

13. Brochure entitled "Peebles Island State Park" distributed by the New York State Office of Parks, Recreation and Historic Preservation.

14. Phelen, op cit., 327. In 1909, Cluett Peabody built a bleachery on Peebles Island.

15. John G. Waite and Diana S. Waite, *Industrial Archeology in Troy, Waterford, Cohoes, Green Island, and Watervliet* (Troy, N.Y.: Hudson–Mohawk Industrial Gateway, 1973), 34. Brief information on the Cluett, Peabody & Co. bleachery is provided.

16. Brochure, op cit.

17. *boatingonthehudson.com*, the web site for the monthly magazine *Boating on the Hudson.*

18. *www.scow.net/scow_photo_gallery.htm.*

Additional sources:

C. R. Roseberry, *Albany: Three Centuries a County* (New York: Tricentennial Commission, 1983).

Cohoes in 76: American Bicentennial 1776–1976 (Cohoes, N.Y.: United States Bicentennial Commission of Cohoes, Inc., 1976).

Oakwood Cemetery

1. Claire K. Schmitt and Norton G. Miller, Warren F. Broderick, John T. Keenan, William D. Niemi, *Natural Areas of Rensselaer County New York*, 2nd edition (Schenectady/Troy, N.Y.: The Rensselaer–Taconic Land Conservancy & Environmental Clearinghouse of Schenectady, Inc., 2002). A map of the cemetery is provided on page 43.

2. A. J. Weise, *History of Lansingburgh, NY: From the Year 1670 to 1877* (Troy, N.Y.: William H. Young, 1877). On page 208 the author points out that Oakwood Cemetery was consecrated on October 16, 1850.

3. Schmitt, op cit. A picture of the cascade by the crematorium can be seen on page 45.

4. DeWitt Clinton, ed., *Picturesque Oakwood: Its Past and Present Associations* (Troy, N.Y.: Frederick S. Hills, 1897). Information is provided on the Gardner Earl Memorial Crematorium and the magnificent grounds and landscape. On page 13 mention is made that: "Rare shrubs and plants abound while trees of rarity in this part of the country are carefully grown and cared for on the grounds. Notable are the umbrella trees of Japan, and the beautiful blue spruce of Colorado."

5. Reed Sparling, "Three Capital District Diversions," *Hudson Valley*, Vol. XXXIII,

No. 12 (April 2005). Information on the history of Oakwood Cemetery and the Gardner Earl Chapel is presented on pages 19–20.

6. Don Rittner, *Images of America: Troy* (Charleston, S.C.: Arcadia Publishing, 1998). A picture of the Gardner Earl Memorial Chapel & Crematorium is shown on page 91. The crematorium was built in 1888–1889 by William and Hannah M. Earl in loving memory of their son.

7. Francis P. Kimball, *The Capital Region of New York State,* Vol. II (New York: Lewis Historical Publishing Company, Inc., 1942). The real story behind Uncle Sam is revealed on pages 314–315.

8. Robert M. Toole, *A Look at Metroland: A new guide to its history and heritage* (Saratoga Springs, N.Y.: R. M. Toole, Landscape Architects, 1976). Background information on "Uncle Sam" Wilson is succinctly presented on page 117.

9. Clinton, op cit. A variety of historical information about the cemetery is provided, especially on General Wool's monument,

10. Kimball, op cit. A picture of General John E. Wool's monument can be seen on page 176.

11. Rachael D. Bliven, *A Resourceful People: A pictorial history of Rensselaer County, New York* (Norfolk, Va.: The Donning Company, 1987). On page 60 is a fascinating picture of the Wool Monument being erected.

12. *www.oakwoodcemetery.org* provides additional information on the cemetery.

Burden Pond Environmental Park

1. Schmitt, *Natural Areas of Rensselaer County*, op cit. A map of the preserve can be seen on page 55.

2. Ibid. On pages 56 and 57 are pictures of the dam at Burden Pond as it looked over a century ago.

3. Phelan, *Hudson Mohawk Gateway: An Illustrated History*, op cit. On page 14 mention is made that Patroon Kiliaen Van Rensselaer purchased the Wynantskill area from Native Americans and in 1656 successfully built a mill there.

4. Don Rittner, *Troy: A Collar City History* (Charleston, S.C.: Arcadia Publishing, 2002). An old map of the lower Wynants Kill, on page 87, illustrates the position of several mills and factories, including Binkerhoff's Nail Factory.

5. Kimball, op cit., 176. "At Troy were turned out in one hundred days the plates for the iron clad Monitor, which battled the Merrimac to a draw."

6. P. Thomas Carroll, Rensselaer County Historian, Burden Iron Museum.

7. Waite, *Industrial Archeology in Troy, Waterford, Cohoes, Green Island, and Watervliet,* op cit. Information on the Burden Iron Works is provided on page 12, including pictures of the blast furnace and the old office building that is now the Burden Museum.

8. Robert M. Vogel, ed., *A Report of the Mohawk–Hudson Area Survey* (Washington, D.C.: Smithsonian Institution Press, 1973). On pages 96–97, the report presents a chronology of the Albany Iron Works, Burden Iron Works, and Bessemer Steel Works.

9. Rittner, *Images of America: Troy*, op cit. On page 40 can be seen a picture of the Burden Iron Wheel, built in 1838–1839. The wheel was 60 feet in diameter, 12 feet wide, with 36 buckets 6 feet 3 inches deep. Running at 1200 horsepower, it was called "the Niagara of waterwheels."

10. R. I. Sweeny, "The Burden Water-Wheel," *Society for Industrial Archeology, no. 2 (April 1973). Reprinted from Transactions*, Vol. 79, 1915, published by the American Society of Civil Engineers.

11. Phelen, op cit. In 1890 the Burden waterwheel ceased operation, and in 1896

the upper works were abandoned. In 1893 the Ferris wheel was designed by George Washington Ferris Jr., a graduate of Rensselaer Polytechnic Institute (RPI), who was no doubt inspired by the Burden waterwheel.

12. Rittner, op cit. It is speculated that George Ferris may have been inspired by Burden's waterwheel to create the first Ferris wheel, which was presented at the 1893 World's Columbia Exposition in Paris. Was it pure coincidence that Ferris's Wheel also had thirty-six buckets?

Additional Source of information:

"Troy: Hub of Industry," *Schenectady & Upstate New York*, Vol. II, no. 3 (Fall 1989), 50–56.

Ann Lee Pond

1. Schmitt, *Natural Areas of Albany County*, op cit. A map of the preserve is on page 40.

2. "Shaker Spirit," *Schenectady & Upstate New York*, Vol. III, no. 1 (Spring 1990). A rare photograph of the original Shaker settlement in Watervliet can be seen on page 93.

3. Allan Keller, *Life along the Hudson,* 2nd edition (Tarrytown, N.Y.: Sleepy Hollow Restorations, Inc., 1985). A picture of the Shaker settlement in Watervliet is on page 201.

4. Schmitt, op cit., 41.

5. Jean S. Olton, compiler, *The Town of Colonie: A Pictorial History* (Colonie, N.Y.: 1980), 52–53. Referring to Town Creek near its confluence with the Mohawk River: "On this stream, the Shakers had one of the largest mills in the town, along with a grist mill."

6. Jerry Grant, Director of Research, Shaker Museum, Old Chatham, New York.

7. John Mylod, *Biography of a River: The People & Legends of the Hudson Valley* (New York: Bonanza Books, 1969), 36. "Mother Lee did not hold with the fighting in the Revolution and often said so. There was at least one instance when, after speaking out against the rebels, she was jailed for her own protection."

8. Edward Deming Andrews, *The People Called Shakers* (New York: Dover Publications, Inc., 1953). Material on the Shaker communities is contained throughout the book. On page 33, Andrews discusses the suspicions of the community at large that Shakers, because of their pacifism, were Tory sympathizers.

9. Grant, op cit.

10. Kimball, *The Capital Region of New York State*, op cit. A brief history of the Shakers is given on page 309, including a reference as to how the name arose: "The sect became known as Shakers because of a whirling dance which accompanied their religious rites."

11. Andrews, op cit. Page 169 describes the Shakers' relationships with Native Americans.

12. Edward Deming Andrews, *The Community Industries of the Shakers* (Charlestown, Mass.: Emporium Publications, 1971), a facsimile reprint of New York State Museum Handbook Number 15, describes industries in various Shaker Communities. Pages 44 and 167 discuss broom and pipe making at the Watervliet community.

13. Andrews, *The People Called Shakers*, op cit. Page 220 tells of a letter of thanks from Governor DeWitt Clinton for generous contributions during the epidemic of 1798.

14. Grant, op cit.

Additional Source of information:

Patricia O'Brien, "A Simpler Way," *Schenectady Magazine*, Vol. 1, no. 3 (Winter 1988), 47–51. Extensive information on the Shaker Community is provided.

Indian Ladder

1. Claire K. Schmitt and Mary S. Brennan, *Natural Areas of Albany County,* 4th edition (Schenectady, N.Y.: Environmental Clearinghouse of Schenectady, 2004). A map of Indian Ladder is presented on page 58.

2. Ibid. The hike along Indian Ladder is detailed on page 59.

3. Barbara McMartin and Peter Kick, *Fifty Hikes in the Hudson Valley* (Woodstock, Vt.: Backcountry Publications, 1988). This book includes a chapter on hiking the Indian Ladder trail (pages 218–221).

4. Jim Cullen, John Mylroie, and Art Palmer, *Karst Hydrogeology and Geomorphology of Eastern New York: A guidebook to the geology field trip* (National Speleological Society Annual Convention, Pittsfield, Massachusetts, 1979). Extensive information on the sites along Indian Ladder is provided on pages 41–49, including several striking photographs.

5. Frank Oppel, compiler, "The Helderbergs (1869)," *New York: Tales of the Empire State* (Secaucus, N.J.: Castle, 1988). On page 265 can be found a description of the two falls in Indian Gulf.

6. Ibid. On page 266 is a description of Minelot Falls in the summer; on page 275 is a description of the fall in winter.

7. Gary L. Donhardt, *Indian Ladder: A History of Life in the Helderbergs* (Collerville, Tenn.: Donhardt and Daughters Publishers, 2001). Much material is contained in this book on the history of Indian Ladder and the region surrounding it.

8. James H. Stoller, *Geological Excursions: A Guide to Localities in the Region of Schenectady and the Mohawk Valley and the Vicinity of Saratoga Springs* (Schenectady, N.Y.: Union Book Co., 1931). An entire chapter on Indian Ladder's geology is presented (pages 78–84).

9. Winifred Goldring, *Guide to the Geology of John Boyd Thacher Park (Indian Ladder Region) and Vicinity: New York State Museum Handbook Number 14* (1933; reprint, Albany, N.Y.: The University of the State of New York, 1997). The author details the geology of Thacher Park and Indian Ladder.

10. Bradford B. Van Diver, *Upstate New York* (Dubuque, Iowa: Kendall/Hunt Publishing Company, 1980). Geological information on Thacher Park is presented on pages 180–183.

11. Thom Engel, authority on the geology of Thacher Park.

Bennett Hill Preserve

1. A brochure on Bennett Hill is available at the kiosk by the parking area at Bennett Hill.

2. Schmitt, *Natural Areas of Albany County*, op cit. Background information on the preserve is furnished on page 69. There is a map on page 68.

3. Peter M. and Judith R. Saidel, *The History of Bennett Hill Farm* (Clarksville, N.Y.: Peter M & Judith R. Saidel, 2002). The Saidels have written the bible on the Bennett Hill Farm.

4. Historic marker in front of the Bennett Hill House.

5. Plaque on Bennett Hill Farm.

6. New Scotland Historical Association. *Images of America: New Scotland Township* (Charleston, S.C.: Arcadia Publishing, 2000). On page 114 mention is made of the Bennett Hill House, a boarding home that could hold up to forty guests. It was part of a 200-acre self-sufficient farm. The proprietor was Mrs. W. H. Rowe

7. Ibid. A picture of the suspension bridge crossing Onesquethaw Creek at Indian

Head is shown on page 77. The bridge was built in 1890 by George C. Ingrahams to enable people to get from Bennett Hill to Clarksville quickly.

Clarksville Cave Preserve

1. Chuck Porter, former Hudson Valley Community College geology professor.
2. Michael Nardacci, ed., *Guide to the Caves and Karst of the Northeast* (National Speleological Society, 1991). A section on Albany caves, written by Ken Davis, appears on page 25.
3. Porter, op cit.
4. Thomas D. Engel, *A Chronicle of Selected Northeastern Caves.: A History Guide for the 1979 NSS Convention Pittsfield, Massachusetts* (n.p.: Thomas D. Engel, 1979), 17.
5. Paul Rubin, "Historic Clarksville Cave," *Northeastern Caver*, XVII, no.5 (1986), 115.

6. Ibid., 114.
7. Engel, op cit., 15.
8. Oppel, "The Helderbergs (1869)," op cit., 271.
9. Engel, op cit., 15.
10. Ibid., 16.
11. Ibid., 16.
12. Oppel, op cit., 271.
13. Nardacci, op cit., 24.
14. Chuck Porter, Ron Grant and Dan Hoyt, "Story behind the Ward–Gregory Link," *The Northeastern Caver*, Vol. XXXV, no 1 (March 2004), 10–12.
15. Clay Perry, Underground Empire: Wonders and Tales of New York Caves (New York: Stephen Daye Press, 1948), 45.
16. John Evans, Peter Quick and Bruce Sloane, eds., *An Introduction to Caves of the Northeast: Guidebook for the 1979 National Speleological Society Convention* (Pittsfield, Mass.: National Speleological Society, 1979), 41
17, Perry, op cit., 44.
18. Mike Warner, Mike Davis and Emily Davis, compilers, "Clarksville Cave Body Recovery," *The Northeastern Caver*, Vol. XXXII, no. 1 (March 2001), 12–20.

Additional Sources of Information:

Paul Rubin and Allison P. Bennett, "Historic Clarksville Cave," *Northeastern Caver*, XXI, no. 4 (Dec. 1990), 113–115, 121–129.

Paul Rubin, "Clarksville Cave—1990," *Northeastern Caver*, Vol. XX, no. 4 (1989), 122–125.

Jim Cullen, *Karst Hydrogeology and Geomorphology of Eastern New York: A guidebook to the geology field trip*, op cit. Some basic facts about the cave are provided on pages 37–40, including a map on page 38

Edmund Niles Huyck Preserve

1. Schmitt, *Natural Areas of Albany County*, op cit. A map of the preserve is presented on page 58.
2. Ibid. Brief information on the preserve is furnished on page 59.
3. Rensselaerville Historical Society, *People Made It Happen Here: History of the Town of Rensselaerville* (Rensselaerville, N.Y.: Rensselaerville Historical Society, 1977). Most of the information presented in the history section of this chapter was gleaned from this informative book.

Part III: Berkshires Region

Balanced Rocks

1. Jim Moore, caver and explorer.

2. Malcolm W. Campbell, Play Hard. *Rest Easy. New England. The Ultimate Active Getaway Guide* (Charlotte, N.C.: Walkabout Press, Inc., 2001), 64. The Balanced Rock in Savoy State Forest is described as "a huge glacial erratic that sits on the edge of a ledge." It's possible that Campbell's description may be of another balanced rock in the state forest. The balanced rock in Savoy State Forest is in a clearing and is not poised on the edge of a ledge.

3. Elizabeth L. Dugger, *Adventure Guide to Massachusetts & Western Connecticut* (Edison, N.J.: Hunter Publishing, Inc., 1999). Mention is made, on page 345, that the balanced rock in Savoy is located in a rugged hiking area.

4. Charles W. G. Smith, *Nature Walks in the Berkshire Hills* (Boston: Appalachian Mountain Club Books, 1997), 182–187. A picture of the balanced rock at Balance Rock State Park can be seen on page 185.

5. A picture of the balanced rock in Lanesboro can be seen in *The Berkshires: Through the Camera of Arthur Palme* (n.p.: Palme–Grove Publishing Company, 1951), pages unnumbered.

6. Berkshire County Historical Society, *Images of America: Pittsfield* (Charleston, S.C.: Arcadia Publishing, 2001). Two interesting early photographs of the boulder are shown. On page 24 a wonderful picture of the rock, with two men sitting on top, can be seen. (For the record, it is not all that easy to climb up to the top of the boulder!) On page 65 a highly unusual picture of the boulder is displayed, taken around 1907, showing two antique automobiles, one on each side of the boulder.

7. Rene Laubach, *A Guide to Natural Places in the Berkshire Hills* (Stockbridge, Mass.: Berkshire House, Publishers, 1992), 145–154.

8. *The Berkshire Hills,* Vol. 3, no. 1 (Sept 1, 1902). A photograph of Balance Rock can be seen.

9. Tyler Resch, ed., Bill Tague's *Berkshires*, Vol. II (Dover, N.H.: Arcadia Publishing, 1998), 11.

10. William H. Tague and Robert B. Kimball, eds., and Richard V. Happel, writer, *Berkshires: Two Hundred Years in Pictures* (Pittsfield, Mass.: The Eagle Publishing Company, 1961). A 100-year-old picture of Balance Rock can be seen on page 53.

11. William H. Tague and Robert B. Kimball, *Berkshires: The First Three Hundred Years, 1676–1976* (Pittsfield, Mass.: The Eagle Publishing Company, 1976). A picture of Balance Rock is displayed on page 53.

12. Ivan Sandrof, *Yesterday's Massachusetts* (Miami, Fla.: E. A. Seemann Publishing, Inc., 1977). On page 109 a picture of Balance Rock in Pittsfield is presented, followed by a picture of a balanced rock in Lanesboro. Because Balance Rock can look totally different when viewed from different angles, the author didn't realize that these two pictures were actually of the same boulder.

13. Roderick Peattie, ed., *The Berkshires: The Purple Hills* (New York: The Vanguard Press, Inc., 1948), 136. The author writes that the boulder is "so perfectly balanced it can be moved with a crowbar." This is unlikely; otherwise the natural formation would not have withstood its interactions with vandals for so long.

14. Resch, op cit., 11.

15. Moore, op cit.

16. Berkshire County Historical Society, op cit., 24.

17. Sandrof, op cit., 110.

18. *The Berkshire Hills*, Vol. 3, no. 2 (Oct. 1, 1902), 110. On page 16 there is a picture of Split Rock "only a few rods north of Balance Rock," with a beech tree sprouting between the two halves.

Shaker Mountain

1. Smith, *Nature Walks in the Berkshire Hills*, op cit., 150–159.

2. Dugger, *Adventure Guide to Massachusetts & Western Connecticut*, op cit. The author gives an excellent description of a hike up to Shaker Mountain on pages 150–151.

3. Stevens, *Hikes & Walks in the Berkshire Hills*, op cit., 117–121. An entire chapter is devoted to Shaker Mountain.

4. Rhonda Ostering and George Ostering, *Hiking Southern New England* (Helena, Mont.: Falcon Press Publishing Co., Inc., 1997). The trails are described on page 46.

5. The Great Trails Council, *Boy Scout's Hancock Shaker Trail* (Unpublished). This twenty-page handout includes maps as well as good descriptions of what you will see along the hike.

6. Dugger, op cit. On page 150 Dugger writes: "The trail up Shaker Mountain ... will take you past ... a water system with mill sites and dams, 150-year old cart roads, sites where charcoal was burned, stone walls, and hilltop holy places."

7. Andrews, *The People Called Shakers*, op cit. The Shaker community is described on page 290.

8. Carney, *A Berkshire Sourcebook*, op cit., 140–141. "The Hancock community was one of nineteen settlements established in New England, New York, Ohio, Indiana and Kentucky. Its isolation was good for such social innovation. In fact, the town of Hancock had first been called Jerico on account of the high natural walls on either side."

9. *The Berkshires: Through the Camera of Arthur Palme*, op cit. Contained in the book is a picture of the Shaker Village in Hancock (pages unnumbered).

10. Samuel Chamberlain, *The Berkshires* (New York: Hastings House, 1956). On page 61 can be seen the circular stone barn that was built in 1826 in Shaker Village. The barn had a circumference of 276 feet and its upper, wooden floor was used to store the carriages.

11. Carney, op cit. A line drawing of the round, stone barn can be seen on page 140.

12. John S. Dyson, *Our Historic Hudson* (Roosevelt, N.Y.: James B. Adler, 1968). On pages 36 and 37 mention is made of the Shakers in relation to presidential candidate Samuel Tilden.

13. Andrews, *The Community Industries of the Shakers*, op cit., describes industries in various Shaker Communities.

14. Patricia Harris, David Lyon, Anna Mundow, and Lisa Oppenheimer, *Massachusetts* (New York: Compass American Guides, 2003). On page 185 is an illustration of how women dressed in the 1870s at the Shaker Village in Hancock.

No Bottom Pond

1. Perry, *Underground Empire: Wonders and Tales of New York Caves*, op cit. On pages 48–51 a fascinating account of the pond's morbid history is related.

2. Ibid., 49.

3. Ibid., 50.

4. Ibid., 50.

5. Ibid., 50.

6. Patricia Edwards Clyne, *Hudson Valley Tales and Trails* (Woodstock, N.Y.: The Overlook Press, 1990), 182–190. Clyne gives a full account of the strange tale of the "Cannibal of Columbia County."

7. Paul Bartholomew, Robert Bartholomew, William Brann and Bruce Hallenbeck, *Monsters of the Northwoods* (Utica, N.Y.: North Country Books, Inc., 1992), 66.

8. Mike Eaton, "Devil's Den and No Bottom Pond: A Day Trip to the Haunts of a Cannibal, Bigfoot, and a Large Black Cat," *Northeastern Caver*, Vol. XXXIII, no. 2 (June 2002), 58.

9. Jim Moore, "No Bottom Pond," *Northeastern Caver*, Vol. XXXII, no. 3 (Sept. 2001), 93–94.

Ice Glen & Laura's Tower

1. Russell Dunn, "Ice Glen Caves: 100 years later," *Northeastern Caver*, Vol. XXII, no. 3 (September 1991). The article presents the experience of hiking through the glen on pages 80–81.

2. Rene Laubach, *A Guide to Natural Places in the Berkshire Hills* (Stockbridge, Mass.: Berkshire Publishers, 1992), 71–77. A chapter on the Ice Glen and Laura's Tower is contained in the book.

3. Charles W. G. Smith, *Nature Walks in the Berkshire Hills* (Boston.: Appalachian Mountain Club Books, 1997), 87–94. The book contains a chapter on the Ice Glen and Laura's Tower.

4. Lauren R. Stevens, *Hikes & Walks in the Berkshire Hills* (Stockbridge, Mass.: Berkshire House Publishers, 1990), 80–81. A description of the Ice Glen is provided.

5. *Massachusetts and Rhode Island Trail Guide*, 7th Edition (Boston.: Appalachian Mountain Club Books, 1995). Brief information and directions are provided on pages 98–99.

6. Stephen Kulik, Pete Salmansohn, Matthew Schmidt, and Heidi Welch, *The Audubon Society Field Guide to the Natural Places of the Northeast: Inland* (New York: Hilltown Press, Inc., 1984), 75–76. Information on the glen is provided.

7. Laubach, op cit., 71–77.

8. Smith, op cit., 87–94.

9. William Carney, *A Berkshire Sourcebook: The history, geography and major landmarks of Berkshire County, Mass.* (Pittsfield, Mass.: The Junior League of Berkshire County, Inc., 1976). The author indicates on page 130 that the suspension bridge crossing the Housatonic River was built by Mary Hopkins in order to link Laurel Hill with the Ice Glen, making it one continuous park. What should be made clear is that Laurel Hill is different from Laurel Mountain and Tower. From the parking area by the suspension bridge, a path leads up a small hill to the top, where "French Bench," designed by sculptor Daniel Chester French, can be seen.

10. Richard Matthews, "Proper Names: An Appellative Atlas of the Berkshires," *Berkshire Magazine*, Vol. X, no. 5 (October/November, 1991), 33.

11. Malcolm W. Campbell, P*lay Hard. Rest Easy. New England: The Ultimate Active Getaway Guide* (Charlotte, N.C.: Walkabout Press, Inc., 2001), 50. The Ice Glen was named "for the microclimate that exists in the ravine—which sometimes lasts well into summer. Ice Glen is testament to the glacial carving. Here, you'll find moss-strewn boulders as large as houses perched atop one another—the place feels like a movie set."

12. Clark W. Bryan, The Book of the Berkshire (1887; reprint, North Egremont, Mass.: Past Perfect Books, 1993), 75. "The ravine is 40 rods long, and is thickly strewn with enormous boulders and the great trunks of fallen trees, all mossy and slippery and in wild confusion, so as to leave cavernous recesses and an often impeded passage for a lively brook." [note: 1 rod = 16.5 feet, which means that Bryan calculates the glen's length as being 660 feet.]

13. Elizabeth L. Dugger, *Adventure Guide to Massachusetts & Western Connecticut*

(Edison, N.J.: Hunter Publishing, Inc., 1999), 353. The Ice Glen is described, with "its steep sides, high boulders, and ice patches under the rocks."

14. Thomas D. Engel, *A Chronicle of Selected Northeastern Caves: A History Guide for the 1979 NSS Convention. Pittsfield, Massachusetts* (n.p.: Thomas D. Engel, 1979). On page 12, Engel indicates that there are approximately twenty talus caves in the Ice Glen.

15. *The Berkshires: Through the Camera of Arthur Palme*, op cit. A picture of a man looking into one of the caves in the Ice Glen is displayed (pages are unnumbered).

16. Barbara Radcliffe Rogers and Stillman Rogers, with Pat Maddell and Juliette Rogers, *Off the Beaten Path: Massachusetts*, 6th edition (Guilford, Conn.: Globe Pequot Press, 2005), 200. "The Ice Glen was carved out by a glacier that left massive boulders where the sun never reaches."

17. *www.berkshireweb.com*

18. New England 13 Berkshires, *members.aol.com/nebrkshr.html*

19. Carney, op cit. On page 23, Carney writes: "Ice Glen, a steep, boulder-clogged gorge in Stockbridge, is a similarly strong landscape passage. Townspeople once passed through it annually, carrying torches. Formations like this, often called gutters or gulfs, occur throughout New England, mystifying and somewhat spooking early settlers. They are now thought to have been cut by the torrential run-off waters of melting glaciers."

20. *www.berkshireweb.com*

21. Clay Perry, *New England's Buried Treasure* (New York: Stephen Daye Press, 1946), 69.

22. Ibid., 66.

Tyringham Cobble

1. Stevens, *Walks in the Berkshire Hills*, op cit., 77–78. The author devotes an entire chapter to the Cobble.

2. Laubach, *A Guide to Natural Places in the Berkshire Hills*, op cit., 64–70. A chapter is devoted to hiking up and down the Cobble.

3. Smith, *Nature Walks in the Berkshire Hills*, op cit. Details on the mountain and hiking up and down its summit are provided on pages 102–109.

4. Michael Tougias and Mark Tougias, *Autumn Rambles of New England: An Explorer's Guide to the Best Fall Colors* (Edison, N.J.: Hunter Publishing Co., Inc., 1998), 64–65. According to the authors, "The exposed rock ridge of the summit is thought to have broken off from nearby Backbone Mountain and flipped over eons ago."

5. Richard Matthews, "Proper Names: An Appellative Atlas of the Berkshires," op cit., 32.

6. Myers, *Tyringham: A Hinterland Settlement*, op cit. The author presents the early history of Tyringham on page 6.

7. Ibid., 6.

8. Ibid., 33.

9. Ibid., 29, 30.

10. Bryan, *The Book of Berkshire*, op cit., 181. "As early as 1792 a society of Shakers was organized in Tyringham, consisting of nine members at first. ... The community soon numbered 100 and once it contained 185. ... but, in 1858, 23 of their number ran away at one time, and in 1874 their number was so reduced that they sold their property in Tyringham and joined the communities at Hancock, Enfield and New Lebanon."

11. Gilder, *Views of the Valley, Tyringham 1739–1989*, op cit. There are pictures of Shakers and Shaker buildings on pages 134–142.

12. Edward Deming Andrews, *The Community Industries of the Shakers*, New York

State Museum Handbook Number 15 (reprint, Charlestown, Mass.: Emporium Publications, 1971). This book describes industries in various Shaker Communities.

13. Meyers, op cit., 80.

14. Ibid., 90.

15. Edward Deming Andrews, The People Called Shakers (New York: Dover Publications, Inc. 1953). The Tyringham Shaker community statistics are noted on page 290.

16. Bryan, op cit., 181.

17. Gilder, op cit., 33.

Additional Sources of Information:

Ray Bearse, ed., *Massachusetts: A Guide to the Pilgrim State*, 2nd edition (Boston: Houghton Mifflin Company, 1971), 428–429.

David Yeaden, *Hidden Corners of New England* (New York: Funk & Wagnalls, 1976), 20–23. The author provides a brief history of the Shakers in Tyringham Valley and a fairly detailed account on Hitson Mansion.

David Emblidge, *Exploring the Appalachian Trail: Hikes in Southern New England* (Mechanicsburg, Pa.: Stackpole Books, 1998). An interesting side bar is reprinted from Tyringham: A Hinterland Settlement by Eloise Meyers. It contains relevant information on page 113 concerning the Shakers at Tyringham.

Ashintully Estate & McLennan Preserve

1. Cornelia Brooke Gilder, *Views of the Valley, Tyringham 1739–1989* (n.p.: Hop Brook Community Club, 1989). Pictures of the Ashintully Estate and Ashintully farm are offered on pages 121 & 122.

2. Christina Tree and William Davis, *The Berkshire Hills & Pioneer Valley of Western Massachusetts: An Explorer's Guide* (Woodstock, Vt.: The Countryman Press, 2004), 69.

3. Charles W. G. Smith, *Nature Walks in the Berkshire Hills* (Boston: Appalachian Mountain Club Books, 1997), 95–101. A chapter is devoted to the hike at the McLennan Preserve.

4. Tree, *The Berkshire Hills & Pioneer Valley of Western Massachusetts*, op cit., 69. Brief information is provided on the Ashintully Garden and the McLennan Reservation.

5. Eloise Myers, *Tyringham: A Hinterland Settlement*, 3rd edition (n.p.: Tyringham Historical Commission, Hinterland Press, 1989), 113.

6. Ibid. Additional information on Ashintully is furnished on page 94.

Additional Source of Information:

Katherine McLennan, widow of John McLennan, provided information on the history of the Ashintully Estate.

Part IV: Schoharie Valley

Vroman's Nose

1. Vincent Schaefer, *Vrooman's Nose* (Fleischmanns, N.Y.: Purple Mountain Press, 1992). This is the definitive book on Vroman's Nose.

2. McMartin, *Fifty Hikes in the Hudson Valley*, op cit., 214–217. A chapter is devoted to the hike.

3. Lester E. Hendrix and Anne Whitbeck Hendrix, compiler and ed., *The Sloughter's History of Schoharie County*. Bicentennial Edition. 1795–1995 (Schoharie, N.Y.: The Tryon Press, 1995). A picture of Vroman's Nose, taken from the river, can

be seen on page 19.

4. *Catskill Mountain Region Guide*, Vol. 18, no. 7 (July, 2003), 38. A beautiful view from the top of Vroman's Nose is presented.

5. Dorwin W. Bulson, *To-wos-scho-hor: The Land of the Unforgotten Indian* (1961), 8. "From the east, this odd projection resembles a dwarfed progeny of Nippletop in the Adirondacks; in the dimness of the day, or in the moonlight, it maintains the pose of an extinct volcano. The pinnacle constitutes a virtual watchtower, commanding a view of several miles in every direction except the quadrant to the rear. Hence it was a setting for Indian deliberations, as well as for smoke signals and reconnaissance."

6. Hendrix, op cit. Mention is made on page 22 that the Karigh Ondontes village was once at the base of the mountain.

7. Paul Grondahl, "The Long Path," *Conservationist*, Vol. 49, no. 6 (July 1995), 18.

8. Perry, *Underground Empire: Wonders and Tales of New York Caves*, op cit. Perry provides an interesting description of Dr. Vincent Schaefer on pages 122–123: "Mr. Schaefer's interests, ranging from his research at the G.E. Laboratories, as assistant to Dr. Irving Langmuir, to crawling into 'rock holes' in search of prehistoric man, and also to study the growth of formations, including 'ice stalagmites' in the Tory Hole, finally led him to get high up above the earth in an airplane with a quantity of dry ice which he dropped into the clouds hovering above Mount Greylock, Massachusetts, to produce the first man-made snowstorm in history."

9. Robert Titus, "The Lost Lakes," *Kaatskill Life*, Vol. 16, no. 2 (summer 2000), 52–57.

10. Hendrix, op cit., 8. "Terrace Mountain and Vroman's Nose became islands in the lake, called Herkimer Lake. The nearest shore from Vroman's Nose was about three-quarters of a mile away, north of West Middleburgh."

11. Robert Titus, "Dance Floors," *Kaatskill Life*, Vol. 13, no. 4, 48–53. The author talks about the planed, flat surfaces at the top of Vroman's Nose, and the effects of the last glaciation on the surface of the bedrock.

Pratt Rock

1. Carol White and David White, *Catskill Day Hikes for All Seasons* (Lake George, N.Y.: Adirondack Mountain Club, Inc., 2002), 160–161.

2. J. Van Vechten Vedder, *Official History of Greene County, New York* (1927; reprint, Cornwallville, N.Y.: Hope Farm Press, 1985), 114–119.

3. Francine Silverman, *The Catskills Alive!* (Edison, N. J.: Hunter Publishing, Inc., 2000). Pratt Rock is referred to on page 325 as "The Mount Rushmore of the Catskills." Silverman also makes the interesting point that the portrait of Zadock Pratt bears a striking resemblance to Abraham Lincoln.

4. Robert Titus, "The Colonel's Tomb," *Kaatskill Life*, Vol. 13, no. 1 (spring 1998), 54–59.

5. Patricia Millen, "Step Back in Time in Prattsville," *Kaatskill Life*, Vol. 9, no. 2 (summer 1994). Mention is made on pages 114–115 of Old Prattsville Day, which was first started in 1992.

6. Titus, "The Colonel's Tomb," op cit.

7. *Prattsville Advocate*, Vol. 3, no. 24 (Saturday, July 8, 1848). The newspaper article mentions that the escarpment was first known as High Rocks.

8. Patricia Millen, *Bare Trees: Zadock Pratt, Master Tanner & the Story of What Happened to the Catskill Mountain Forests* (Hensonville, N.Y., Black Dome Press Corp., 1995). This book tells the history of Zadock Pratt and the tanning industry in the nineteenth century. There are good line drawings and photos supporting the text.

9. Field Horne, T*he Greene County Catskills: A History* (Hensonville, N.Y.: Black Dome Press Corp, 1994). Information is provided on Zadock Pratt's life on page 59.

10. Adams, *The Catskills: An Illustrated Historical Guide with Gazetteer*, op cit. Interesting facts about Zadock Pratt are presented on pages 144–145.

11. Evers, *The Catskills: From Wilderness to Woodstock*, op cit. Evers devotes an entire chapter, on pages 341–350, to the fascinating history of "Colonel Pratt of Prattsville."

12. Patricia Edwards Clyne, "Hemlock, Hides, and Chutzpah," *Hudson Valley* (September 1997), 25–31.

13. Lee McAllister, *Hiking the Catskills: a guide for exploring the natural beauty of America's romantic & magical mountains and "off the beaten path"* (New York: New York–New Jersey Trail Conference, 1989). The author mentions on page 26 that Zadock Pratt was ahead of his time as a conservationist. Pratt realized that the hillsides were being laid to waste from over-harvesting. He began replanting trees, but apparently not in time to stop the collapse of Prattsville as a tannery village.

14. Joanne Michaels, *An Explorer's Guide to the Hudson Valley & Catskill Mountains: including Saratoga Springs & Albany* (Woodstock, Vt.: The Countryman Press, 2004). Information on the Zadock Pratt Museum is presented on page 184. The museum is contained in Zadock Pratt's former house and shows life as it was lived in the 1850s.

Part V: Hudson Valley Region

Lindenwald & Martin Van Buren Nature Trail

1. The National Park Service rangers on site and the website *(MAVA_info@nps.gov)* provide background information on the history of Martin Van Buren and Lindenwald, as well as specific information about the site and hours.

2. Raymond C. Houghton, *A Revolutionary Day along Historic US Route 9* (Delmar, N.Y.: Cyber Haus Computer Learning Center, 2002). Pages 52–54 mention the origin of the term ok, meaning "Old Kinderhook," which was used in reference to Martin Van Buren.

3. Allan Keller, *Life along the Hudson* (Tarrytown, N.Y.: Sleepy Hollow Press, 1985). Page 242 describes the relationships of Peter Van Ness, Aaron Burr, and Washington Irving to the house that was later the residence of Martin Van Buren.

4. Frank L. Amoroso, "Kinderhook 1609–1976" *(www.kinderhookconnection.com)*. Page 4 describes the history of Martin Van Buren and mentions that, after Van Buren died, Lindenwald was won in a card game by Lawrence Jerome, father to Jenny Jerome, who later became Winston Churchill's mother.

5. Robert Lopez, "Big Plans for Van Buren Site," *Times Union*, Section D–1, April 24, 2005. The writer describes the then-current renovations at the site and possible plans for acquisition of lands formerly owned by the Van Buren family that would be used for recreational purposes such as hiking, biking and horseback riding. The article also provides additional historical background.

6. Houghton, op cit. The history of the Knox Trail (named after General Knox) is described.

Rogers Island

1. Shirley W. Dunn, *The Mohicans and Their Land, 1609–1730* (Fleischmanns, N.Y.: Purple Mountain Press, 1994), 183. "The sale included Ten Points Island, later known as Vastrick or Rogers Island." This is a reference to land that was transferred from the Mohicans to the director of Rensselaerswyck.

Notes

2. Arthur G. Adams, *The Hudson River Guidebook* (New York: Fordham University Press, 1996), 247.

3. R. Lionel De Lisser, Picturesque Catskills, Greene County (1894; reprint with foreword and index by Alf Evers, Cornwallville, N.Y.: Hope Farm Press, 1971), 19–20. The author provides extensive details on the battle that occurred on Rogers Island.

4. Ibid., 20.

5. Field Horne, *The Greene County Catskills: A History* (Hensonville, N.Y.: Black Dome Press Corp., 1994). A 1910 photo on page 132 shows ice cutters at work at Rogers Island.

6. Walter F. Burmeister, *Appalachian Waters 2: The Hudson River and Its Tributaries* (Oakton, Va.: Appalachian Books, 1974). Information is provided, on page 64, on the Rip Van Winkle Bridge that straddles Rogers Island.

Additional Source of Information:

Russell Dunn, "Tribal Warfare," *Hudson Valley*, Vol. XXIX, no. 6 (October 2000). A full account of Rogers Island's history is provided on pages 23, 77, 78.

Olana

1. Stan Lichens, *The Romantic Landscape: Photographs in the Tradition of the New York Hudson Valley Painters* (Petaluma, Calif.: Pomegranate Communications, Inc., 2004). Several pictures of Olana are presented on pages 69 and 79.

2. The New York State Office of Parks, Recreation and Historic Preservation's "State Historic Site" brochure provides an overview of Olana and information about hours and directions.

3. *www.hvnet.com/HOUSES/olana*. The Hudson Valley Network 2004 website provides relevant information and pictures of Olana.

4. Linda McLean, Director, Olana State Historic Site.

5. Arthur G. Adams, *The Catskills: An Illustrated Historical Guide with Gazetteer* (New York: Fordham University Press, 1990), 192. Adams tells of Church's extensive travels and his studies with Thomas Cole, and describes the famous Church painting, Niagara Falls.

6. Richard E. Slavin III, in "Frederic Church and Olana," *Conservationist*, Vol. 28, no. 6 (June/July 1974), 25–30, describes the history of Olana and Frederic Church.

7. Lisa Berg, "The Home and Final Work of Art of Frederic Church," *Kutri's Korner, Great Art and Artists*, 1999 website (www.kaiku.com). Page 2 recounts an exhibition of the Church painting Heart of the Andes where visitors paid twenty-five cents for admission to see the painting.

8. McLean, op cit.

9. Tim Mulligan, *The Hudson River Valley: A History & Guide* (New York: Random House, 1985), 49. Church is quoted as saying, "About one hour this side of Albany is the center of the world—I own it." Church was obviously very proud of his accomplishment.

10. Gerald L. Carr, *Olana Landscapes: The World of Frederic E. Church* (New York: Rizzoli International Publications, Inc. 1989). This book provides a photographic view of many of the scenes in Olana as Church had intended them to be seen; the accompanying text helps to explain the logic behind Church's methodology.

Additional Source of Information:

Kenneth Myers, *The Catskills: Painters, Writers, and Tourists in the Mountains* (Yonkers, N.Y.: The Hudson River Museum of Westchester, 1987). Page 109 lists Church's artworks that relate to Catskill scenery and provides background information about Church.

Montgomery Place

1. The Historic Hudson Valley brochure 2004 and website *(www.hudsonvalley.org)* provides background information on Montgomery Place.

2. Ibid.

3. Arthur G. Adams, *Hudson River Guidebook*, 2nd edition (New York: Fordham University Press, 1996), 231. The causeway created by the Hudson River Railway is described.

4. Lichens, *The Romantic Landscape*, op cit. On page 16 can be seen a picture of the water lily pond, and on page 44 a picture of a vase surrounded by magnificent colors.

5. Katherine M. Babbitt, Janet *Montgomery: Hudson River Squire* (Monroe, N.Y.: Library Research Associates, Inc., 1975). The story of General Richard Montgomery's funeral procession on the Hudson River passing Chateau de Montgomery, and Janet Montgomery's reaction to the occasion, is recounted on pages 37–38.

6. Adams, *Hudson River Guidebook*, op cit. On page 231 is a description of Skillpot Island.

7. Jacquetta M. Haley, ed., *Pleasure Grounds: Andrew Jackson Downing and Montgomery Place* (Tarrytown, N.Y.: Sleepy Hollow Press, 1988). Haley mentions on page 11 that the land was originally farmed by the Van Benthuysen family.

8. Babbitt, op cit., 13.

9. Ibid., 34. Babbitt describes the building of Chateau de Montgomery (Montgomery Place).

10. Historic Hudson Valley brochure, op cit.

11. Babbitt, op cit., 37, 38.

12. Ibid., 37, 38.

13. Haley, op cit., 12.

14. Ibid., 14, 15. Downing participated in the capacity of a friend, rather than as an employed landscape gardener, in influencing the design of the gardens.

15. Ibid., 18.

Ravena Falls

1. Schmitt, *Natural Areas of Albany County*, op cit. Background information on the preserve is presented on page 79, and there is a map on page 78.

2. Chuck Friday, local authority on the mills of Ravena and Greene County.

3. Ibid.

4. Informational sign next to bridge.

5. Town of New Baltimore Bicentennial Committee, *The Heritage of New Baltimore* (New Baltimore, N.Y.: Town of New Baltimore, 1976), 102.

6. Schmitt, op cit., 79.

7. Town of New Baltimore Bicentennial Committee, op cit., 104.

8. Ibid.

Additional Sources of Information:

Old newspaper clippings related to Ravena Falls are contained in the Vedder Research Library at the Bronck House Museum on Rt. 9W in Coxsackie.

Hudson River School Art Trail

1. "Hudson River School Art Trail" brochure, Cedar Grove project, Thomas Cole National Historic Site.

2. Elizabeth Jacks, Director, Cedar Grove.

3. Ibid.

4. Ernest Ingersoll, *Handy Guide to the Hudson River and Catskill Mountains*

Notes

(1910; reprint, Astoria, N.Y.: J.C. & A.L. Fawcett, Inc., 1989), 193.

5. Ruth Piwonka, "Mount Merino: Views of Mount Merino, South Bay, and the City of Hudson, Painted by Henry Ary and His Contemporaries" (Kinderhook, N.Y.: Columbia County Historical Society, 1978), pages unnumbered. Piwonka mentions that Mount Merino was called Rorabuch in earlier times. Although Piwonka admits that the meaning of this word is obscure, she thinks that it "may be derived from Dutch words meaning stirring and bay or may derive from a now lost Indian place name."

6. Captain Franklin Ellis, *History of Columbia County, New York, with Illustrations of Some of Its Prominent Men and Pioneers* (1878; reprint, Old Chatham, N.Y.: Sachem Press, 1974), 360. Ellis talks about the "bold elevation of Mount Merino, two hundred and fifty feet above the river."

7. Margaret B. Schram, *Hudson's Merchants and Whalers: The Rise and Fall of a River Port, 1783-1850* (Hensonville, N.Y.: Black Dome Press Corp., 2004), 87.

8. Jacques Milbert, *Picturesque Itinerary of the Hudson River and the Peripheral parts of North America* (Ridgewood, N.J.: The Gregg Press, 1968), 37. "Mount Merino, [was] crowned by a fort and with a very broad base." Milbert goes on to give a brief account of hiking to Mount Merino and then sketching the harbor while a storm was blowing in.

9. Historic marker at park.

10. Anonymous, *Columbia County at the End of the Century: A historical record of its formation and settlements, its resources, its institutions, its industries and its people*, Vol. I. (Hudson, N.Y.: The Record Printing & Publishing Co., 1900), 311. Old, full-page pictures of the Promenade can be seen on pages 296, 298, and 304.

11. Schram, op cit., 48.

12. Anonymous, op cit., 311.

13. Historic Design Associates, *Historic Hudson: Rehabilitation through Urban Renewal in the Lower Warren Street Historic Area of Hudson, New York* (Hudson, N.Y.: Raymond Parish & Pine, Inc., 1974), 4.

14. Columbia County Historical Society, *www.cchs.org*

15. Robert A. Gildersleeve, *Catskill Mountain House Trail Guide: In the Footsteps of the Hudson River School* (Hensonville, N.Y.: Black Dome Press Corp., 2005), 172.

16. Gildersleeve, op cit., 62.

17. Adams, *The Catskills,* op cit., 189.

18. Ibid., 377.

19. Roland Van Zandt, *The Catskill Mountain House: Cradle of the Hudson River School* (1966; reprint, Hensonville, N.Y.: Black Dome Press Corp., 1993), 109.

20. Raymond Beecher, *Kaaterskill Clove: Where Nature Met Art* (Hensonville, N.Y.: Black Dome Press Corp., 2004), 40.

21. John K. Howat, *The Hudson River and Its Painters* (1972; reprint, New York: American Legacy Press, 1983), 33.

22. Cedar Grove Website *(www.thomascole.org)*.

23. Adams, *The Catskills*, op cit., 189.

24. Ibid., 190.

25. Beecher, op cit., 48.

Additional Sources of Information:

Albany Institute of History and Art, *www.albanyinstitute.org*.

Ruth Piwonka, *Mt. Merino Catalogue of Exhibits* (Kinderhook N.Y.: NYS Council on the Arts and Columbia County Historical Society, 1976 and 1977).

Bob Gildersleeve, "Hiking at North–South Lake," *Catskill Center News*, Vol. 34, no. 2. On page 2 the author talks about the trail to Artist Rock and Sunset Rock.

Catskill Mountain House Escarpment

1. Bruce Wadsworth and the Schenectady Chapter of the Adirondack Mountain Club, *Guide to Catskill Trails 8*, 2nd edition (Lake George, N.Y.: Adirondack Mountain Club, Inc., 1988). Detailed information and mileages are provided on pages 74–79 under "Escarpment Trail (southern section)," from Schutt's Road to North Point.

2. E. O. Wilson, "It Won't Bite," *Kaatskill Life*, Vol. 14, no. 4 (Winter 1999–2000). A picture of Alligator Rock can be seen on page 9.

3. The Mountain Top Historical Society, *Kaaterskill: From the Catskill Mountain House to the Hudson River School* (Hensonville, N.Y.: Black Dome Press Corp., 1993). On page 97, Alligator Rock is described as follows: "The photos showed this open mouth with uprighted stones placed so as to make a fairly complete set of teeth."

4. Gildersleeve, *Catskill Mountain House Trail Guide*, op cit. A picture/postcard of the rock can be seen on page 72.

5. Howard Stone, *25 Bicycle Tours in the Hudson Valley: Scenic Rides from Saratoga to West Point* (Woodstock, Vt.: Backcountry Publications, 1989), 94. "The viewpoint is the top of an escarpment that plunges sharply about 1,500 feet to the floor of the Hudson Valley. The view unfolds without warning—suddenly a 50-mile sweep of the river lies beneath you in a silvery ribbon. Its closest point is about 7 miles away, yet it looks almost close enough to throw a stone into."

6. Van Zandt, *The Catskill Mountain House*, op cit. Van Zandt's book provides a fascinating history, in great detail, of the Mountain House.

7. Gildersleeve, op cit. A postcard of this unusual rock can be seen on page 46.

8. Ibid. A drawing of views of the valley from Boulder Rock is displayed on page 48.

9. The Mountain Top Historical Society, op cit., 96. Boulder Rock "sat precisely on the line dividing the Kaaterskill and Mountain House properties."

10. Alf Evers, *The Catskills: From Wilderness to Woodstock* (Woodstock, N.Y.: The Overlook Press, 1982), 496–509, provides a full account of what came to be known as the "Fried Chicken Wars."

Saugerties Lighthouse

1. *www.saugertieslighthouse.com*

2. Russell Patton, Jr., "Lighting the Way," Kaatskill Life, Vol. 13, no. 2 (summer 1998), 53–55. Background information is provided on the Saugerties Lighthouse, with several photographs included.

3. Peggy Turco, *Walks and Rambles in the Western Hudson Valley* (Woodstock, Vt.: Backcountry Publications, 1996). The hike is described on pages 141–145 in the chapter "Ruth Reynolds Glunt Nature Preserve."

4. Jeff Anzevino, Scenic Hudson, Inc.

5. Patton, op cit., 53.

6. Videotape of the lighthouse's restoration can be viewed at the Saugerties Lighthouse Museum, which is located within the lighthouse. Supplemental materials are also available on site.

7. Ruth Reynolds Glunt, "Never Let the Light Go Out!" *Conservationist* (December-January, 1972–1973). In this article on the lighthouses of the Hudson River, two pictures of the Saugerties Lighthouse are presented on pages 24–25.

8. Harold Faber, *My Times in the Hudson Valley: The Insider's Guide to Historic Homes, Scenic Drives, Restaurants, Museums, Farm Produce & Points of Interest* (Hensonville, N.Y.: Black Dome Press Corp., 1997), 159. "Opposite it [The Coast Guard Station] on the north side is the old lighthouse, a two-story stuccoed red brick building with a glass cupola on top that once flashed the warning light for river pilots." A photo

of the lighthouse taken by Allen Bryan can be seen on page 160. A photo of the lighthouse under construction, taken by Cara Lee, can be found on page 163.

9. Patton, op cit., 54.

10. John Mylod, *Biography of a River: The People & Legends of the Hudson Valley* (New York: Bonanza Books,1969), 4. "A lighthouse helped to keep ships off the mud flats there for more than a century, but like similar 'lights' at Tarrytown and Hudson it has been replaced recently by an automatic buoy."

11. Kimball, *The Capital Region of New York State*, Vol. I, op cit., page 148. "Sawyer's Creek is an English translation of the Dutch Zaagertjes, meaning 'saw mill man,' referring to a miller who had an 'establishment on the stream.'"

Overlook Mountain

1. McMartin, *Fifty Hikes in the Hudson Valley*, op cit. Background information on Overlook Mountain and the hike is provided on pages 126–129.

2. Carol White and David White, *Catskill Day Hikes for All Seasons* (Lake George, N.Y.: Adirondack Mountain Club, Inc., 2002). Background information on the hike is furnished on pages 91–94.

3. The New York–New Jersey Trail Conference, *New York Walk Book* (Garden City, N.Y.: Anchor Books, 1971), 148.

4. Peggy Turco, *Walks and Rambles in the Western Hudson Valley: Landscape, Ecology, & Folklore in Orange & Ulster Counties* (Woodstock, Vt.: Backcountry Publications, 1996), 179–183.

5. Dick Voloshen, Overlook Project Director, *Overlook Fire Tower Guide* (Woodstock, N.Y., revised 2004).

6. Ibid.

7. Evers, *The Catskills: From Wilderness to Woodstock*, op cit., 471. On pages 470–480 an entire chapter is devoted to the Overlook Mountain House.

8. T. Morris Longstreth, *The Catskills* (1918; reprint, Hensonville, N.Y.: Black Dome Press Corp., 2003). On pages 26–29 a visit up to Meads and to the top of Overlook Mountain is recounted.

9. Alf Evers, *In Catskill Country: Collected Essays on Mountain History, Life and Lore* (Woodstock, N.Y.: The Overlook Press, 1995), 110. "Rocky features on the mountaintop were quickly converted into a great stone turtle, a pulpit, a Poet's Glen, a Lover's Retreat. ... An extensive body of Indian lore and legend was improvised to add romantic charm to caves and rocks within the Overlook Park."

10. Evers, *The Catskills: From Wilderness to Woodstock*, op cit., 473.

11. Ibid., 687.

12 Adams, *The Catskills: An Illustrated Historical Guide with Gazetteer*, op cit. A picture of Meads Mountain House is shown on page 126.

13. Voloshen, op cit.

14. Ibid.

15. Robert Titus, "Ulster Blues," *Kaatskill Life*, Vol. 10, no. 2 (summer 1995), 72–77.

Additional Source of Information:

Frank Knight, "Open Space Institute: Protecting the Land for People and Wildlife," *Kaatskill Life*, Vol. 19, no. 3 (fall 2004). The author advances the argument on page 35 that Overlook Mountain is "regarded by many as the birthplace of the Hudson River School of Painters."

Sky Top & Mohonk Lake

1. Joan LaChance, Mohonk archivist.

2. Benjamin H. Matteson and Joan A. LaChance, *The Summerhouses of Mohonk* (Mohonk Lake, N.Y.: Mohonk Mountain House, 1998). This work provides extensive information on the fascinating summerhouses of Mohonk.

3. LaChance, op cit.

4. Benjamin H. Matteson and Joan A. LaChance, *The Story of Sky Top and Its Four Towers* (Lake Mohonk, N.Y.: Mohonk Mountain House, 1998), 12.

5. Lachance, op cit.

6. Larry E. Burgess, *Mohonk, Its People and Spirit: A History of One Hundred Years of Growth and Service* (Fleischmanns, N.Y.: Purple Mountain Press, 1980). A photo of the slender wooden observation tower on Eagle Cliff can be seen on page 27.

7. Edward G. Henry, *Gunks Trails: A Ranger's Guide to the Shawangunk Mountains* (Hensonville, N.Y.: Black Dome Press Corp., 2003), 65.

8. Kiosk near the Albert K. Smiley Memorial Tower.

9. Jack Fagan, *Scenes and Walks in the Northern Shawangunks* (New York: New York–New Jersey Trail Conference, 1998), 67.

10. Ibid., 67.

11. Burgess, op cit., 15.

12. Henry, op cit., 63.

13. Carol A. Johnson and Marion W. Ryan, *Images of America: New Paltz* (Charleston, S.C.: Arcadia Publishing, 2001), 9, provides information on the derivation of the word "paltz."

14. Henry, op cit., 65.

15. Jeffrey Perls, *Shawangunk Trail Companion: A Complete Guide to Hiking, Mountain Biking, Cross-Country Skiing, and More, Only 90 Miles from New York City* (Woodstock, Vt.: Backcountry Guides, 2003), 129.

16. Fagan, op cit., 65.

17. Robi Josephson, *Images of America: Mohonk Mountain House and Preserve* (Charleston, S.C.: Arcadia Publishing, 2002), 42.

18. *Mohonk Preserve Trail Map: Northern Section.* (Creative Solutions, 2004).

19. Josephson, op cit., 7.

20. Ibid., 38, 39.

21. Henry, op cit., 65.

Additional Source of Information:

Steve Weiman, *A Rock with a View: Trails of the Shawangunk Mountains* (New Paltz, N.Y.: n.p., 1995).

Bibliography

Ackerman, Elizabeth Barclay, ed. *The Heritage of New Baltimore.* New Baltimore, N.Y.: Town of New Baltimore Bicentennial Committee, 1976.

Adams, Arthur G. *The Hudson River Guidebook.* New York: Fordham University Press, 1996.

———.*The Catskills: An Illustrated Historical Guide with Gazetteer.* New York: Fordham University Press, 1990.

Adams, Arthur G., Roger Coco, Harriet Greenman, and Leon R. A. Greenman. *Guide to the Catskills: with trail guides and maps.* New York: Walking News, Inc., 1975.

Albany Institute of History and Art web site: *www.albanyinstitute.org*

Albright, Tim. Lecture "A Picture and Postcard History of the Indian Ladder Region" presented at the Thacher Nature Center, November 21, 2002.

Allen, George. "Exploring Van Hornsville," *Northeastern Caver*, Vol. XXIV, no. 4 (Dec. 1993).

Andrews, Edward Deming. *The People Called Shakers: A Search for the Perfect Society.* New York: Dover Publications, Inc. 1953.

Appalachian Mountain Club. *Massachusetts & Rhode Island Trail Guide.* 7th Edition. Boston.: Appalachian Mountain Club Books, 1995.

Babbitt, Katherine M. Janet Montgomery: *Hudson River Squire.* Monroe, N.Y.: Library Research Associates, Inc., 1975.

Bartholomew, Paul, Robert Bartholomew, William Brann and Bruce Hallenbeck. *Monsters of the Northwoods.* Utica, N.Y.: North Country Books, Inc., 1992.

Bearse, Ray. Massachusetts: *A Guide to the Pilgrim State,* 2nd edition. Boston: Houghton Mifflin Company, 1971.

Beecher, Raymond. *Kaaterskill Clove: Where Nature Met Art.* Hensonville, N.Y.: Black Dome Press Corp., 2004.

Beers, J. B. & Co. *History of Greene County, New York: with biographical sketches of its prominent men.* 1884. Reprint, Saugerties, N.Y.: Hope Farm Press, 1969.

Benjamin, Vernon. "The Tawagonshi Agreement of 1613. A chain of Friendship in the Dutch Valley." *Hudson Valley Regional Review* (March 2000).

Bennet, John, and Seth Masia. *Walks in the Catskills.* New York: The East Woods Press, Inc., 1974.

Bennett, Dean B. *The Forgotten Nature of New England.* Camden, Me.: Down East Books, 1996.

Berkshire County Historical Society. *Images of America: Pittsfield.* Charleston, S.C.: Arcadia Publishing, 2001.

The Berkshire Hills (newspaper). Vol. 3, no. 2 (Oct. 1, 1902); Vol. 2, no. 1, (Oct. 1, 1905); Vol. 3, no. 1 (Sept 1, 1902).

Bicentennial Commission of Saratoga. *Enjoy Saratoga County.* 1974.

Bliven, Rachel D., et al. *A Resourceful People: A pictorial history of Rensselaer County, New York.* Norfolk, Va.: The Donning Company, 1987.

Brady, John, and Brian White. *Fifty Hikes in Massachusetts.* Woodstock, Vt.: Backcountry Publications, 1983.

Brandow, John Henry. *The Story of Old Saratoga and New York's Share in the Revolution,* 2nd edition. Albany, N.Y.: The Brandow Printing Company, 1919.

Brown, Chris W. III. *Guide to New York Waterways and Lake Champlain.* Gretna, La.: Pelican Publishing Company, Inc., 1998.

Bryan, Clark W. *The Book of Berkshire*. 1887. Reprint, North Egremont, Mass.: Past Perfect Books, 1993.

Bulson, Dorwin W. *To-wos-scho-hor: The Land of the Unforgotten Indian*. 1961.

Burgess, Larry E. *Mohonk, Its People and Spirit: A History of One Hundred Years of Growth and Service*. Fleischmanns, N.Y.: Purple Mountain Press, 1980.

Burmeister, Walter F. *Appalachian Waters 2: The Hudson River and Its Tributaries*. Oakton, Va.: Appalachian Books, 1974.

Campbell, Malcolm W. *Play Hard. Rest Easy. New England: The Ultimate Active Getaway Guide*. Charlotte, N.C.: Walkabout Press, Inc., 2001.

Carney, William. *The Berkshire Sourcebook: The history, geography and major landmarks of Berkshire County, Mass.* Pittsfield, Mass.: The Junior League of Berkshire County, Inc., 1976.

Carr, Gerald L. *Olana Landscapes: The World of Frederic E. Church*. New York: Rizzoli International Publications, Inc., 1989.

Chamberlain, Samuel. *The Berkshires*. New York: Hastings House, 1956.

Clinton, DeWitt, ed. *Picturesque Oakwood: Its Past and Present Associations*. Troy, N.Y.: Frederick S. Hills, 1897.

Clyne, Patricia Edwards. *Hudson Valley Tales and Trails*. Woodstock, N.Y.: The Overlook Press, 1990.

———. "Hemlock, Hides, and Chutzpah," *Hudson Valley* (September 1997).

Cohoes in 76: American Bicentennial 1776–1976. Cohoes, N.Y.: United States Bicentennial Commission of Cohoes, Inc., 1976.

Columbia County at the End of the Century: A historical record of its formation and settlements, its resources, its institutions, its industries, and its people. Vol. I. Hudson, N.Y.: The Record Printing & Publishing Co., 1900.

Columbia County Historical Society web site: *www.cchs.org*

Cooper, James Fenimore. *The Leatherstocking Saga, including Last of the Mohicans*. New York: Pantheon Books, 1954.

Cullen, Jim, John Mylroie and Art Palmer. *Karst Hydrogeology and Geomorphology of Eastern New York: A guidebook to the geology field trip*. National Speleological Society Annual Convention, Pittsfield, Massachusetts, 1979.

Cushing, H.P., and R. Ruedemann. *Geology of Saratoga Springs and Vicinity. Museum Bulletin # 169*. Albany, N.Y.: The University of the State of New York, 1914.

De Lisser, R. Lionel. *Picturesque Catskills, Greene County*. 1894. Reprint, Cornwallville, N.Y.: Hope Farm Press, 1971.

Donhardt, Gary L. *Indian Ladder: A History of Life in the Helderbergs*. Collierville, Tenn.: Donhardt and Daughters Publishers, 2001.

Doyle, Roseann. "Queen of the Spas," *Mohawk Valley, USA*, Vol. 2, no. 5 (summer 1981).

Dugger, Elizabeth L. *Adventure Guide to Massachusetts & Western Connecticut*. Edison, N.J.: Hunter Publishing, Inc., 1999.

Dumont, Kevin. *1991 NSS Convention Guide to the Caves and Karst of the Northeast*. National Speleological Society, 1991

Dunn, Russell. *Catskill Region Waterfall Guide: Cool Cascades of the Catskills & Shawangunks*. Hensonville, N.Y.: Black Dome Press Corp., 2004.

———. "Ice Glen Caves: 100 Years Later." *Northeastern Caver*, Vol. XXII, no. 3 (Sept. 1991).

———. "No Bottom Pond." *Northeastern Caver*, Vol. XXII, no. 4 (December, 1991).

———. "Tribal Warfare." *Hudson Valley*, Vol. XXIX, no. 6 (October, 2000).

Dunn, Shirley W. *The Mohicans and Their Land: 1609–1730*. Fleischmanns, N.Y.: Purple Mountain Press, 1994.

Dunn, Violet, ed. *Saratoga County Heritage*. Saratoga, NY: Saratoga County, 1974.

Bibliography

Dyson, John S. *Our Historic Hudson*. Roosevelt, N.Y.: James B. Adler, 1968.

Eaton, Mike. "Devil's Den and No Bottom Pond: A Day Trip to the Haunts of a Cannibal, Bigfoot, and a Large Black Cat." *Northeastern Caver,* Vol. XXXIII, no. 2 (June 2002).

Ellis, Captain Franklin. *History of Columbia County, New York, with Illustrations of some of its Prominent Men and Pioneers.* 1878. Reprint, Old Chatham, N.Y.: Sachem Press, 1974.

Emblidge, David. *Exploring the Appalachian Trail: Hikes in Southern New England.* Mechanicsburg, Pa.: Stackpole Books, 1998.

Engel, Thomas D. *A Chronicle of Selected Northeastern Caves: A History Guide for the 1979 NSS Convention.* Pittsfield, Mass.: Thomas D. Engel, 1979.

Evans, John, Peter Quick and Bruce Sloane. *An Introduction to Caves of the Northeast: Guidebook for the 1979 National Speleological Society Convention.* Pittsfield, Mass.: National Speleological Society, 1979.

Evers, Alf. *In Catskill Country: Collected Essays on Mountain History, Life and Lore.* Woodstock, N.Y.: The Overlook Press, 1995.

———.*The Catskills: From Wilderness to Woodstock.* Woodstock, N.Y.: The Overlook Press, 1982.

Faber, Harold. *My Times in the Hudson Valley: The Insider's Guide to Historic Homes, Scenic Drives, Restaurants, Museums, Farm Produce & Points of Interest.* Hensonville, N.Y.: Black Dome Press Corp., 1997.

Fagan, Jack. *Scenes and Walks in the Northern Shawangunks.* New York: New York–New Jersey Trail Conference, 1998.

———. *Time and the Mountain: A Guide to the Geology of the Northern Shawangunk Mountains.* New Paltz, N. Y.: The Mohonk Preserve, Inc., 1996.

Friday, Chuck. Unpublished research and materials.

Gazda, William M. *Place Names in New York.* Schenectady, N.Y.: Gazda Associates, Inc., 1997.

Gilder, Cornelia Brooke. *Views of the Valley, Tyringham 1739–1989.* Hop Brook Community Club, 1989.

Gildersleeve. Robert A. *Catskill Mountain House Trail Guide: In the Footsteps of the Hudson River School.* Hensonville, N.Y.: Black Dome Press Corp., 2005.

———. "Hiking at North–South Lake." *Catskill Center News,* Vol. 34, no. 2.

Glunt, Ruth Reynolds. "Never Let the Light Go Out!" *Conservationist* (Dec.-Jan., 1972–1973).

Goldring, Winifred. *Guide to the Geology of John Boyd Thacher Park (Indian Ladder Region) and Vicinity: New York State Museum Handbook Number 14.* 1933. Reprint, Albany, N.Y.: The University of the State of New York, 1997.

The Great Trails Council. *Boy Scout's Hancock Shaker Trail.* Unpublished.

Gresham Publishing Company, ed. *History and Biography of Washington County and the Towns of Queensbury, New York, with Historical Notes on the Various Towns.* Richmond, Ind.: Gresham Publishing Company, 1894.

Grondahl, Paul. "The Long Path." *Conservationist,* Vol. 49, no. 6 (July 1995).

Haley, Jacquetta M., ed. *Pleasure Grounds: Andrew Jackson Downing and Montgomery Place.* Tarrytown, N.Y.: Sleepy Hollow Press, 1988.

Harris, Patricia, David Lyon, Anna Mundow and Lisa Oppenheimer. *Massachusetts.* New York: Compass American Guides, 2003.

Hendrix, Lester E., and Anne Whitbeck, eds. *The Sloughter's History of Schoharie County. Bicentennial Edition. 1795–1995.* Schoharie, N.Y.: The Tryon Press, 1995.

Henry, Edward G. *Gunks Trails: A Ranger's Guide to the Shawangunk Mountains.* Hensonville, N.Y.: Black Dome Press Corp., 2003.

Historic Design Associates. *Historic Hudson: Rehabilitation through Urban Renewal in the Lower Warren Street Historic Area of Hudson, New York*. Hudson, N.Y.: Raymond Parish & Pine, Inc., 1974.

Horne, Field. *The Greene County Catskills: A History*. Hensonville, N.Y.: Black Dome Press Corp., 1994.

Howat, John K. *The Hudson River and Its Painters*. 1972. Reprint, New York: American Legacy Press, 1983.

Howell and Tenny. *History of the County of Albany, NY: From 1609 to 1886, with Portraits, Biographies and Illustrations*. 1886. Reprint, Salem, Mass.: Higginson Book Company, n.d.

Illustrated History of Montgomery and Fulton Counties. N.p.: Heart of the Lake Publishings, 1981.

Ingersoll, Ernest. *Handy Guide to the Hudson River and Catskill Mountains*. 1910. Reprint, Astoria, N.Y.: J.C. & A.L. Fawcett, Inc., 1989.

Johnson, Carol A., and Marion W. Ryan. *Images of America: New Paltz*. Charleston, S.C.: Arcadia Publishing, 2001.

Joki, Robert. *Saratoga Lost: Images of Victorian America*. Hensonville, N.Y.: Black Dome Press Corp., 1998.

Josephson, Robi. *Images of America: Mohonk Mountain House and Preserve*. Charleston, S.C.: Arcadia Publishing, 2002.

Keller, Allan. *Life along the Hudson 2nd edition*. Tarrytown, N.Y.: Sleepy Hollow Press, 1985.

Kimball, Francis. *The Capital Region of New York State,* Vol. II. New York: Lewis Historical Publishing Co., Inc., 1942.

Knight, Frank. "Open Space Institute: Protecting the Land for People and Wildlife." *Kaatskill Life*, Vol. 19, no. 3 (fall 2004).

Kulik, Stephen, Pete Salmansohn, Matthew Schmidt and Heidi Welch. *The Audubon Society Field Guide to the Natural Places of the Northeast: Inland*. New York: Hilltown Press, Inc., 1984.

Laubach, Rene. *A Guide to Natural Places in the Berkshire Hills*. Stockbridge, Mass.: Berkshire House Publishers, 1992.

Lewis, Cynthia C., and Thomas J. Lewis. *Best Hikes with Children in the Catskills & Hudson River Valley*. Seattle, Wash.: The Mountaineers, 1992.

Lichens, Stan. *The Romantic Landscape: Photographs in the Tradition of the New York Hudson Valley Painters*. Petaluma, Calif.: Pomegranate Communications, Inc., 2004.

Lord, Thomas Reeves. *Stories of Lake George Fact and Fancy*. Remberton, N.J.: Pinelands Press, 1987.

Longstreth, T. Morris. *The Catskills*. 1918. Reprint, Hensonville, N.Y.: Black Dome Press Corp., 2003.

Matteson, Benjamin H., and Joan A. LaChance. *The Story of Sky Top and Its Four Towers*. Lake Mohonk, N.Y.: Mohonk Mountain House, 1998.

———. *The Summerhouses of Mohonk*. Mohonk Lake, N.Y.: Mohonk Mountain House, 1998.

Matthews, Richard. "Proper Names: An Appellative Atlas of the Berkshires." *Berkshire Magazine,* Vol. X, no. 5 (October/November, 1991).

McAllister, Lee. *Hiking the Catskills: a guide for exploring the natural beauty of America's romantic & magical mountains and "off the beaten path."* New York: The New York–New Jersey Trail Conference, 1989.

McLaughlin, Donald. "The Noses: Mohawk Valley Gateway." *Mohawk Valley USA*, Vol. 1, no. 3 (December 1980).

Bibliography

McMartin, Barbara, & Peter Kick. *Fifty Hikes in the Hudson Valley.* Woodstock, Vt.: Backcountry Publications, 1988.

McMartin, Barbara, and Edythe Robbins. *Discover the Eastern Adirondacks.* Woodstock, Vt.: Backcountry Publications, 1988.

Michaels, Joanne. *An Explorer's Guide to the Hudson Valley & Catskill Mountains: including Saratoga Springs & Albany.* Woodstock, Vt.: The Countryman Press, 2004.

Milbert, Jacques. *Picturesque Itinerary of the Hudson River and the Peripheral parts of North America.* Ridgewood, N.J.: The Gregg Press, 1968.

Millen, Patricia. "Step Back in Time in Prattsville." *Kaatskill Life,* Vol. 9, no. 2 (summer 1994).

Moore, Jim. "No Bottom Pond." *Northeastern Caver,* Vol. XXXII, no. 3 (Sept. 2001).

Mountain Top Historical Society. *Kaaterskill: From the Catskill Mountain House to the Hudson River School.* Hensonville, N.Y.: Black Dome Press Corp., 1998.

Mulligan, Tim. *The Hudson River Valley: A History & Guide.* New York: Random House, 1985.

Myers, Eloise. *Tyringham, a Hinterland Settlement.* 3rd edition. N.p.: Tyringham Historical Commission, Hinterland Press, 1989.

Myers, Kenneth. *The Catskills: Painters, Writers, and Tourists in the Mountains.* Yonkers, N.Y.: The Hudson River Museum of Westchester, 1987.

Mylod, John. *Biography of a River: The People & Legends of the Hudson Valley.* New York: Bonanza Books, 1969.

Nardacci, Michael, ed. *Guide to the Caves and Karst of the Northeast.* National Speleological Society, 1991.

New Scotland Historical Association. *Images of America: New Scotland Township.* Charleston, S.C.: Arcadia Publishing, 2000.

New York: A Guide to the Empire State. N.p.: Oxford University Press, 1940.

New York–New Jersey Trail Conference. *New York Walk Book.* 5th edition. Garden City, N.Y.: Anchor Press, 1971.

O'Brien, Patricia. "A Simpler Way." *Schenectady Magazine,* Vol. 1, no. 3 (winter 1988).

Olton, Jean S., compiler. *The Town of Colonie: A Pictorial History.* Colonie, N.Y.: 1980.

Oppel, Frank, compiler. "The Helderbergs (1869)." *New York State: Tales of the Empire State.* Secaucus, N.J.: Castle, 1988.

Ostering, Rhonda, and George Ostering. *Hiking Southern New England.* Helena, Mont.: Falcon Press Publishing Co., Inc., 1997.

Palme, Arthur. *The Berkshires: Through the Camera of Arthur Palme.* N.p.: Palme–Grove Publishing Company, 1951.

Palmer, Leland R. "Vischer Ferry: Nature and Historic Preserve." *Mohawk Valley USA,* Vol. 4, no. 2 (summer 1983).

Parker, Joseph A. *Looking Back: A History of Troy & Rensselaer County, 1925–1982.* Troy, N.Y.: J. A. Parker, 1982.

Patton, Russ Jr. "Lighting the Way." *Kaatskill Life,* Vol. 13, no. 2 (summer 1998).

Peattie, Roderick, ed. *The Berkshires: The Purple Hills.* New York: Vanguard Press, Inc., 1948.

Perry, Clay. *New England's Buried Treasure.* New York: Stephen Daye Press, 1946.

———. *Underground Empire: Wonders and Tales of New York Caves.* New York, N.Y.: Stephen Daye Press, 1948.

Perls, Jeffrey. *Shawangunks Trail Companion: A Complete Guide to Hiking, Mountain Biking, Cross-Country Skiing, and More Only 90 Miles from New York City.* Woodstock, Vt.: Backcountry Guides, 2003.

Phelan, Thomas, and P. Thomas Carroll. *Hudson Mohawk Gateway: An Illustrated History.* Sun Valley, Calif.: American Historical Press, 2001.

Phelps, Stephen. "The Indomitable Emma Willard." *Conservationist*, March/April 1979.

Piwonka, Ruth. *Mount Merino: Views of Mount Merino, South Bay, and the City of Hudson, Painted by Henry Ary and His Contemporaries.* Kinderhook, N.Y.: Columbia County Historical Society, 1978.

———. "Mt. Merino Catalogue of Exhibits." Kinderhook N.Y.: NYS Council on the Arts and Columbia County Historical Society, 1976 and 1977.

Porter, Chuck, Ron Grant and Dan Hoyt. "Story behind the Ward–Gregory Link." *Northeastern Caver*, Vol. XXXV, no 1 (March 2004).

Rensselaerville Historical Society. *People Made It Happen Here: History of the Town of Rensselaerville.* Rensselaerville, N.Y.: Rensselaerville Historical Society, 1977.

Resch, Tyler. *Bill Tague's Berkshires.* Vol. II. Dover, N.H.: Arcadia Publishing, 1998.

Rittner, Don. *Images of America: Troy.* Charleston, S.C.: Arcadia Publishing, 1998.

———. *Troy: A Collar City History.* Charleston, S.C.: Arcadia Publishing, 2002.

Rogers, Barbara Radcliffe, Stillman Rogers, Pat Maddell and Juliette Rogers. *Off the Beaten Path: Massachusetts.* 6th edition. Guilford, Conn.: Globe Pequot Press, 2005.

Roseberry, C.R. *Albany: Three Centuries a County.* Albany, N.Y.: Tricentennial Commission, 1983.

———. *From Niagara to Montauk: The Scenic Pleasures of New York State.* Albany, N.Y.: State University of New York Press, 1982.

Roy, Jennifer. *Saratoga: The Family Place to Be.* Utica, N.Y.: Nicholas K. Burns, 2001.

Rubin, Paul. "Clarksville Cave—1990." *Northeastern Caver*, Vol. XX, no. 4. (1989).

———. "Historic Clarksville Cave." *Northeastern Caver*, XVII, no. 5. (1986).

Rubin, Paul, and Allison P. Bennett. "Historic Clarksville Cave." *Northeastern Caver*, Vol. XXI no. 4 (Dec. 1990).

Saidel, Peter M., and Judith R. Saidel. *The History of Bennett Hill Farm.* Clarksville, N.Y.: Peter M. & Judith R. Saidel, 2002.

Sandrof, Ivan. *Yesterday's Massachusetts.* N.p.: E.A. Seemann Publishing, Inc., 1977.

Schaefer, Vincent J. *Vrooman's Nose.* Fleischmanns, N.Y.: Purple Mountain Press, 1992.

Schenectady & Upstate New York. "Shaker Spirit." Vol. III, no. 1 (spring 1990).

Schenectady & Upstate New York. "Troy: Hub of Industry." Vol. II, no. 3 (fall 1989).

Scherer, John L. *Images of America: Clifton Park.* Dover, N.H.: Arcadia Publishing, 1996.

Schmitt, Claire K., and Mary S. Brennan. *Natural Areas of Albany County.* 4th edition. Schenectady, N.Y.: Environmental Clearinghouse of Schenectady, 2004.

Schmitt, Claire K, Norton G. Miller, Warren F. Broderick, John T. Keenan and William D. Niemi. *Natural Areas of Rensselaer County, New York.* 2nd edition. Schenectady/Troy, N.Y.: The Rensselaer–Taconic Land Conservancy & Environmental Clearinghouse of Schenectady, Inc., 2002.

Schmitt, Claire K., and Judith S. Wolk. *Natural Areas of Saratoga County.* Schenectady, N.Y.: Environmental Clearinghouse of Schenectady, 1998.

Schram, Margaret B. *Hudson's Merchants and Whalers: The Rise and Fall of a River Port, 1783–1850.* Hensonville, N.Y.: Black Dome Press Corp., 2004.

Schuman, Michael. A. *New York State's Special Places: day trips, weekends, and outings in the Empire State.* Woodstock, Vt.: The Countryman Press, 1988.

Silverman, Francine. *The Catskills Alive!* Edison, N.J.: Hunter Publishing, Inc., 2000.

Slavin, Richard E. III. "Frederic Church and Olana." *Conservationist*, Vol. 28, no. 6 (June-July 1974).

Smith, Charles W. G. *Nature Walks in the Berkshire Hills.* Boston: Appalachian Mountain Club, 1997.

Snell, Charles W., and Francis F. Wilson. *Saratoga National Historical Park, New York.* 1950. Reprint, Washington, D.C.: Department of the Interior, 1961.

Bibliography

Sparling, Reed. "Three Capital District Diversions." *Hudson Valley,* Vol. XXXIII, No. 12 (April 2005).

Stevens, Lauren R. *Hikes & Walks in the Berkshire Hills.* Stockbridge, Mass.: Berkshire House Publishers, 1990.

Stoller, James H. *Geological Excursions: A Guide to Localities in the Region of Schenectady and the Mohawk Valley and in the Vicinity of Saratoga Springs.* Schenectady, N.Y.: Union Book Co., 1931.

Stone, Howard. *25 Bicycle Tours in the Hudson Valley: Scenic Rides from Saratoga to West Point.* Woodstock, Vt.: Backcountry Publications, 1989.

Stone, William L. *Reminiscences of Saratoga and Ballston.* N.p.: Virtue & Yorston, 1875.

——. *Visits to the Saratoga Battle-Grounds, 1780–1880.* 1895. Reprint, Kennikat Press, 1970.

Swanner, Grace Maguire, MD. *Saratoga Queen of Spas: a History of the Saratoga Spa and the Mineral Springs of the Saratoga and Ballston Areas.* Utica, N.Y.: North Country Books, 1988.

Sweeny, F.R.I. "The Burden Water-Wheel." *Transactions.* 1915. Reprint, Society for Industrial Archeology, no. 2 (April 1973).

Sylvester, Nathaniel Bartlett. *History of Saratoga County, New York.* Philadelphia: Everts & Ensign, 1878.

Tague, William H., and Robert B. Kimball, eds., with text by Richard V. Happel. Revised by Tyler Resch with the assistance of Judy Katz. *Berkshire: The First Three Hundred Years, 1676–1976.* Pittsfield, Mass.: The Eagle Publishing Company, 1976.

Tague, William H. and Robert B. Kimball, eds. with text by Richard V. Happel. *Berkshires: Two Hundred Years in Pictures.* Pittsfield, Mass.: The Eagle Publishing Company, 1961.

Thurheimer, David C. *Landmarks of the Revolution in New York State.* N.p.: NYS American Revolution Bicentennial Commission, 1976.

Thurston, Elisha P., compiler. *History of the Town of Greenwich.* Salem, N.Y.: H.D. Morris, Book & Job Printer, 1876.

Titus, Robert. "Dance Floors." *Kaatskill Life,* Vol. 13, no. 4 (winter 1998–1999).

——. "The Colonel's Tomb." *Kaatskill Life,* Vol. 13, no. 1 (spring 1998).

——. "The Lost Lakes" *Kaatskill Life,* Vol. 16, no. 2 (summer 2001).

——. "Ulster Blues." *Kaatskill Life,* Vol. 10, no. 2 (summer 1995).

Toole, Robert M. *A Look at Metroland: A new guide to its history and heritage.* Saratoga Springs, N.Y.: R.M. Toole, Landscape Architects, 1976.

Tougias, Michael, and Mark Tougias. *Autumn Rambles of New England: An Explorer's Guide to the Best Fall Colors.* Edison, N.J.: Hunter Publishing Co., Inc., 1998.

Town of New Baltimore Bicentennial Committee. *The Heritage of New Baltimore.* New Baltimore, N.Y.: Town of New Baltimore, 1976.

Tree, Christina, and William Davis. *The Berkshire Hills & Pioneer Valley of Western Massachusetts: An Explorer's Guide.* Woodstock, Vt.: The Countryman Press, 2004.

Turco, Peggy. *Walks and Rambles in the Western Hudson Valley: Landscape, Ecology & Folklore in Orange & Ulster Counties.* Woodstock, Vt.: Backcountry Publications, 1996.

VanDerwerker, J.B. *Early Days in Saratoga County.* Interlaken, N.Y.: Empire State Books, 1994.

Van Diver, Bradford B. *Roadside Geology of New York.* Missoula, Mont.: Mountain Press Publishing Company, 1985.

——. *Upstate New York.* Dubuque, Iowa: Kendall/Hunt Publishing Company, 1980.

Van Zandt, Roland. *The Catskill Mountain House: Cradle of the Hudson River School.* 1966; reprint, Hensonville, N.Y.: Black Dome Press Corp., 1993.

Vedder, J. Van Vechten. *Official History of Greene County.* 1927. Reprint, Cornwallville, N.Y.: Hope Farm Press, 1985.

Vogel, Robert M., ed. *A Report of the Mohawk-Hudson Area Survey.* Washington, D.C.: Smithsonian Institution Press, 1973.

Von Riedesel, Baroness Friederike. *Letters and Journals Relating to the War of the Revolution.* 1867. Reprint, Gansevoort, N. Y.: Corner House Historical Publications, 2001.

Wadsworth, Bruce, and the Schenectady Chapter of the Adirondack Mountain Club. *Guide to Catskill Trails 8.* 2nd edition. Lake George, N.Y.: Adirondack Mountain Club, Inc., 1988.

Waite, John G., and Diana S. Waite. *Industrial Archeology in Troy, Waterford, Cohoes, Green Island, and Watervliet.* Troy, N.Y.: Hudson–Mohawk Industrial Gateway, 1973.

Warner, Mike, and Emily Davis, compilers, with reports from Emily Davis. "Clarksville Cave Body Recovery." *Northeastern Caver*, Vol. XXXII, no. 1 (March, 2001).

Washington County Historical Society. *History of Washington County, New York: Some Chapters in the History of the Town of Easton, NY.* Washington County, N.Y.: Washington County Historical Society, 1959.

Washington, William R., and Patricia S. Smith. *Crossroads and Canals: The History of Clifton Park, Saratoga County, New York.* n.d. Reprint, Albany, N.Y.: Fort Orange Press, 1985.

Weiman, Steve. *A Rock with a View: Trails of the Shawangunk Mountains.* New Paltz, N.p., 1995.

Weise, A.J. *History of Lansingburgh, N.Y.: From the Year 1670 to 1877.* Troy, N.Y.: William H. Young, 1877.

———. *History of the Seventeen Towns of Rensselaer County: from the colonization of the manor of Rensselaerwyck to the present time.* Troy, N.Y.: J. M. Francis & Tucker, 1880.

White, Carol, and David White. *Catskill Day Hikes for All Seasons.* Lake George, N.Y.: Adirondack Mountain Club, Inc., 2002.

Williams, Stephen. "Stark's Knob Takes Tourists to Hudson River Overlook." *The Sunday Gazette*, February 25, 2001.

Wilson, E.O. "It Won't Bite." *Kaatskill Life*, Vol. 14, no. 4 (winter 1999–2000).

Yeadon, David. *Hidden Corners of New England.* New York: Funk & Wagnalls, 1976.

Index

Index

Index

Index